Prayer

by

ELLEN G. WHITE

Pacific Press® Publishing Association
Nampa, Idaho
Oshawa, Ontario, Canada
www.pacificpress.com

Cover design by Willie Duke
Cover illustration by Lee Christiansen
Inside design by Steve Lanto

ISBN 13: 978-0-8163-1909-1
ISBN 10: 0-8163-1909-X

09 10 11 • 6 5 4

Preface

The scriptures admonish us to "pray without ceasing." This does not mean that we are to spend all of our time on our knees in formal prayer. It does mean that we must live and serve our Lord in the atmosphere of prayer.

Prayer is the channel of communication between our souls and God. God speaks to us through His Word; we respond to Him through our prayers, and He always listens to us. We cannot weary or burden Him by our frequent heart-to-heart communications.

We have come to serious times. Events in our world call upon every follower of Christ to be totally in earnest in our relationship with God. To strengthen this relationship and satisfy our emotional and spiritual needs, we must learn the power of prayer. We must plead with the Lord, like the disciples of old, saying, "Lord, teach us to pray."

That God is willing and ready to hear and to respond to our heartfelt prayers under all circumstances is profoundly reassuring. He is a loving Father who is interested both when things are going well and when the vicissitudes of life deal us devastating, tough, and terrible blows. When we feel like crying out, "God, where are You?" it is good to know that He is just a prayer away.

One writer has said, "More things are wrought by prayer than this world dreams of." It is also true of the church. "A revival of true godliness among us is the greatest and most urgent of all our needs. To seek this should be our first work" (1SM, 121). God will do things for us when we pray that He will not do if we do not pray (GC, 525). We acknowledge that we need the outpouring of the Holy Spirit. But this can be accomplished only as we pray individually and collectively. When God's people pray earnestly, sincerely, individually, and collectively, God will answer. Great things will happen in and among God's people. And the world will feel the impact as the Holy Spirit comes to equip and empower His people.

We believe this book will find a ready reception among people of all backgrounds. As we read the selections from Ellen G. White on the vital subject of prayer, we will find our hearts strangely and warmly stirred. These messages will hit home to our souls. Conviction on many points expressed will find lodgment in our hearts, evoking an echoing response to measure up to God's call to a deeper and richer prayer life.

"Our heavenly Father waits to bestow upon us the fullness of His blessing. It is our privilege to drink largely at the fountain of boundless love. What a wonder it is that we pray so little. God is ready and willing to hear the sincere prayer of the humblest of His children. . . . Why should the sons and daughters of God be reluctant to pray, when prayer is the key in the hand of faith to unlock heaven's storehouse where are treasured the boundless resources of Omnipotence?" (SC, 94, 95).

Contents

1

God Invites Us to Pray

LINKED WITH GOD THROUGH PRAYER.—It is a wonderful thing that we can pray effectually; that unworthy, erring mortals possess the power of offering their requests to God. What higher power can man desire than this,—to be linked with the infinite God? Feeble, sinful man has the privilege of speaking to his Maker. We may utter words that reach the throne of the Monarch of the universe. We may speak with Jesus as we walk by the way, and He says, I am at thy right hand.

We may commune with God in our hearts; we may walk in companionship with Christ. When engaged in our daily labor, we may breathe out our heart's desire, inaudible to any human ear; but that word cannot die away into silence, nor can it be lost. Nothing can drown the soul's desire. It rises above the din of the street, above the noise of machinery. It is God to whom we are speaking, and our prayer is heard.

Ask, then; ask, and ye shall receive. Ask for humility, wisdom, courage, increase of faith. To every sincere prayer an answer will come. It may not come just as you desire, or at the time you look for it; but it will come in the way and at the time that will best meet your need. The prayers you offer in loneliness, in weariness, in trial, God answers, not always according to your expectations, but always for your good.—(*Gospel Workers,* 258.)

JESUS INVITES US TO PRAY.—The Lord gives us the privilege of seeking Him individually in earnest prayer, of unburdening our souls to Him, keeping nothing from Him who has invited us, "Come unto Me, all ye that labor and are heavy-laden, and I will give you rest." Oh, how grateful we should be that Jesus is willing and able to bear all our infirmities and strengthen and heal all our diseases if it will be for our good and for His glory.—(*Medical Ministry,* 16.)

"Come unto Me," is His invitation. Whatever your anxieties and trials, spread out your case before the Lord.—(*The Desire of Ages,* 329.)

TELL JESUS ALL YOUR NEEDS.—There are few who rightly appreciate or improve the precious privilege of prayer. We should go to Jesus and tell Him all our needs. We may bring Him our little cares and perplexities as well as our greater troubles. Whatever arises to disturb or distress us, we should take it to the Lord in prayer. When we feel that we need the presence of Christ at every step, Satan will have little opportunity to intrude his temptations. It is his studied effort to keep us away from our best and most sympathizing friend. We should make no one our confidant but Jesus. We can safely commune with Him of all that is in our hearts.—(*Testimonies for the Church,* vol. 5, 200, 201.)

OPENING THE HEART TO A FRIEND.—Prayer is the opening of the heart to God as to a friend. Not that it is necessary in order to make known to God what we are, but in order to enable us to receive Him. Prayer does not bring God down to us, but brings us up to Him.

When Jesus was upon the earth, He taught His disciples how to pray. He directed them to present their daily needs before God, and to cast all their care upon Him. And the assurance He gave them that their petitions should be heard, is assurance also to us.—(*Steps to Christ,* 93.)

GOD WELCOMES US TO HIS AUDIENCE CHAMBER.—We come to God by special invitation, and He waits to welcome us to His audience chamber. The first disciples who followed Jesus were not satisfied with a hurried conversation with Him by the way; they said, "Rabbi, . . . where dwellest Thou? . . . They came and saw where He dwelt, and abode with Him that day." John 1:38, 39. So we may be admitted into closest intimacy and communion with God. "He that dwelleth in the secret place of the Most High shall abide under the shadow of the Almighty." Psalm 91:1. Let those who desire the blessing of God knock and wait at the door of mercy with firm assurance, saying, For Thou, O Lord, hast said, "Everyone that asketh receiveth; and he that seeketh findeth; and to him that knocketh it shall be opened."—(*Thoughts From the Mount of Blessing,* 131.)

AN EXALTED PRIVILEGE.—When in trouble, when assailed by fierce temptations, they [God's children] have the privilege of prayer. What an exalted privilege! Finite beings, of dust and ashes, admitted through the mediation of Christ, into the audience-chamber of the Most High. In such exercises the soul is brought into a sacred nearness with God, and is renewed in knowledge, and true holiness, and fortified against the assaults of the enemy.—(*An Appeal to Mothers,* 24.)

PRAYER IS BOTH A SPIRITUAL NECESSITY AND A PRIVILEGE.—Those who have professed to love Christ, have not comprehended the relation which exists between them and God, . . . They do not realize what a great privilege and necessity are prayer, repentance, and the doing of the words of Christ.—(*Selected Messages,* bk. 1, 134.)

PRAYER ENABLES US TO LIVE IN THE SUNSHINE OF HIS PRESENCE.— It is our privilege to open our hearts, and let the sunshine of Christ's presence in. My brother, my sister, face the light. Come into actual, personal contact with Christ, that you may exert an influence that is uplifting and reviving. Let your faith be strong and pure and steadfast. Let gratitude to God fill your hearts. When you rise in the morning, kneel at your bedside, and ask God to give you strength to fulfil the duties of the day, and to meet its temptations. Ask Him to help you to bring into your work Christ's sweetness of character. Ask Him to help you to speak words that will inspire those around you with hope and courage, and draw you nearer to the Saviour.—(*Sons and Daughters of God,* 199.)

OUR PRAYERS NEVER BURDEN OR WEARY GOD.—There is no time or place in which it is inappropriate to offer up a petition to God. There is nothing that can prevent us from lifting up our hearts in the spirit of earnest prayer. In the crowds of the street, in the midst of a business engagement, we may send up a petition to God and plead for divine guidance, as did Nehemiah when he made his request before King Artaxerxes. A closet of communion may be found wherever we are. We should have the door of the heart open continually and our invitation going up that Jesus may come and abide as a heavenly guest in the soul.

Although there may be a tainted, corrupted atmosphere around us, we need not breathe its miasma, but may live in the pure air of heaven. We may close every door to impure imaginings and unholy thoughts by lifting the soul into the presence of God through sincere prayer. Those whose hearts are open to receive the support and blessing of God will walk in a holier atmosphere than that of earth and will have constant communion with heaven.

We need to have more distinct views of Jesus and a fuller comprehension of the value of eternal realities. The beauty of holiness is to fill the hearts of God's children; and that this may be accomplished, we should seek for divine disclosures of heavenly things.

Let the soul be drawn out and upward, that God may grant us a breath of the heavenly atmosphere. We may keep so near to God that in every unexpected trial our thoughts will turn to Him as naturally as the flower turns to the sun.

Keep your wants, your joys, your sorrows, your cares, and your fears before God. You cannot burden Him; you cannot weary Him. He who numbers the hairs of your head is not indifferent to the wants of His children. "The Lord is very pitiful, and of tender mercy" (James 5:11). His heart of love is touched by our sorrows and even by our utterances of them. Take to Him everything that perplexes the mind. Nothing is too great for Him to bear, for He holds up worlds. He rules over all the affairs of the universe.

Nothing that in any way concerns our peace is too small for Him to notice. There is no chapter in our experience too dark for Him to read; there is no perplexity too difficult for Him to unravel. . . . The relations between God and each soul are as distinct and full as though there were not another soul upon the earth to share His watchcare, not another soul for whom He gave His beloved Son.—(*Steps to Christ*, 99, 100.)

A FORETASTE OF HEAVEN.—Rest yourself wholly in the hands of Jesus. Contemplate His great love, and while you meditate upon His self-denial, His infinite sacrifice made in our behalf in order that we should believe in Him, your heart will be filled with holy joy, calm peace, and indescribable love. As we talk of Jesus, as we call upon Him in prayer, our confidence that He is our personal, loving Saviour will strengthen and His character will appear more and more lovely. . . . We may enjoy rich feasts of love, and as we fully believe that we are His by adoption, we may have a foretaste of heaven. Wait upon the Lord in faith. The Lord draws out the soul in prayer, and gives us to feel His precious love. We have a nearness to Him, and can hold sweet communion with Him. We obtain distinct views of His tenderness and compassion, and our hearts are broken and melted with contemplation of the love that is given to us. We feel indeed an abiding Christ in the soul. We abide in Him, and feel at home with Jesus. The promises flow into the soul. Our peace is like a river, wave after wave of glory rolls into the heart, and indeed we sup with Jesus and He with us. We have a realizing sense of the love of God, and we rest in His love.

No language can describe it, it is beyond knowledge. We are one with Christ, our life is hid with Christ in God. We have the assurance that when He who is our life shall appear, then shall we also appear with Him in glory. With strong confidence, we can call God our Father.—(*SDA Bible Commentary,* vol. 3, 1147, 1148.)

PRAYER BRINGS FRESHNESS TO SPIRITUAL LIFE.—Our life is to be bound up with the life of Christ; we are to draw constantly from Him, partaking of Him, the living Bread that came down from heaven, drawing from a fountain ever fresh, ever giving forth its abundant treasures. If we keep the Lord ever before us, allowing our hearts to go out in thanksgiving and praise to Him, we shall have a continual freshness in our religious life. Our prayers will take the form of a conversation with God as we would talk with a friend. He will speak His mysteries to us personally. Often there will come to us a sweet joyful sense of the presence of Jesus. Often our hearts will burn within us as He draws nigh to commune with us as He did with Enoch. When this is in truth the experience of the Christian, there is seen in his life a simplicity, a humility, meekness, and lowliness of heart, that show to all with whom he associates that he has been with Jesus and learned of Him.—(*Christ's Object Lessons,* 129, 130.)

A PLACE TO FLEE THAT IS ALWAYS OPEN.—The way to the throne of God is always open. You cannot always be on your knees in prayer, but your silent petitions may constantly ascend to God for strength and guidance. When tempted, as you will be, you may flee to the secret place of the Most High. His everlasting arms will be underneath you.—(*In Heavenly Places,* 86.)

THE SECRET OF SPIRITUAL POWER.—Prayer is the breath of the soul. It is the secret of spiritual power. No other means of grace can be substituted and the health of the soul be preserved. Prayer brings the heart into immediate contact with the Wellspring of life, and strengthens the sinew and muscle of the religious experience. Neglect the exercise of prayer, or engage in prayer spasmodically, now and then, as seems convenient, and you lose your hold on God. The spiritual faculties lose their vitality, the religious experience lacks health and vigor. . . .

It is a wonderful thing that we can pray effectually, that unworthy, erring mortals possess the power of offering their requests to God. What higher power can man desire than this,—to be linked with the infinite God? Feeble, sinful man has the privilege of speaking to his Maker. We may utter words that reach the throne of the Monarch of the universe. We may speak with Jesus as we walk by the way, and He says, I am at thy right hand.—(*Messages to Young People,* 249, 250.)

SECRET PRAYER THE SOUL OF RELIGION.—Do not neglect secret prayer, for it is the soul of religion. With earnest, fervent prayer plead for purity of soul. Plead as earnestly, as eagerly, as you would for your mortal life, were it at stake. Remain before God until unutterable longings are begotten within you for salvation, and the sweet evidence is obtained of pardoned sin.—(*Spiritual Gifts,* bk. 2, 264.)

EVERY SINCERE PRAYER IS HEARD.—As yet the disciples were unacquainted with the Saviour's unlimited resources and power. He said to them, "Hitherto have ye asked nothing in My name." John 16:24. He explained that the secret of their success would be in asking for strength and grace in His name. He would be present before the Father to make request for them. The prayer of the humble suppliant He presents as His own desire in that soul's behalf. Every sincere prayer is heard in heaven. It may not be fluently expressed; but if the heart is in it, it will ascend to the sanctuary where Jesus ministers, and He will present it to the Father without one awkward, stammering word, beautiful and fragrant with the incense of His own perfection.

The path of sincerity and integrity is not a path free from obstruction, but in every difficulty we are to see a call to prayer.

There is no one living who has any power that he has not received from God, and the source whence it comes is open to the weakest human being. "Whatsoever ye shall ask in My name," said Jesus, "that will I do, that the Father may be glorified in the Son. If ye shall ask anything in My name, I will do it."

"In My name," Christ bade His disciples pray. In Christ's name His followers are to stand before God. Through the value of the sacrifice made for them, they are of value in the Lord's sight. Because of the imputed righteousness of Christ they are accounted precious. For Christ's sake the Lord pardons those that fear Him. He does not see in them the vileness of the sinner. He recognizes in them the likeness of His Son, in whom they believe.—(*The Desire of Ages,* 667.)

ANGELS MARK OUR PRAYERS AND INFLUENCE US FOR GOOD.—When you rise in the morning, do you feel your helplessness and your need of strength from God? and do you humbly, heartily make known your wants to your heavenly Father? If so, angels mark your prayers, and if these prayers have not gone forth out of feigned lips, when you are in danger of unconsciously doing wrong and exerting an influence which will lead others to do wrong, your guardian angel will be by your side, prompting you to a better course, choosing your words for you, and influencing your actions.

If you feel in no danger, and if you offer no prayer for help and strength to resist temptations, you will be sure to go astray; your neglect of duty will be marked in the book of God in heaven, and you will be found wanting in the trying day.—(*Testimonies for the Church,* vol. 3, 363, 364.)

LIKE MOSES, WE MAY ENJOY INTIMATE COMMUNION WITH GOD.— That hand that made the world, that holds the mountains in their places, takes this man of dust,—this man of mighty faith,—and mercifully covers him in a cleft of the rock, while the glory of God and all His goodness pass before him. Can we marvel that the "excellent glory" reflected from Omnipotence shone in the face of

Moses with such brightness that the people could not look upon it? The impress of God was upon him, making him appear as one of the shining angels from the throne.

This experience, above all else the assurance that God would hear his prayer, and that the divine presence would attend him, was of more value to Moses as a leader than the learning of Egypt, or all his attainments in military science. No earthly power or skill or learning can supply the place of God's immediate presence. In the history of Moses we may see what intimate communion with God it is man's privilege to enjoy. To the transgressor it is a fearful thing to fall into the hands of the living God. But Moses was not afraid to be alone with the Author of that law which had been spoken with such awful grandeur from Mount Sinai; for his soul was in harmony with the will of his Maker.

Prayer is the opening of the heart to God as to a friend. The eye of faith will discern God very near, and the suppliant may obtain precious evidence of the divine love and care for him.— (*Gospel Workers,* 34, 35.)

PRAY WITH HOLY BOLDNESS.—"If ye abide in me, and my words abide in you, ye shall ask what ye will, and it shall be done unto you." When you pray, present this promise. It is our privilege to come to Him with holy boldness. As in sincerity we ask Him to let His light shine upon us, He will hear and answer us.—(*Child Guidance,* 499.)

Heaven is open to our petitions, and we are invited to come "boldly unto the throne of grace, that we may obtain mercy, and find grace to help in time of need." We are to come in faith, believing that we shall obtain the very things we ask of him.—(*Signs of the Times,* April 18, 1892.)

ASK FOR OUR NEEDS.—Every promise in the word of God furnishes us with subject matter for prayer, presenting the pledged word of Jehovah as our assurance. Whatever spiritual blessing we need, it is our privilege to claim through Jesus. We may tell the Lord, with the simplicity of a child, exactly what we need. We may state to Him our temporal matters, asking Him for bread and raiment as well as for the bread of life and the robe of Christ's righteousness. Your heavenly Father knows that you have need of all these things, and you are invited to ask Him concerning them. It is through the name of Jesus that every favor is received. God will honor that name, and will supply your necessities from the riches of His liberality.—(*Thoughts From the Mount of Blessing,* 133.)

ASK AND BELIEVE.—As you ask the Lord to help you, honor your Saviour by believing that you do receive His blessing. All power, all wisdom, are at our command. We have only to ask.

Walk continually in the light of God. Meditate day and night upon His character. Then you will see His beauty and rejoice in His goodness. Your heart will glow with a sense of His love. You will be uplifted as if borne by everlasting arms. With the power and light that God imparts, you can comprehend more and accomplish more than you ever before deemed possible.—(*Ministry of Healing,* 514.)

GO FORWARD, TRUSTING GOD.—We are to encourage in one another that living faith which Christ has made it possible for every believer to have. The work is to be carried forward as the Lord prepares the way. When He brings His people into strait places, then it is their privilege to assemble together for prayer, remembering that all things come of God. Those who have not yet shared in the trying experiences that attend the work in these last days will soon have to pass through scenes that will severely test their confidence in God. It is at the time His people see no way to advance, when the Red Sea is before them and the pursuing army behind, that God bids them: "Go forward." Thus He is working to test their faith. When such experiences come to you, go forward, trusting in Christ. Walk step by step in the path He marks out. Trials will come, but go forward. This will give you an experience that will strengthen your faith in God and fit you for truest service.—(*Testimonies for the Church,* vol. 9, 273.)

2

Our Need of Prayer

PRAYER IS AS ESSENTIAL TO LIFE AS DAILY FOOD.—Daily prayer is as essential to growth in grace, and even to spiritual life itself, as is temporal food to physical well-being. We should accustom ourselves to often lift the thoughts to God in prayer. If the mind wanders, we must bring it back; by persevering effort, habit will finally make it easy. We cannot for one moment separate ourselves from Christ with safety. We may have His presence to attend us at every step, but only by observing the conditions which He has Himself laid down.—(*Messages to Young People,* 115.)

PRAYER IS A SPIRITUAL NECESSITY.—Although Christ had given the promise to His disciples that they should receive the Holy Spirit, this did not remove the necessity of prayer. They prayed all the more earnestly; they continued in prayer with one accord. Those who are now engaged in the solemn work of preparing a people for the coming of the Lord, should also continue in prayer.—(*Gospel Workers,* 371.)

They [Jesus' disciples] had not heeded the repeated warning, "Watch and pray." At first they had been much troubled to see their Master, usually so calm and dignified, wrestling with a sorrow that was beyond comprehension. They had prayed as they heard the strong cries of the sufferer. They did not intend to forsake their Lord, but they seemed paralyzed by a stupor which they might have shaken off if they had continued pleading with God. They did not realize the necessity of watchfulness and earnest prayer in order to withstand temptation.—(*The Desire of Ages,* 688.)

The experience of the disciples in the Garden of Gethsemane contains a lesson for the Lord's people today. . . . They did not realize the necessity of watchfulness and earnest prayer in order to withstand temptation. Many today are fast asleep, as were the disciples. They are not watching and praying lest they enter into temptation. Let us often read and give careful study to those portions of God's Word that have special reference to these last days, pointing out the dangers that will threaten God's people.—(*In Heavenly Places,* 97.)

PRAYER IS THE LIFE OF THE SOUL.—Prayer is a necessity; for it is the life of the soul. Family prayer, public prayer, have their place; but it is secret communion with God that sustains the soul life.—(*Education,* 258.)

PRAYER NECESSARY FOR SPIRITUAL HEALTH.—Several times each day precious, golden moments should be consecrated to prayer and the study of the Scriptures, if it is only to commit a text to memory, that spiritual life may exist in the soul. The varied interests of the cause furnish us with food for reflection and inspiration for our prayers. Communion with God is highly essential for spiritual health, and here only may be obtained that wisdom and correct judgment so necessary in the performance of every duty.—(*Testimonies for the Church,* vol. 4, 459.)

CHRIST'S EXAMPLE SHOWS THE NECESSITY OF PRAYER.—If those who sound the solemn notes of warning for this time could realize their accountability to God, they would see the necessity for fervent prayer. When the cities were hushed in midnight slumber, when every man had gone to his own house, Christ, our example, would repair to the Mount of Olives, and there, amid the overshadowing trees, would spend the entire night in prayer. He who was Himself without the taint of sin,—a treasure-house of blessing; whose voice was heard in the fourth watch of the night by the terrified disciples upon the stormy sea, in heavenly benediction; and whose word could summon the dead from their graves,—He it was who made supplication with strong crying and tears. He prayed not for Himself, but for those whom He came to save. As He became a suppliant, seeking at the hand of His Father fresh supplies of strength, and coming forth refreshed and invigorated as man's substitute, He identified Himself with suffering humanity, and gave them an example of the necessity of prayer.

His nature was without the taint of sin. As the Son of man, He prayed to the Father, showing that human nature requires all the divine support which man can obtain that he may be braced for duty and prepared for trial. As the Prince of Life, He had power with God, and prevailed for His people. This Saviour, who prayed for those that felt no need of prayer, and wept for those that felt no need of tears, is now before the throne, to receive and present to His Father the petitions of those for whom He prayed on earth. The example of Christ is for us to follow. Prayer is a necessity in our labor for the salvation of souls. God alone can give the increase of the seed we sow.—(*Gospel Workers,* 28, 29.)

JESUS URGED THE NECESSITY OF PRAYER.—He [Jesus] urged upon men the necessity of prayer, repentance, confession, and the abandonment of sin. He taught them honesty, forbearance, mercy, and compassion, enjoining upon them to love not only those who loved them, but those who hated them, who treated them despitefully. In this He was revealing to them the character of the Father, who is long-suffering, merciful, and gracious, slow to anger, and full of goodness and truth.—(*Christian Education,* 74.)

PRAYER A NECESSITY TO DANIEL.—Daniel was subjected to the severest temptations that can assail the youth of today; yet he was true to the religious instruction received in early life. He was surrounded with influences calculated to subvert those who would vacillate between principle and inclination; yet the word of God presents him as a faultless character. Daniel dared not trust to his own moral power. Prayer was to him a necessity. He made God his strength, and the fear of God was continually before him in all the transactions of his life.—(*Fundamentals of Christian Education,* 78.)

SPIRITUAL ADVANCE DEPENDS ON PRAYER.—If there were more praying among us, more exercise of a living faith, and less dependence upon some one else to have an experience for us, we would be far in advance of where we are today in spiritual intelligence. What we need is a deep, individual heart and soul experience. Then we shall be able to tell what God is doing and how He is working. We need to have a living experience in the things of God; and we are not safe unless we have this. There are some who have a good experience, and they tell you about it; but when you come to weigh it up, you see that it is not a correct experience, for it is not in accordance with a plain Thus saith the Lord. If ever there was a time in our history when we needed to humble our individual souls before God, it is today. We need to come to God with faith in all that is promised in the Word, and then walk in all the light and power that God gives.—(*Review and Herald,* July 1, 1909.)

PRAYER NEEDED DAILY.—Religion must begin with emptying and purifying the heart, and must be nurtured by daily prayer.—(*Testimonies for the Church,* vol. 4, 535.)

It is just as convenient, just as essential, for us to pray three times a day as it was for Daniel. Prayer is the life of the soul, the foundation of spiritual growth. In your home, before your family, and before your workmen, you should testify to this truth. And when you are privileged to meet with your brethren in the church, tell them of the necessity of keeping open the channel of communication between God and the soul. Tell them that if they will find heart and voice to pray, God will find answers to their prayers.

Tell them not to neglect their religious duties. Exhort the brethren to pray. We must seek if we would find, we must ask if we would receive, we must knock if we would have the door opened unto us.—(*Signs of the Times,* February 10, 1890.)

In the service of the Jewish priesthood we are continually reminded of the sacrifice and intercession of Christ. All who come to Christ today are to remember that His merit is the incense that mingles with the prayers of those who repent of their sins and receive pardon and mercy and grace. Our need of Christ's intercession is constant. Day by day, morning and evening, the humble heart needs to offer up prayers to which will be returned answers of grace and peace and joy. "By him therefore let us offer the sacrifice of praise to God continually, that is, the fruit of our lips giving thanks to his name. But to do good and to communicate forget not: for with such sacrifice God is well pleased."—(*SDA Bible Commentary,* vol. 6, 1078.)

Like the patriarchs of old, those who profess to love God should erect an altar to the Lord wherever they pitch their tent. If ever there was a time when every house should be a house of prayer, it is now. Fathers and mothers should often lift up their hearts to God in humble supplication for themselves and their children. Let the father, as priest of the household, lay upon the altar of God the morning and evening sacrifice, while the wife and children unite in prayer and praise. In such a household Jesus will love to tarry.

From every Christian home a holy light should shine forth. Love should be revealed in action. It should flow out in all home intercourse, showing itself in thoughtful kindness, in gentle, unselfish courtesy. There are homes where this principle is carried out—homes where God is worshiped and truest love reigns. From these homes morning and evening prayer ascends to God as sweet incense, and His mercies and blessings descend upon the suppliants like the morning dew.—(*Patriarchs and Prophets,* 144.)

In following Christ, looking unto Him who is the Author And Finisher of your faith, you will feel that you are working under

His eye, that you are influenced by His presence, and that He knows your motives. At every step you will humbly inquire: Will this please Jesus? Will it glorify God? Morning and evening your earnest prayers should ascend to God for His blessing and guidance. True prayer takes hold upon Omnipotence and gives us the victory. Upon his knees the Christian obtains strength to resist temptation.—(*Testimonies for the Church,* vol. 4, 615, 616.)

As the priests morning and evening entered the holy place at the time of incense, the daily sacrifice was ready to be offered upon the altar in the court without. This was a time of intense interest to the worshipers who assembled at the tabernacle. Before entering into the presence of God through the ministration of the priest, they were to engage in earnest searching of heart and confession of sin. They united in silent prayer, with their faces toward the holy place. Thus their petitions ascended with the cloud of incense, while faith laid hold upon the merits of the promised Saviour prefigured by the atoning sacrifice. The hours appointed for the morning and the evening sacrifice were regarded as sacred, and they came to be observed as the set time for worship throughout the Jewish nation. And when in later times the Jews were scattered as captives in distant lands, they still at the appointed hour turned their faces toward Jerusalem and offered up their petitions to the God of Israel. In this custom Christians have an example for morning and evening prayer. While God condemns a mere round of ceremonies, without the spirit of worship, He looks with great pleasure upon those who love Him, bowing morning and evening to seek pardon for sins committed and to present their requests for needed blessings.—(*Patriarchs and Prophets,* 353, 354.)

PRAYER CONNECTS US TO HEAVEN.—Those who will put on the whole armor of God and devote some time every day to meditation and prayer and to the study of the Scriptures will be connected with heaven and will have a saving, transforming influence upon those around them. Great thoughts, noble aspirations, clear perceptions of truth and duty to God, will be theirs. They will be yearning for purity, for light, for love, for all the graces of heavenly birth. Their earnest prayers will enter into that within the veil. This class will have a sanctified boldness to come into the presence of the Infinite One. They will feel that heaven's light and glories are for them, and they will become refined, elevated, ennobled by this intimate acquaintance with God. Such is the privilege of true Christians.—(*Testimonies for the Church,* vol. 5, 112, 113.)

PRAYER TO BE FIRST ACTIVITY OF THE DAY.—Consecrate yourself to God in the morning; make this your very first work. Let your prayer be, "Take me, O Lord, as wholly Thine. I lay all my plans at Thy feet. Use me today in Thy service. Abide with me, and let all my work be wrought in Thee." This is a daily matter. Each morning consecrate yourself to God for that day. Surrender all your plans to Him, to be carried out or given up as His providence shall indicate. Thus day by day you may be giving your life into the hands of God, and thus your life will be molded more and more after the life of Christ.—(*Steps to Christ,* 70.)

The very first outbreathing of the soul in the morning should be for the presence of Jesus. "Without Me," He says, "ye can do nothing." It is Jesus that we need; His light, His life, His spirit, must be ours continually. We need Him every hour. And we should pray in the morning that as the sun illuminates the landscape, and fills the world with light, so the Sun of Righteousness may shine into the chambers of mind and heart, and make us all light in the Lord. We cannot do without His presence one moment. The enemy knows when we undertake to do without our Lord, and he is there, ready to fill our minds with his evil suggestions that we may fall from our steadfastness; but it is the desire of the Lord that from moment to moment we should abide in Him, and thus be complete in Him.—(*My Life Today,* 15.)

PRAYER IS A DUTY.—Nothing tends more to promote health of body and of soul than does a spirit of gratitude and praise. It is a positive duty to resist melancholy, discontented thoughts and feelings—as much a duty as it is to pray.—(*Ministry of Healing,* 251.)

PRAYER MOST NEEDED WHEN WE LEAST FEEL LIKE PRAYING.—When we feel the least inclined to commune with Jesus, let us pray the most. By so doing we shall break Satan's snare, the clouds of darkness will disappear, and we shall realize the sweet presence of Jesus.—(*Lift Him Up,* 372.)

DARKNESS ENCLOSES THOSE WHO NEGLECT PRAYER.—If the Saviour of men, the Son of God, felt the need of prayer, how much more should feeble, sinful mortals feel the necessity of fervent, constant prayer.

Our heavenly Father waits to bestow upon us the fullness of His blessing. It is our privilege to drink largely at the fountain of boundless love. What a wonder it is that we pray so little! God is ready and willing to hear the sincere prayer of the humblest of His children, and yet there is much manifest reluctance on our part to make known our wants to God. What can the angels of heaven think of poor helpless human beings, who are subject to temptation, when God's heart of infinite love yearns toward them, ready to give them more than they can ask or think, and yet they pray so little and have so little faith? The angels love to bow before God; they love to be near Him. They regard communion with God as their highest joy; and yet the children of earth, who need so much the help that God only can give, seem satisfied to walk without the light of His Spirit, the companionship of His presence.

The darkness of the evil one encloses those who neglect to pray. The whispered temptations of the enemy entice them to sin; and it is all because they do not make use of the privileges that God has given them in the divine appointment of prayer. Why should the sons and daughters of God be reluctant to pray, when prayer is the key in the hand of faith to unlock heaven's storehouse, where are treasured the boundless resources of Omnipotence?—(*Steps to Christ,* 93–95.)

AVOID NEGLECTING PRAYER.—Watch, brethren, the first dimming of your light, the first neglect of prayer, the first symptom of spiritual slumber.—(*Testimonies for the Church,* vol. 4, 124.)

You need to watch, lest the busy activities of life lead you to neglect prayer when you most need the strength prayer would give. Godliness is in danger of being crowded out of the soul through overdevotion to business. It is a great evil to defraud the soul of the strength and heavenly wisdom which are waiting your demand. You need that illumination which God alone can give. No one is fitted to transact his business unless he has this wisdom.—(*Testimonies for the Church,* vol. 5, 560.)

SATAN DECEIVES THOSE WHO DO NOT PRAY.—All who do not earnestly search the Scriptures and submit every desire and purpose of life to that unerring test, all who do not seek God in prayer for a knowledge of His will, will surely wander from the right path and fall under the deception of Satan.—(*Testimonies for the Church,* vol. 5, 192.)

TEMPTATION MAKES PRAYER A NECESSITY.—The strength acquired in prayer to God, united with individual effort in training the mind to thoughtfulness and caretaking, prepares the person for daily duties and keeps the spirit in peace under all circumstances, however trying. The temptations to which we are daily exposed make prayer a necessity. In order that we may be kept by the power of God through faith, the desires of the mind should be continually ascending in silent prayer for help, for light, for strength, for knowledge. But thought and prayer cannot take the place of earnest, faithful improvement of the time. Work and prayer are both required in perfecting Christian character.

We must live a twofold life—a life of thought and action, of silent prayer and earnest work. . . . God requires us to be living epistles, known and read of all men. The soul that turns to God for its strength, its support, its power, by daily, earnest prayer, will have noble aspirations, clear perceptions of truth and duty, lofty purposes of action, and a continual hungering and thirsting after righteousness.—(*God's Amazing Grace,* 317.)

PRAYER NEEDED NOW MORE THAN IN THE EARLY DAYS.—We must be much in prayer if we would make progress in the divine life. When the message of truth was first proclaimed, how much we prayed. How often was the voice of intercession heard in the chamber, in the barn, in the orchard, or the grove. Frequently we spent hours in earnest prayer, two or three together claiming the promise; often the sound of weeping was heard and then the voice of thanksgiving and the song of praise. Now the day of God is nearer than when we first believed, and we should be more earnest, more zealous, and fervent than in those early days. Our perils are greater now than then. Souls are more hardened. We need now to be imbued with the spirit of Christ, and we should not rest until we receive it.—(*Testimonies for the Church,* vol. 5, 161, 162.)

SEEK THE LORD WITH ALL THE HEART.—Our prayers should be full of tenderness and love. When we yearn for a deeper, broader realization of the Saviour's love, we shall cry to God for more wisdom. If ever there was a need of soul-stirring prayers and sermons, it is now. The end of all things is at hand. O that we could see as we should the necessity of seeking the Lord with all the heart! Then we should find Him. May God teach His people how to pray.—(*God's Amazing Grace,* 92.)

PRAYER IS NOT TIME WASTED.—Every morning take time to begin your work with prayer. Do not think this wasted time; it is time that will live through eternal ages. By this means success and spiritual victory will be brought in. The machinery will respond to the touch of the Master's hand. God's blessing is certainly worth asking for, and the work cannot be done aright unless the beginning is right. The hands of every worker must be strengthened, his heart must be purified, before the Lord can use him effectively.—(*Testimonies for the Church,* vol. 7, 194.)

FEW APPRECIATE THE PRIVILEGE OF PRAYER.—We should watch and work and pray as though this were the last day that would be granted us. How intensely earnest, then, would be our life. How closely would we follow Jesus in all our words and deeds.

There are few who rightly appreciate or improve the precious privilege of prayer. We should go to Jesus and tell Him all our needs. We may bring Him our little cares and perplexities as well as our greater troubles. Whatever arises to disturb or distress us, we should take it to the Lord in prayer. When we feel that we need the presence of Christ at every step, Satan will have little opportunity to intrude his temptations. It is his studied effort to keep us away from our best and most sympathizing friend. We should make no one our confidant but Jesus. We can safely commune with Him of all that is in our hearts.—(*Testimonies for the Church,* vol. 5, 200, 201.)

MORE PRAYER NEEDED AS THE END APPROACHES.—Confederacies will increase in number and power as we draw nearer to the end of time. These confederacies will create opposing influences to the truth, forming new parties of professed believers who will act out their own delusive theories. The apostasy will increase. "Some shall depart from the faith, giving heed to seducing spirits, and doctrines of devils" (1 Tim. 4:1). Men and women have confederated to oppose the Lord God of heaven, and the church is only half awake to the situation. There needs to be much more of prayer, much more of earnest effort, among professed believers.—(*Selected Messages,* bk. 2, 383.)

If there was ever a time when we should watch and pray in real earnest, it is now. There may be supposable things that appear as good things, and yet they need to be carefully considered with much prayer, for they are specious devices of the enemy to lead souls in a path which lies so close to the path of truth that it will be scarcely distinguishable from the path which leads to holiness and heaven. But the eye of faith may discern that it is diverging from the right path, though almost imperceptibly. At first it may be thought positively right, but after a while it is seen to be widely divergent from the path of safety, from the path which leads to holiness and heaven.—(*Testimonies to Ministers,* 229.)

VICTORY THROUGH DAILY PRAYER.—Through daily prayer to God, they will have wisdom and grace from Him to bear the conflicts and stern realities of life, and come off victorious. Fidelity, and serenity of mind, can only be retained by watchfulness and prayer.—(*Messages to Young People,* 80.)

VICTORY REQUIRES EARNEST PRAYER.—The victory is not won without much earnest prayer, without the humbling of self at every step. Our will is not to be forced into co-operation with divine agencies, but it must be voluntarily submitted.—(*Thoughts From the Mount of Blessing,* 142.)

WE MUST TAKE TIME TO PRAY.—We should now acquaint ourselves with God by proving His promises. Angels record every prayer that is earnest and sincere. We should rather dispense with selfish gratifications than neglect communion with God. The deepest poverty, the greatest self-denial, with His approval, is better than riches, honors, ease, and friendship without it. We must take time to pray.—(*The Great Controversy,* 622.)

SPEND MUCH TIME IN PRAYER.—Let much time be spent in prayer and close searching of the word. Let all obtain the real facts of faith in their own souls through belief that the Holy Spirit will be imparted to them because they have a real hungering and thirsting after righteousness. . . . Let there be more praying, believing, and receiving, and more working together with God.—(*Testimonies for the Church,* vol. 6, 65, 66.)

PRAY AS NEVER BEFORE.—Look unto Jesus in simplicity and faith. Gaze upon Jesus until the spirit faints under the excess of light. We do not half pray. We do not half believe. "Ask, and it shall be given you." Luke 11:9. Pray, believe, strengthen one another. Pray as you never before prayed that the Lord will lay His hand upon you, that you may be able to comprehend the length and breadth and depth and height, and to know the love of Christ, which passeth knowledge, that you may be filled with all the fullness of God.—(*Testimonies for the Church,* vol. 7, 214.)

Pray, yes, pray as you have never prayed before, that you may not be deluded by Satan's devices, that you may not be given up to a heedless, careless, vain spirit, and attend to religious duties to quiet your own conscience.—(*Testimonies for the Church,* vol. 2, 144.)

PRAY ALWAYS.—"Pray always;" that is, be ever in the spirit of prayer, and then you will be in readiness for your Lord's coming.—(*Testimonies for the Church,* vol. 5, 235.)

NEED OF MUCH PRAYER.—There is now need of much prayer. Christ commands, "Pray without ceasing;" that is, keep the mind uplifted to God, the source of all power and efficiency.—(*Testimonies to Ministers,* 510.)

ACTIVITY NO SUBSTITUTE FOR PRAYER.—As activity increases and men become successful in doing any work for God, there is danger of trusting to human plans and methods. There is a tendency to pray less, and to have less faith. Like the disciples, we are in danger of losing sight of our dependence on God, and seeking to make a savior of our activity. We need to look constantly to Jesus, realizing that it is His power which does the work. While we are to labor earnestly for the salvation of the lost, we must also take time for meditation, for prayer, and for the study of the word of God. Only the work accomplished with much prayer, and sanctified by the merit of Christ, will in the end prove to have been efficient for good.—(*The Desire of Ages,* 362.)

PRAYER NEEDED TO TAKE UNPOPULAR STANDS.—It takes moral courage, firmness, decision, perseverance, and very much prayer to step out on the unpopular side. We are thankful that we can come to Christ as the poor suffering ones came to Christ in the temple.—(*Evangelism,* 240).

PRAYER NEEDED TO DO GOD'S WORK.—Much prayer and the most vigorous exercise of the mind are necessary if we would be prepared to do the work which God would entrust to us. Many never attain to the position which they might occupy, because they wait for God to do for them that which He has given them power to do for themselves. All who are fitted for usefulness in this life must be trained by the severest mental and moral discipline, and then God will assist them by combining divine power with human effort.—(*Testimonies for the Church,* vol. 4, 611.)

PRAYER NEEDED TO UNDERSTAND TRUTH.—The themes of redemption are momentous themes, and only those who are spiritually minded can discern their depth and significance. It is our safety, our life, our joy, to dwell upon the truths of the plan of salvation. Faith and prayer are necessary in order that we may behold the deep things of God. Our minds are so bound about with narrow ideas, that we catch but limited views of the experience it is our privilege to have. How little do we comprehend what is meant by the prayer of the apostle, when he says, "That he would grant you, according to the riches of his glory, to be strengthened with might by his spirit in the inner man; that Christ may dwell in your hearts by faith; that ye, being rooted and grounded in love, may be able to comprehend with all saints what is the breadth, and length, and depth, and height; and to know the love of Christ, which passeth knowledge, that ye might be filled with all the fullness of God. Now unto him that is able to do exceeding abundantly above all that we ask or think, according to the power that worketh in us, unto him be glory in the church by Christ Jesus throughout all ages, world without end. Amen."—(*Review and Herald,* November 17, 1891.)

PRAYER NEEDED IN THE HOME.—Affection cannot be lasting, even in the home circle, unless there is a conformity of the will and disposition to the will of God. All the faculties and passions are to be brought into harmony with the attributes of Jesus Christ. If the father and mother in the love and fear of God unite their interests to have authority in the home, they will see the necessity of much prayer, much sober reflection. And as they seek God, their eyes will be opened to see heavenly messengers present to protect them in answer to the prayer of faith. They will overcome the weaknesses of their character and go on unto perfection.— (*The Adventist Home,* 315, 316.)

PRAYER NEEDED TO MAINTAIN CONNECTION WITH GOD.—Neglect the exercise of prayer, or engage in prayer spasmodically, now and then, as it is deemed convenient, and you lose your connection with God. The Christian life becomes dry, and the spiritual faculties have no vitality. The religious experience lacks health and vigor.—(*Signs of the Times,* July 31, 1893.)

PRAYER NEEDED FOR SPIRITUAL STRENGTH.—The reason why some are restless is, that they do not go to the only true source for happiness. They are ever trying to find out of Christ that enjoyment which is found alone in Him. In Him are no disappointed hopes. Oh how is the precious privilege of prayer neglected! The reading of the word of God prepares the mind for prayer. One of the greatest reasons why many have so little disposition to draw near to God by prayer is, that they have unfitted themselves for this sacred work by reading fascinating stories, which have excited the imagination and aroused unholy passions. The word of God becomes distasteful; the hour of prayer is not thought of. Prayer is the strength of the Christian. When alone, he is not alone; he feels the presence of One who has said, "Lo, I am with you alway."— (*Review and Herald,* March 11, 1880.)

PRAYER NEEDED TO ENTER HEAVEN.—There is no such thing as our entering the heavenly portals through indulgence and folly, amusement, selfishness, but only by constant watchfulness and unceasing prayer. Spiritual vigilance on our part individually is the price of safety. Swerve not to Satan's side a single inch, lest he gain advantage over you.—(*SDA Bible Commentary,* vol., 6, 1094.)

PRAYER KEEPS US FAITHFUL.—Without unceasing prayer and diligent watching, we are in danger of growing careless, and of deviating from the right path. The adversary seeks continually to obstruct the way to the mercy-seat, that we may not by earnest supplication and faith obtain grace and power to resist temptation.—(*Review and Herald,* December 8, 1904.)

PRAY FOR THE SPIRIT.—If we are to learn of Christ, we must pray as the apostles prayed when the Holy Spirit was poured upon them. We need a baptism of the Spirit of God. We are not safe for one hour while we are failing to render obedience to the Word of God.—(*Fundamentals of Christian Education,* 537.)

WEAKNESS TURNED TO STRENGTH THROUGH PRAYER.—They [many of God's people] do not see the importance of self-knowledge and self-control. They do not watch and pray, lest they enter into temptation. If they would watch, they would become acquainted with their weak points, where they are most likely to be assailed by temptation. With watchfulness and prayer their weakest points can be so guarded as to become their strongest points, and they can encounter temptation without being overcome. Every follower of Christ should daily examine himself, that he may become perfectly acquainted with his own conduct.—(*Testimonies for the Church,* vol. 2, 511.)

PRAY IN ALL CIRCUMSTANCES.—In your business, in companionship for leisure hours, and in alliance for life, let all the associations you form be entered upon with earnest, humble prayer. You will thus show that you honor God, and God will honor you. Pray when you are fainthearted. When you are desponding, close the lips firmly to men; do not shadow the path of others; but tell everything to Jesus. Reach up your hands for help. In your weakness lay hold of infinite strength. Ask for humility, wisdom, courage, increase of faith, that you may see light in God's light and rejoice in His love.—(*The Ministry of Healing,* 513.)

3

God Hears Prayer

GOD HEARS THE PRAYER OF THE HUMBLE.—Our heavenly Father waits to bestow upon us the fullness of His blessing. It is our privilege to drink largely at the fountain of boundless love. What a wonder it is that we pray so little! God is ready and willing to hear the sincere prayer of the humblest of His children, and yet there is much manifest reluctance on our part to make known our wants to God. What can the angels of heaven think of poor helpless human beings, who are subject to temptation, when God's heart of infinite love yearns toward them, ready to give them more than they can ask or think, and yet they pray so little and have so little faith? The angels love to bow before God; they love to be near Him. They regard communion with God as their highest joy; and yet the children of earth, who need so much the help that God only can give, seem satisfied to walk without the light of His Spirit, the companionship of His presence.—(*Steps to Christ,* 94.)

Those who have a humble, trusting, contrite heart, God accepts, and hears their prayer; and when God helps, all obstacles will be overcome. How many men of great natural abilities and high scholarships have failed when placed in positions of responsibility, while those of feebler intellect, with less favorable surroundings, have been wonderfully successful. The secret was: The former trusted to themselves, while the latter united with Him who is wonderful in counsel and mighty in working to accomplish what He will.—(*Testimonies for the Church,* vol. 4, 538, 539.)

GOD HEARS AND ANSWERS PRAYER.—God hears prayer. Christ has said, "If ye shall ask anything in My name, I will do it." Again He says, "If any man serve Me, him will My Father honor." John 14:14; 12: 26. If we live according to His word, every precious promise He has given will be fulfilled to us. We are undeserving of His mercy, but as we give ourselves to Him, He receives us. He will work for and through those who follow Him.—(*Ministry of Healing,* 226, 227.)

The Lord will certainly hear and answer the prayers of His workers if they will seek Him for counsel and instruction.—(*Evangelism,* 399.)

God hears the prayers of all who seek Him in truth. He has the power that we all need. He fills the heart with love, and joy, and peace, and holiness.—(*Testimonies for the Church,* vol. 9, 169.)

I saw that every prayer which is sent up in faith from an honest heart will be heard of God and answered, and the one that sent up the petition will have the blessing when he needs it most, and it will often exceed his expectations. Not a prayer of a true saint is lost if sent up in faith from an honest heart.—(*Testimonies for the Church,* vol. 1, 121.)

GOD LISTENS TO EVERY PRAYER.—The infinite God, said Jesus, makes it your privilege to approach Him by the name of Father. Understand all that this implies. No earthly parent ever pleaded so earnestly with an erring child as He who made you pleads with the transgressor. No human, loving interest ever followed the impenitent with such tender invitations. God dwells in every abode; He hears every word that is spoken, listens to every prayer that is offered, tastes the sorrows and disappointments of every soul, regards the treatment given to father, mother, sister, friend, and neighbor. He cares for our necessities, and His love and mercy and grace are continually flowing to satisfy our need.—(*Signs of the Times,* October 28, 1903.)

GOD HEARS EVERY SINCERE PRAYER.—The Bible shows us God in His high and holy place, not in a state of inactivity, not in silence and solitude, but surrounded by ten thousand times ten thousand and thousands of thousands of holy intelligences, all waiting to do His will. Through channels which we cannot discern He is in active communication with every part of His dominion. But it is in this speck of a world, in the souls that He gave His only-begotten Son to save, that His interest and the interest of all heaven is centered. God is bending from His throne to hear the cry of the oppressed. To every sincere prayer He answers, "Here am I." He uplifts the distressed and downtrodden. In all our afflictions He is afflicted. In every temptation and every trial the angel of His presence is near to deliver.—(*The Desire of Ages,* 356.)

As yet the disciples were unacquainted with the Saviour's unlimited resources and power. He said to them, "Hitherto have ye asked nothing in My name." John 16:24. He explained that the secret of their success would be in asking for strength and grace in His name. He would be present before the Father to make request for them. The prayer of the humble suppliant He presents as His own desire in that soul's behalf. Every sincere prayer is heard in heaven. It may not be fluently expressed; but if the heart is in it, it will ascend to the sanctuary where Jesus ministers, and He will present it to the Father without one awkward, stammering word, beautiful and fragrant with the incense of His own perfection.

The path of sincerity and integrity is not a path free from obstruction, but in every difficulty we are to see a call to prayer.

There is no one living who has any power that he has not received from God, and the source whence it comes is open to the weakest human being. "Whatsoever ye shall ask in My name," said Jesus, "that will I do, that the Father may be glorified in the Son. If ye shall ask anything in My name, I will do it."

"In My name," Christ bade His disciples pray. In Christ's name His followers are to stand before God. Through the value of the sacrifice made for them, they are of value in the Lord's sight. Because of the imputed righteousness of Christ they are accounted precious. For Christ's sake the Lord pardons those that fear Him. He does not see in them the vileness of the sinner. He recognizes in them the likeness of His Son, in whom they believe.—(*The Desire of Ages*, 667.)

NO SINCERE PRAYER IS LOST.—Make your requests known to your Maker. Never is one repulsed who comes to Him with a contrite heart. Not one sincere prayer is lost. Amid the anthems of the celestial choir, God hears the cries of the weakest human being. We pour out our heart's desire in our closets, we breathe a prayer as we walk by the way, and our words reach the throne of the Monarch of the universe. They may be inaudible to any human ear, but they cannot die away into silence, nor can they be lost through the activities of business that are going on. Nothing can drown the soul's desire. It rises above the din of the street, above the confusion of the multitude, to the heavenly courts. It is God to whom we are speaking, and our prayer is heard. You who feel the most unworthy, fear not to commit your case to God.—(*In Heavenly Places*, 82.)

GOD HEARS JESUS' INTERCESSION MINGLED WITH OUR PRAYERS.—Christ has pledged Himself to be our substitute and surety, and He neglects no one. There is an inexhaustible fund of perfect obedience accruing from His obedience. In heaven His merits, His self-denial and self-sacrifice, are treasured as incense to be offered up with the prayers of His people. As the sinner's sincere, humble prayers ascend to the throne of God, Christ mingles with them the merits of His own life of perfect obedience. Our prayers are made fragrant by this incense. Christ has pledged Himself to intercede in our behalf, and the Father always hears His Son.—(*Sons and Daughters of God,* 22.)

GOD ALWAYS RESPONDS, THOUGH WE MAY NOT REALIZE IT.—If we come to God, feeling helpless and dependent, as we really are, and in humble, trusting faith make known our wants to Him whose knowledge is infinite, who sees everything in creation, and who governs everything by His will and word, He can and will attend to our cry, and will let light shine into our hearts. Through sincere prayer we are brought into connection with the mind of the Infinite. We may have no remarkable evidence at the time that the face of our Redeemer is bending over us in compassion and love, but this is even so. We may not feel His visible touch, but His hand is upon us in love and pitying tenderness.—(*Steps to Christ,* 97.)

GOD'S ANSWERS ARE NOT ALWAYS WHAT WE EXPECT.—Ask, then; ask, and ye shall receive. Ask for humility, wisdom, courage, increase of faith. To every sincere prayer an answer will come. It may not come just as you desire, or at the time you look for it; but it will come in the way and at the time that will best meet your need. The prayers you offer in loneliness, in weariness, in trial, God answers, not always according to your expectations, but always for your good.—(*Messages to Young People,* 250.)

GOD HEARS PRAYERS FOR THE CONVERSION OF SOULS.—When those who know the truth practice the self-denial enjoined in God's word, the message will go with power. The Lord will hear our prayers for the conversion of souls. God's people will let their light shine forth, and unbelievers, seeing their good works, will glorify our heavenly Father.—(*Counsels on Stewardship,* 302.)

BELIEVE THAT GOD HEARS YOUR PRAYERS.—The people of God must move understandingly. They should not be satisfied until every known sin is confessed; then it is their privilege and duty to believe that Jesus accepts them. They must not wait for others to press through the darkness and obtain the victory for them to enjoy. Such enjoyment will last only till the meeting closes. But God must be served from principle instead of from feeling. Morning and night obtain the victory for yourselves in your own family. Let not your daily labor keep you from this. Take time to pray, and as you pray, believe that God hears you. Have faith mixed with your prayers. You may not at all times feel the immediate answer; but then it is that faith is tried. You are proved to see whether you will trust in God, whether you have living, abiding faith. "Faithful is He that calleth you, who also will do it." Walk the narrow plank of faith. Trust all on the promises of the Lord. Trust God in darkness. That is the time to have faith. But you often let feeling govern you. You look for worthiness in yourselves when you do not feel comforted by the Spirit of God, and despair because you cannot find it. You do not trust enough in Jesus, precious Jesus. You do not make His worthiness to be all, all. The very best you can do will not merit the favor of God. It is Jesus' worthiness that will save you, His blood that will cleanse you. But you have efforts to make. You must do what you can on your part. Be zealous and repent, then believe.—(*Testimonies for the Church,* vol. 1, 167.)

4

Prayer and Soul Winning

PRAYER AN IMPORTANT PART OF SUCCESS IN SOUL WINNING.—If the members of the churches would but put to work the powers of mind that they have, in well-directed efforts, in well-matured plans, they might do a hundredfold more for Christ than they are now doing. If they went forth with earnest prayer, with meekness and lowliness of heart, seeking, personally to impart to others the knowledge of salvation, the message might reach the inhabitants of the earth.—(*Review and Herald,* April 11, 1893).

We are to come to God in faith, and pour out our supplications before Him, believing that He will work in our behalf, and in behalf of those we are seeking to save. We are to devote more time to earnest prayer.—(*SDA Bible Commentary,* vol. 3, 1146, 1147.)

Select another and still another soul, daily seeking guidance from God, laying everything before Him in earnest prayer, and working in divine wisdom. As you do this, you will see that God will give the Holy Spirit to convict, and the power of truth to convert, the soul.—(*Medical Ministry,* 245).

Bear in mind that the success of reproof depends greatly upon the spirit in which it is given. Do not neglect earnest prayer that you may possess a lowly mind, and that angels of God may go before you to work upon the hearts you are trying to reach, and so soften them by heavenly impressions that your efforts may avail. —(*Testimonies for the Church,* vol. 2, 53.)

If several should meet together with one accord, with hearts burdened for perishing souls, and should offer earnest, fervent prayers, they would prove effectual.—(*Review and Herald,* August 23, 1892.)

PRAYING FOR SOULS WILL BRING US CLOSER TO GOD.—As we seek to win others to Christ, bearing the burden of souls in our prayers, our own hearts will throb with the quickening influence of God's grace; our own affections will glow with more divine fervor; our whole Christian life will be more of a reality, more earnest, more prayerful.—(*Christ's Object Lessons,* 354).

When self dies, there will be awakened an intense desire for the salvation of others,—a desire which will lead to persevering efforts to do good. There will be a sowing beside all waters; and earnest supplication, importunate prayers, will enter heaven in behalf of perishing souls.—(*Gospel Workers,* 470).

COME TOGETHER TO PRAY FOR THE CONVERSION OF SOULS.—If in one place there are only two or three who know the truth, let them form themselves into a band of workers. Let them keep their bond of union unbroken, pressing together in love and unity, encouraging one another to advance, each gaining courage and strength from the assistance of the others. . . . As they work and pray in Christ's name, their numbers will increase.—(*Testimonies for the Church,* vol. 7, 21.)

Let the Los Angeles church have special seasons of prayer daily for the work that is being done. The blessing of the Lord will come to the church members who thus participate in the work, gathering in small groups daily to pray for its success. Thus the believers will obtain grace for themselves, and the work of the Lord will be advanced.—(*Evangelism*, 111, 112.)

We should hold convocations for prayer, asking the Lord to open the way for the truth to enter the strongholds where Satan has set up his throne, and dispel the shadow he has cast athwart the pathway of those who he is seeking to deceive and destroy. —(*Testimonies for the Church*, vol. 6, 80.)

Oh, that the earnest prayer of faith may arise everywhere, Give me souls buried now in the rubbish of error, or I die! Bring them to the knowledge of the truth as it is in Jesus.—(*This Day With God*, 171).

EVERYONE CAN PRAY FOR SOULS.—Not all are called to personal labor in foreign fields, but all can do something by their prayers and their gifts to aid the missionary work.—(*Testimonies for the Church*, vol. 6, 29.)

Brethren and sisters, have you forgotten that your prayers should go out, like sharp sickles, with the laborers in the great harvest field?—(*Testimonies for the Church*, vol. 3, 162.)

Let those who are spiritual converse with these souls. Pray with and for them. Let much time be spent in prayer and close searching of the word. Let all obtain the real facts of faith in their own souls through belief that the Holy Spirit will be imparted to them because they have a real hungering and thirsting after righteousness.—(*Testimonies for the Church*, vol. 6, 65.)

When the gospel net is cast, let there be a watching by the net, with tears and earnest prayer. Let the workers determine not to become discouraged; and not to let go the net until it is drawn ashore, with the fruit of their labor.—(*Signs of the Times,* March 16, 1882.)

How can we honor God, how can we vindicate His word, unless we are much in prayer appealing to Him to manifest His power in behalf of the perishing?—(*Review and Herald,* August 23, 1892.)

PERSONAL SOULWINNING EFFORTS MADE SUCCESSFUL BY PRAYER.— I determined that my efforts should never cease till these dear souls, for whom I had so great an interest, yielded to God. Several entire nights were spent by me in earnest prayer for those whom I had sought out and brought together for the purpose of laboring and praying with them. . . .

At every one of our little meetings I continued to exhort and pray for each one separately, until every one had yielded to Jesus, acknowledging the merits of His pardoning love. Every one was converted to God.—(*Testimonies for the Church,* vol. 1, 33, 34.)

PRAYER FOR SOULS TAKES THE MIND FROM ITS OWN SMALL CON- CERNS.—Solicit prayer for the souls for whom you labor; present them before the church as objects for the supplication. It will be just what the church needs, to have their minds called from their little, petty difficulties, to feel a great burden, a personal inter- est, for a soul that is ready to perish.—(*Medical Ministry,* 244, 245.)

PRAY FOR GREATER EFFICIENCY IN SOUL WINNING.—Oh, let it be seen, my brethren, that Jesus is abiding in the heart, sustaining, strengthening, comforting. It is your privilege to be endowed, from day to day, with a rich measure of His Holy Spirit, and to have broadened views of the importance and scope of the message we are proclaiming to the world. The Lord is willing to reveal to you won- drous things out of His law. Wait before Him with humility of heart.

Pray most earnestly for an understanding of the times in which we live, for a fuller conception of His purpose, and for increased efficiency in soul saving.—(*Testimonies to Ministers,* 513, 514.)

There are many souls yearning unutterably for light, for assurance and strength beyond what they have been able to grasp. They need to be sought out and labored for patiently, perseveringly. Beseech the Lord in fervent prayer for help. Present Jesus because you know Him as your personal Saviour. Let His melting love, His rich grace, flow forth from human lips. You need not present doctrinal points unless questioned. But take the Word, and with tender, yearning love for souls, show them the precious righteousness of Christ, to whom you and they must come to be saved.—(*Evangelism,* 442.)

The disciples prayed with intense earnestness for a fitness to meet men and in their daily intercourse to speak words that would lead sinners to Christ. Putting away all differences, all desire for the supremacy, they came close together in Christian fellowship. They drew nearer and nearer to God, and as they did this they realized what a privilege had been theirs in being permitted to associate so closely with Christ. Sadness filled their hearts as they thought of how many times they had grieved Him by their slowness of comprehension, their failure to understand the lessons that, for their good, He was trying to teach them.

These days of preparation were days of deep heart searching. The disciples felt their spiritual need and cried to the Lord for the holy unction that was to fit them for the work of soul saving. They did not ask for a blessing for themselves merely. They were weighted with the burden of the salvation of souls. They realized that the gospel was to be carried to the world, and they claimed the power that Christ had promised.—(*Acts of the Apostles,* 37.)

MUCH PRAYER IS NEEDED TO KNOW HOW TO APPROACH INDIVIDUALS WITH TRUTH.—It is not everyone who can labor judiciously for the salvation of souls. There is much close thinking to be done. We must not enter into the Lord's work haphazard and expect success. The Lord needs men of mind, men of thought. Jesus calls for co-workers, not blunderers. God wants right-thinking and intelligent men to do the great work necessary to the salvation of souls.

Mechanics, lawyers, merchants, men of all trades and professions, educate themselves that they may become masters of their business. Should the followers of Christ be less intelligent, and while professedly engaged in His service be ignorant of the ways and means to be employed? The enterprise of gaining everlasting life is above every earthly consideration. In order to lead souls to Jesus there must be a knowledge of human nature and a study of the human mind. Much careful thought and fervent prayer are required to know how to approach men and women upon the great subject of truth.—(*Testimonies for the Church*, vol. 4, 67.)

PRAYER ACCOMPLISHES MORE IN SOUL WINNING THAN WORDS ALONE.—Satan is on your track. He is an artful opponent, and the malignant spirit which you meet in your work is inspired by him. Those whom he controls echo his words. If the veil could be rent away from their eyes, those thus worked would see Satan plying all his arts to win them from the truth. In rescuing souls from his devices, far more will be accomplished by Christlike, humble prayer than by many words without prayer.—(*Colporteur Ministry*, 81.)

God calls for modest, quiet, sober-minded youth, and men of mature age, who are well balanced with principle, who can pray as well as talk, who will rise up before the aged, and treat gray hairs with respect.

The cause of God is suffering for want of laborers of understanding and mental power. My brethren and sisters, the Lord has blessed you with intellectual faculties capable of vast improvement. Cultivate your talents with persevering earnestness. Train and discipline the mind by study, by observation, by reflection. You cannot meet the mind of God unless you put to use every power. The mental faculties will strengthen and develop if you will go to work in the fear of God, in humility, and with earnest prayer. A resolute purpose will accomplish wonders. Be open, firm, decided Christians. Exalt Jesus, talk of His love, tell of His power, and thus let your light shine forth to the world.—(*Life Sketches*, 275.)

PRAY FOR SOULS.—Begin to pray for souls; come near to Christ, close to His bleeding side. Let a meek and quiet spirit adorn your lives, and let your earnest, broken, humble petitions ascend to Him for wisdom that you may have success in saving not only your own soul, but the souls of others. Pray more than you sing. Do you not stand in greater need of prayer than of singing? Young men and women, God calls upon you to work, work for Him. Make an entire change in your course of action. You can do work that those who minister in word and doctrine cannot do. You can reach a class whom the minister cannot affect.—(*Testimonies for the Church*, vol. 1, 513.)

Let us also pray earnestly in behalf of those whom we expect to visit, by living faith bringing them, one by one, into the presence of God.—(*Christian Service*, 169.)

Work among the lowly, the poor, and the oppressed. We should pray for and with the helpless ones who have not strength of will to control the appetites that passion has degraded. Earnest, persevering effort must be made for the salvation of those in whose hearts an interest is awakened.—(*Testimonies for the Church*, vol. 6, 84.)

5

God's Promises Concerning Prayer

GOD PROMISES TO HEAR AND ANSWER PRAYER.—Christ is the connecting link between God and man. He has promised His personal intercession by employing His name. He places the whole virtue of His righteousness on the side of the suppliant. Christ pleads for man, and man, in need of divine help, pleads for himself in the presence of God, using the power of the influence of the One who gave His life for the world. As we acknowledge before God our appreciation of Christ's merits, fragrance is given to our intercessions. Oh, who can value this great mercy and love! As we approach God through the virtue of Christ's merits, we are clothed with His priestly vestments. He places us close by His side, encircling us with His human arm, while with His divine arm He grasps the throne of the Infinite. He puts His merits, as sweet incense, in a censer in our hands, in order to encourage our petitions. He promises to hear and answer our supplications.—(*SDA Bible Commentary,* vol. 6, 1078.)

The simple prayers indited by the Holy Spirit will ascend through the gates ajar, the open door which Christ has declared: I have opened, and no man can shut. These prayers, mingled with the incense of the perfection of Christ, will ascend as fragrance to the Father, and answers will come.—(*Testimonies for the Church,* vol. 6, 467.)

I saw that every prayer which is sent up in faith from an honest heart will be heard of God and answered, and the one that sent up the petition will have the blessing when he needs it most, and it will often exceed his expectations. Not a prayer of a true saint is lost if sent up in faith from an honest heart.—(*Testimonies for the Church,* vol. 1, 121.)

To pray as Nehemiah prayed in his hour of need is a resource at the command of the Christian under circumstances when other forms of prayer may be impossible. Toilers in the busy walks of life, crowded and almost overwhelmed with perplexity, can send up a petition to God for divine guidance. Travelers by sea and land, when threatened with some great danger, can thus commit themselves to Heaven's protection. In times of sudden difficulty or peril the heart may send up its cry for help to One who has pledged Himself to come to the aid of His faithful, believing ones whenever they call upon Him. In every circumstance, under every condition, the soul weighed down with grief and care, or fiercely assailed by temptation, may find assurance, support, and succor in the unfailing love and power of a covenant-keeping God.—(*Prophets and Kings,* 631, 632.)

IF WE ASK, GOD WILL ANSWER.—It is a part of God's plan to grant us, in answer to the prayer of faith, that which He would not bestow did we not thus ask.—(*The Great Controversy,* 525.)

God hears prayer. Christ has said, "If ye shall ask anything in My name, I will do it." Again He says, "If any man serve Me, him will My Father honor." John 14:14; 12:26. If we live according to His word, every precious promise He has given will be fulfilled to us. We are undeserving of His mercy, but as we give ourselves to Him, He receives us. He will work for and through those who follow Him.—(*Ministry of Healing*, 226, 227.)

As you ask the Lord to help you, honor your Saviour by believing that you do receive His blessing. All power, all wisdom, are at our command. We have only to ask.—(*Ministry of Healing*, 514.)

God has a heaven full of blessings that He wants to bestow on those who are earnestly seeking for that help which the Lord alone can give.—(*Sons and Daughters of God*, 123.)

JESUS PRESENTS OUR POORLY-WORDED PRAYERS TO THE FATHER.— Every sincere prayer is heard in heaven. It may not be fluently expressed; but if the heart is in it, it will ascend to the sanctuary where Jesus ministers, and He will present it to the Father without one awkward, stammering word, beautiful and fragrant with the incense of His own perfection.—(*The Desire of Ages*, 667.)

STRENGTH TO OVERCOME TEMPTATION GIVEN TO THOSE WHO PRAY.—All are accountable for their actions while in this world upon probation. All have power to control their actions if they will. If they are weak in virtue and purity of thoughts and acts, they can obtain help from the Friend of the helpless. Jesus is acquainted with all the weaknesses of human nature, and, if entreated, will give strength to overcome the most powerful temptations. All can obtain this strength if they seek for it in humility.— (*Child Guidance*, 466, 467.)

GOD ANSWERS OUR PRAYERS WHEN AND HOW HE SEES BEST.— Every saint who comes to God with a true heart, and sends his honest petitions to Him in faith, will have his prayers answered. Your faith must not let go of the promises of God, if you do not see or feel the immediate answer to your prayers. Be not afraid to trust God. Rely upon His sure promise: "Ask, and ye shall receive." God is too wise to err, and too good to withhold any good thing from His saints that walk uprightly. Man is erring, and although his petitions are sent up from an honest heart, he does not always ask for the things that are good for himself, or that will glorify God. When this is so, our wise and good Father hears our prayers, and will answer, sometimes immediately; but He gives us the things that are for our best good and His own glory. God gives us blessings; if we could look into His plan, we would clearly see that He knows what is best for us and that our prayers are answered. Nothing hurtful is given, but the blessing we need, in the place of something we asked for that would not be good for us, but to our hurt.

I saw that if we do not feel immediate answers to our prayers, we should hold fast our faith, not allowing distrust to come in, for that will separate us from God. If our faith wavers, we shall receive nothing from Him. Our confidence in God should be strong; and when we need it most, the blessing will fall upon us like a shower of rain.—(*Testimonies for the Church*, vol. 1, 120, 121.)

GOD SUPPLIES WISDOM IN ANSWER TO PRAYER.—The Lord has given us the promise, "If any of you lack wisdom, let him ask of God, that giveth to all men liberally, and upbraideth not; and it shall be given him." It is in the order of God that those who bear responsibilities should often meet together to counsel with one another, and to pray earnestly for that wisdom which He alone can impart. Unitedly make known your troubles to God. Talk less; much precious time is lost in talk that brings no light. Let brethren unite in fasting and prayer for the wisdom that God has promised to supply liberally.—(*Testimonies to Ministers*, 499.)

CHRIST'S GRACE IS AVAILABLE EVEN BEFORE WE PRAY.—Even before the prayer is uttered, . . . grace from Christ goes forth to meet the grace that is working upon the human soul.—(*Christ's Object Lessons*, 206.)

W<small>E MAY CLAIM</small> H<small>IS PROMISES BOLDLY.</small>—"If ye abide in me, and my words abide in you, ye shall ask what ye will, and it shall be done unto you." When you pray, present this promise. It is our privilege to come to Him with holy boldness. As in sincerity we ask Him to let His light shine upon us, He will hear and answer us. But we must live in harmony with our prayers. They are of no avail if we walk contrary to them. I have seen a father who, after reading a portion of scripture and offering prayer, would often, almost as soon as he had risen from his knees, begin to scold his children. How could God answer the prayer he had offered? And if, after scolding his children, a father offers prayer, does that prayer benefit the children? No; not unless it is a prayer of confession to God.—(*Child Guidance,* 499.)

A<small>NGELS WILL ASSIST US IN ANSWER TO PRAYER.</small>—When about to speak passionately, close your mouth. Don't utter a word. Pray before you speak, and heavenly angels will come to your assistance and drive back the evil angels, who would lead you to dishonor God, reproach His cause, and weaken your own soul.—(*Testimonies for the Church,* vol. 2, 82.)

A<small>NGELS WILL COME TO OUR SIDE IN ANSWER TO PRAYER.</small>—The guardianship of the heavenly host is granted to all who will work in God's ways and follow His plans. We may in earnest, contrite prayer call the heavenly helpers to our side. Invisible armies of light and power will work with the humble, meek, and lowly one.—(*Selected Messages,* bk. 1, 97.)

T<small>HE GOSPEL WILL MAKE RAPID PROGRESS AS A RESULT OF PRAYER.</small>—God would work mightily for His people today if they would place themselves wholly under His guidance. They need the constant abiding of the Holy Spirit. If there were more prayer in the councils of those bearing responsibilities, more humbling of the heart before God, we should see abundant evidence of divine leadership, and our work would make rapid progress.—(*Testimonies for the Church,* vol. 8, 238.)

PRAYER WILL BRING POWER TO OVERCOME.—We must have on the whole armor of God and be ready at any moment for a conflict with the powers of darkness. When temptations and trials rush in upon us, let us go to God and agonize with Him in prayer. He will not turn us away empty, but will give us grace and strength to overcome, and to break the power of the enemy.—(*Early Writings,* 46.)

BLESSINGS WILL BE PROPORTIONATE TO OUR FAITH.—Pray in faith. And be sure to bring your lives into harmony with your petitions, that you may receive the blessings for which you pray. Let not your faith weaken, for the blessings received are proportionate to the faith exercised. "According to your faith be it unto you." "All things, whatsoever ye shall ask in prayer, believing, ye shall receive." Matthew 9:29; 21:22. Pray, believe, rejoice. Sing praises to God because He has answered your prayers. Take Him at His word. "He is faithful that promised." Hebrews 10:23. Not one sincere supplication is lost. The channel is open; the stream is flowing. It carries with it healing properties, pouring forth a restoring current of life and health and salvation. —(*Testimonies for the Church,* vol. 7, 274.)

6

The Prayer of Faith

PRAYER IS HEAVEN'S MEANS OF SUCCESS IN OVERCOMING SIN.—
There are many who, though striving to obey God's commandments, have little peace or joy. This lack in their experience is the
result of a failure to exercise faith. They walk as it were in a salt
land, a parched wilderness. They claim little, when they might
claim much; for there is no limit to the promises of God. Such
ones do not correctly represent the sanctification that comes
through obedience to the truth. The Lord would have all His sons
and daughters happy, peaceful, and obedient. Through the exercise of faith the believer comes into possession of these blessings.
Through faith, every deficiency of character may be supplied, every defilement cleansed, every fault corrected, every excellence
developed.

Prayer is heaven's ordained means of success in the conflict
with sin and the development of Christian character. The divine
influences that come in answer to the prayer of faith will accomplish in the soul of the suppliant all for which he pleads. For the
pardon of sin, for the Holy Spirit, for a Christlike temper, for
wisdom and strength to do His work, for any gift He has prom-

ised, we may ask; and the promise is, "Ye shall receive."—(*The Acts of the Apostles,* 563, 564.)

GOD LONGS TO DO GREAT THINGS FOR US.—Our part is to pray and believe. Watch unto prayer. Watch, and co-operate with the prayer-hearing God. Bear in mind that "we are labourers together with God." 1 Cor. 3:9. Speak and act in harmony with your prayers. It will make an infinite difference with you whether trial shall prove your faith to be genuine, or show that your prayers are only a form.

When perplexities arise, and difficulties confront you, look not for help to humanity. Trust all with God. The practice of telling our difficulties to others only makes us weak, and brings no strength to them. It lays upon them the burden of our spiritual infirmities, which they cannot relieve. We seek the strength of erring, finite man, when we might have the strength of the unerring, infinite God.

You need not go to the ends of the earth for wisdom, for God is near. It is not the capabilities you now possess or ever will have that will give you success. It is that which the Lord can do for you. We need to have far less confidence in what man can do and far more confidence in what God can do for every believing soul. He longs to have you reach after Him by faith. He longs to have you expect great things from Him. He longs to give you understanding in temporal as well as in spiritual matters. He can sharpen the intellect. He can give tact and skill. Put your talents into the work, ask God for wisdom, and it will be given you.—(*Christ's Object Lessons,* 146.)

PRAYER AND FAITH WILL DO WONDERFUL THINGS.—I fear that there is not that faith that is essential. Shall we not brace ourselves against disappointments and temptations to be discouraged? God is merciful, and with the truth rejoicing, purifying, ennobling the life, we can do a sound and solid work for God. Prayer and faith will do wonderful things. The Word must be our weapon of warfare. Miracles can be wrought through the Word; for it is profitable for all things.—(*Evangelism,* 489.)

FAITH TO BE MIXED WITH OUR PRAYERS.—The people of God must move understandingly. They should not be satisfied until every known sin is confessed; then it is their privilege and duty to believe that Jesus accepts them. They must not wait for others to press through the darkness and obtain the victory for them to enjoy. Such enjoyment will last only till the meeting closes. But God must be served from principle instead of from feeling. Morning and night obtain the victory for yourselves in your own family. Let not your daily labor keep you from this. Take time to pray, and as you pray, believe that God hears you. Have faith mixed with your prayers. You may not at all times feel the immediate answer; but then it is that faith is tried. You are proved to see whether you will trust in God, whether you have living, abiding faith. "Faithful is He that calleth you, who also will do it." Walk the narrow plank of faith. Trust all on the promises of the Lord. Trust God in darkness. That is the time to have faith. But you often let feeling govern you. You look for worthiness in yourselves when you do not feel comforted by the Spirit of God, and despair because you cannot find it. You do not trust enough in Jesus, precious Jesus. You do not make His worthiness to be all, all. The very best you can do will not merit the favor of God. It is Jesus' worthiness that will save you, His blood that will cleanse you. But you have efforts to make. You must do what you can on your part. Be zealous and repent, then believe.

Confound not faith and feeling together. They are distinct. Faith is ours to exercise. This faith we must keep in exercise. Believe, believe. Let your faith take hold of the blessing, and it is yours. Your feelings have nothing to do with this faith. When faith brings the blessing to your heart, and you rejoice in the blessing, it is no more faith, but feeling.—(*Testimonies for the Church,* vol. 1, 167.)

PRAYER AND FAITH LAY HOLD OF GOD'S POWER.—True faith and true prayer—how strong they are! They are as two arms by which the human suppliant lays hold upon the power of Infinite Love.

Faith is trusting in God,—believing that He loves us, and knows what is for our best good. Thus, instead of our own way, it leads us to choose His way. In place of our ignorance, it accepts His wisdom; in place of our weakness, His strength; in place of our sinfulness, His righteousness. Our lives, ourselves, are already His; faith acknowledges His ownership, and accepts its blessings. Truth, uprightness, purity, are pointed out as secrets of life's success. It is faith that puts us in possession of these. Every good impulse or aspiration is the gift of God; faith receives from God the life that alone can produce true growth and efficiency.—(*Gospel Workers,* 259.)

OUR LIVES ARE TO BE IN HARMONY WITH OUR PETITIONS.—Pray in faith. And be sure to bring your lives into harmony with your petitions, that you may receive the blessings for which you pray. Let not your faith weaken, for the blessings received are proportionate to the faith exercised. "According to your faith be it unto you." "All things, whatsoever ye shall ask in prayer, believing, ye shall receive." Matthew 9:29; 21:22. Pray, believe, rejoice. Sing praises to God because He has answered your prayers. Take Him at His word. "He is faithful that promised." Hebrews 10:23. Not one sincere supplication is lost. The channel is open; the stream is flowing. It carries with it healing properties, pouring forth a restoring current of life and health and salvation. —(*Testimonies for the Church,* vol. 7, 274.)

GOD ACCEPTS THE PRAYER OF FAITH.—The humble, intelligent prayer of faith, that comes from unfeigned lips, is wholly acceptable to God. It is the heart-felt prayer that is heard in heaven and rewarded by an answer on earth. "But to this man will I look, even to him that is poor, and of a contrite spirit, and that trembleth at my word." "For thus saith the high and lofty One, that inhabiteth eternity, whose name is Holy; I dwell in the high and holy place, with him also that is of a contrite and a humble spirit, to revive the spirit of the humble, and to revive the heart of the contrite ones." "The sacrifices of God are a broken spirit; a broken and a contrite heart, O God, thou wilt not despise."—(*Signs of the Times,* December 3, 1896.)

PRESS YOUR PETITIONS IN FAITH.—God will be to us everything we will let Him be. Our languid, half-hearted prayers will not bring us returns from heaven. Oh, we need to press our petitions! Ask in faith, wait in faith, receive in faith, rejoice in hope, for everyone that seeketh findeth. Be in earnest in the matter. Seek God with all the heart. People put soul and earnestness into everything they undertake in temporal things, until their efforts are crowned with success. With intense earnestness learn the trade of seeking the rich blessings that God has promised, and with persevering, determined effort you shall have His light and His truth and His rich grace.

In sincerity, in soul hunger, cry after God. Wrestle with the heavenly agencies until you have the victory. Put your whole being into the Lord's hands, soul, body, and spirit, and resolve to be His loving, consecrated agency, moved by His will, controlled by His mind, infused by His Spirit.

Tell Jesus your wants in the sincerity of your soul. You are not required to hold a long controversy with, or preach a sermon to, God, but with a heart of sorrow for your sins, say, "Save me, Lord, or I perish." There is hope for such souls. They will seek, they will ask, they will knock, and they will find. When Jesus has taken away the burden of sin that is crushing the soul, you will experience the blessedness of the peace of Christ.—(*Our High Calling,* 131.)

GOD ANSWERS THE PRAYER OF FAITH WITH POWER.—When men are as devoted as Elijah was and possess the faith that he had, God will reveal Himself as He did then. When men plead with the Lord as did Jacob, the results that were seen then will again be seen. Power will come from God in answer to the prayer of faith.—(*Gospel Workers,* 255.)

UNDERSTAND THE SCIENCE OF PRAYER.—Prayer and faith are closely allied, and they need to be studied together. In the prayer of faith there is a divine science; it is a science that everyone who would make his lifework a success must understand. Christ says, "What things soever ye desire, when ye pray, believe that ye receive them, and ye shall have them." Mark 11:24. He makes it plain that our asking must be according to God's will; we must ask for the things that He has promised, and whatever we receive must be used in doing His will. The conditions met, the promise is unequivocal.

For the pardon of sin, for the Holy Spirit, for a Christlike temper, for wisdom and strength to do His work, for any gift He has promised, we may ask; then we are to believe that we receive, and return thanks to God that we have received.—(*Education,* 257, 258.)

PRIVATE PRAYERS SUSTAIN THE SOUL LIFE.—We need look for no outward evidence of the blessing. The gift is in the promise, and we may go about our work assured that what God has promised He is able to perform, and that the gift, which we already possess, will be realized when we need it most.

To live thus by the word of God means the surrender to Him of the whole life. There will be felt a continual sense of need and dependence, a drawing out of the heart after God. Prayer is a necessity; for it is the life of the soul. Family prayer, public prayer, have their place; but it is secret communion with God that sustains the soul life.

It was in the mount with God that Moses beheld the pattern of that wonderful building which was to be the abiding place of His glory. It is in the mount with God—in the secret place of communion—that we are to contemplate His glorious ideal for humanity. Thus we shall be enabled so to fashion our character building that to us may be fulfilled His promise, "I will dwell in them, and walk in them; and I will be their God, and they shall be My people." 2 Corinthians 6:16.

It was in hours of solitary prayer that Jesus in His earth life received wisdom and power. Let the youth follow His example in finding at dawn and twilight a quiet season for communion with their Father in heaven. And throughout the day let them lift up their hearts to God. At every step of our way He says, "I the Lord thy God will hold thy right hand, . . . Fear not; I will help thee." Isaiah 41:13. Could our children learn these lessons in the morning of their years, what freshness and power, what joy and sweetness, would be brought into their lives!—(*Education,* 258, 259.)

ASKING IN FAITH BRINGS RICH BLESSINGS.—In the words we speak to the people and in the prayers we offer, God desires us to give unmistakable evidence that we have spiritual life. We do not enjoy the fullness of blessing which the Lord has prepared for us, because we do not ask in faith. If we would exercise faith in the word of the living God we should have the richest blessings. We dishonor God by our lack of faith; therefore we can not impart life to others by bearing a living, uplifting testimony. We cannot give that which we do not possess.—(*Testimonies for the Church,* vol. 6, 63.)

ASK IN FAITH; THEN RECEIVE.—There is strength to be obtained of God. He can help. He can give grace and heavenly wisdom. If you ask in faith, you will receive; but you must watch unto prayer. Watch, pray, work, should be your watchword.—(*Testimonies for the Church,* vol. 2, 427.)

FAITH CLAIMS THE BLESSING BEFORE IT IS REALIZED AND FELT.— I have frequently seen that the children of the Lord neglect prayer, especially secret prayer, altogether too much; that many do not exercise that faith which it is their privilege and duty to exercise, often waiting for that feeling which faith alone can bring. Feeling is not faith; the two are distinct. Faith is ours to exercise, but joyful feeling and the blessing are God's to give. The grace of God comes to the soul through the channel of living faith, and that faith it is in our power to exercise.

True faith lays hold of and claims the promised blessing before it is realized and felt. We must send up our petitions in faith within the second veil and let our faith take hold of the promised blessing and claim it as ours. We are then to believe that we receive the blessing, because our faith has hold of it, and according to the Word it is ours. "What things soever ye desire, when ye pray, believe that ye receive them, and ye shall have them." Mark 11:24. Here is faith, naked faith, to believe that we receive the blessing, even before we realize it. When the promised blessing is realized and enjoyed, faith is swallowed up. But many suppose they have much faith when sharing largely of the Holy Spirit and that they cannot have faith unless they feel the power of the Spirit. Such confound faith with the blessing that comes through faith. The very time to exercise faith is when we feel destitute of the Spirit. When thick clouds of darkness seem to hover over the mind, then is the time to let living faith pierce the darkness and scatter the clouds. True faith rests on the promises contained in the Word of God, and those only who obey that Word can claim its glorious promises. "If ye abide in Me, and My words abide in you, ye shall ask what ye will, and it shall be done unto you." John 15:7. "Whatsoever we ask, we receive of Him, because we keep His commandments, and do those things that are pleasing in His sight." 1 John 3:22.—(*Early Writings*, 72, 73.)

Do not falter if no immediate answer is given.—Your faith must not let go of the promises of God, if you do not see or feel the immediate answer to your prayers. Be not afraid to trust God. Rely upon His sure promise: "Ask, and ye shall receive." God is too wise to err, and too good to withhold any good thing from His saints that walk uprightly.—(*Testimonies for the Church*, vol. 1, 120.)

Pray; then leave the results with God.—Work in faith, and leave results with God. Pray in faith, and the mystery of His providence will bring its answer. At times it may seem that you cannot succeed. But work and believe, putting into your efforts faith, hope, and courage. After doing what you can, wait for the Lord, declaring His faithfulness, and He will bring His word to pass. Wait, not in fretful anxiety, but in undaunted faith and unshaken trust.—(*Testimonies for the Church,* vol. 7, 245.)

PRAY WITH CONFIDENCE.—It is the heartfelt prayer of faith that is heard in heaven and answered on earth. God understands the needs of humanity. He knows what we desire before we ask Him. He sees the soul's conflict with doubt and temptation. He marks the sincerity of the suppliant. He will accept the humiliation and affliction of the soul. "To this man will I look," He declares, "even to him that is poor and of a contrite spirit, and trembleth at my word."

It is our privilege to pray with confidence, the Spirit inditing our petitions. With simplicity we should state our needs to the Lord, and claim His promise.—(*God's Amazing Grace,* 92.)

JESUS IS AS WILLING TO LISTEN TO PRAYER TODAY AS WHEN HE WAS ON EARTH.—Worldly wisdom teaches that prayer is not essential. Men of science claim that there can be no real answer to prayer; that this would be a violation of law, a miracle, and that miracles have no existence. The universe, say they, is governed by fixed laws, and God Himself does nothing contrary to these laws. Thus they represent God as bound by His own laws—as if the operation of divine laws could exclude divine freedom. Such teaching is opposed to the testimony of the Scriptures. Were not miracles wrought by Christ and His apostles? The same compassionate Saviour lives today, and He is as willing to listen to the prayer of faith as when He walked visibly among men.—(*The Great Controversy,* 525.)

THE PRAYER OF FAITH EXPRESSES THE SIMPLE WANTS OF THE SOUL.—Prayer is not an expiation for sin; it has no virtue or merit of itself. All the flowery words at our command are not equivalent to one holy desire. The most eloquent prayers are but idle words if they do not express the true sentiments of the heart. But the prayer that comes from an earnest heart, when the simple wants of the soul are expressed, as we would ask an earthly friend for a favor, expecting it to be granted—this is the prayer of faith. God does not desire our ceremonial compliments, but the unspoken cry of the heart broken and subdued with a sense of its sin and utter weakness finds its way to the Father of all mercy.—(*Thoughts From the Mount of Blessing*, 86, 87.)

PRAYER MOVES GOD TO ACTION.—By your fervent prayers of faith you can move the arm that moves the world. You can teach your children to pray effectually as they kneel by your side. Let your prayers arise to the throne of God, "Spare thy people, O Lord, and give not thine heritage to reproach, that the heathen should rule over them: wherefore should they say among the people, Where is their God?"

God is at work. He doeth wonders, and although He is high and lifted up, prayer can reach His throne. He that is turning and overturning, He that can do marvelous things, will regard the contrite prayer of faith from the humblest of His children.—(*Review and Herald*, April 23, 1889.)

GOD CANNOT ANSWER PRAYERS THAT ARE NOT ASKED.—Prayer and faith will do what no power on earth can accomplish. We are seldom, in all respects, placed in the same position twice. We continually have new scenes and new trials to pass through, where past experience cannot be a sufficient guide. We must have the continual light that comes from God. Christ is ever sending messages to those who listen for His voice.

It is a part of God's plan to grant us, in answer to the prayer of faith, that which He would not bestow did we not thus ask.—(*My Life Today*, 15.)

MINISTERS TO BE UNTIRING IN PRAYER.—Ministers should seek a heart preparation before entering upon the work of helping others, for the people are far in advance of many of the ministers. They should untiringly wrestle in prayer until the Lord blesses them. When the love of God is burning on the altar of their hearts, they will not preach to exhibit their own smartness, but to present Christ who taketh away the sins of the world.—(*Testimonies for the Church,* vol. 5, 166.)

THE REMEDY FOR DISCOURAGEMENT IS FAITH, PRAYER, AND WORK.—For all who are disheartened there is but one remedy,— faith, prayer, and work.—(*Testimonies for the Church,* vol. 6, 438.)

PRAYER IS THE WEAPON BY WHICH WE RESIST THE ENEMY.—Christ is our only hope. Come to God in the name of Him who gave His life for the life of the world. Rely upon the efficacy of His sacrifice. Show that His love, His joy, is in your soul, and that because of this, your joy is full. In God is our strength. Pray much. Prayer is the life of the soul. The prayer of faith is the weapon by which we may successfully resist every assault of the enemy.—(*Signs of the Times,* August 24, 1904.)

PRAYER NOT LOST, EVEN IF NOT ANSWERED AS WE EXPECT.—The prayer of faith is never lost; but to claim that it will be always answered in the very way and for the particular thing we have expected, is presumption.—(*Testimonies for the Church,* vol. 1, 231.)

THE COMFORTER COMES IN ANSWER TO THE PRAYER OF FAITH.— At all times and in all places, in all sorrows and in all afflictions, when the outlook seems dark and the future perplexing, and we feel helpless and alone, the Comforter will be sent in answer to the prayer of faith. Circumstances may separate us from every earthly friend; but no circumstance, no distance, can separate us from the heavenly Comforter. Wherever we are, wherever we may go, He is always at our right hand to support, sustain, uphold, and cheer.— (*The Desire of Ages,* 669, 670.)

ANGELS CARRY OUR PRAYERS TO THE HEAVENLY SANCTUARY.— Angels hear the offering of praise and the prayer of faith, and they bear the petitions to Him who ministers in the sanctuary for His people, and pleads His merits in their behalf. True prayer takes hold upon Omnipotence, and gives men the victory. Upon his knees the Christian obtains strength to resist temptation.—(*Review and Herald*, February 1, 1912.)

EARNEST PRAYER WILL BAFFLE SATAN'S STRONGEST EFFORTS.— Man is Satan's captive and is naturally inclined to follow his suggestions and do his bidding. He has in himself no power to oppose effectual resistance to evil. It is only as Christ abides in him by living faith, influencing his desires and strengthening him with strength from above, that man may venture to face so terrible a foe. Every other means of defense is utterly vain. It is only through Christ that Satan's power is limited. This is a momentous truth that all should understand. Satan is busy every moment, going to and fro, walking up and down in the earth, seeking whom he may devour. But the earnest prayer of faith will baffle his strongest efforts. Then take "the shield of faith," brethren, "wherewith ye shall be able to quench all the fiery darts of the wicked."—(*Testimonies for the Church*, vol. 5, 294.)

THE PRAYER OF FAITH PREVAILS AGAINST SATAN.—The prayer of faith is the great strength of the Christian and will assuredly prevail against Satan. This is why he insinuates that we have no need of prayer. The name of Jesus, our Advocate, he detests; and when we earnestly come to Him for help, Satan's host is alarmed. It serves his purpose well if we neglect the exercise of prayer, for then his lying wonders are more readily received.—(*Testimonies for the Church*, vol. 1, 296.)

CHAPTER

7

Prayer and Obedience

PRAY AND WORK.—We are not to sit in calm expectancy of oppression and tribulation, and fold our hands, doing nothing to avert the evil. Let our united cries be sent up to heaven. Pray and work, and work and pray. But let none act rashly. Learn as never before that you must be meek and lowly in heart.—(*Selected Messages,* bk. 2, 370, 371.)

We must pray and work and believe. The Lord is our efficiency.—(*Evangelism,* 438.)

You will have to wrestle with difficulties, carry burdens, give advice, plan and execute, constantly looking to God for help. Pray and labor, labor and pray; as pupils in the school of Christ, learn of Jesus.—(*Testimonies to Ministers,* 498, 499.)

PRAYER IS HEAVEN'S PLAN FOR SUCCESS AGAINST SIN.—There are many who, though striving to obey God's commandments, have little peace or joy. This lack in their experience is the result of a failure to exercise faith. They walk as it were in a salt land, a parched

64

wilderness. They claim little, when they might claim much; for there is no limit to the promises of God. Such ones do not correctly represent the sanctification that comes through obedience to the truth. The Lord would have all His sons and daughters happy, peaceful, and obedient. Through the exercise of faith the believer comes into possession of these blessings. Through faith, every deficiency of character may be supplied, every defilement cleansed, every fault corrected, every excellence developed.

Prayer is heaven's ordained means of success in the conflict with sin and the development of Christian character. The divine influences that come in answer to the prayer of faith will accomplish in the soul of the suppliant all for which he pleads. For the pardon of sin, for the Holy Spirit, for a Christlike temper, for wisdom and strength to do His work, for any gift He has promised, we may ask; and the promise is, "Ye shall receive."—(*Acts of the Apostles,* 563, 564.)

DAILY TEMPTATIONS MAKE PRAYER A NECESSITY.—The strength acquired in prayer to God, united with individual effort in training the mind to thoughtfulness and care-taking, prepares the person for daily duties and keeps the spirit in peace under all circumstances, however trying. The temptations to which we are daily exposed make prayer a necessity. In order that we may be kept by the power of God through faith, the desires of the mind should be continually ascending in silent prayer for help, for light, for strength, for knowledge. But thought and prayer cannot take the place of earnest, faithful improvement of the time. Work and prayer are both required in perfecting Christian character.—(*Testimonies for the Church,* vol. 4, 459.)

DAILY PRAYER TURNS MISTAKES INTO VICTORIES.—If one who daily communes with God errs from the path, if he turns a moment from looking steadfastly unto Jesus, it is not because he sins wilfully; for when he sees his mistake, he turns again, and fastens his eyes upon Jesus, and the fact that he has erred, does not make him less dear to the heart of God. He knows that he has communion with the Saviour; and when reproved for his mistake in some matter of judgment, he does not walk sullenly, and complain of God, but turns the mistake into a victory. He learns a lesson from the words of the Master, and takes heed that he be not again deceived.—(*Review and Herald,* May 12, 1896.)

CHRIST IS THE MEDIUM OF PRAYER BETWEEN US AND GOD.—Christ is the connecting link between God and man. He has promised His personal intercession. He places the whole virtue of His righteousness on the side of the suppliant. He pleads for man, and man, in need of divine help, pleads for himself in the presence of God, using the influence of the One who gave His life for the life of the world. As we acknowledge before God our appreciation of Christ's merits, fragrance is given to our intercessions. As we approach God through the virtue of the Redeemer's merits, Christ places us close by His side, encircling us with His human arm, while with His divine arm He grasps the throne of the Infinite. He puts His merits, as sweet incense, in the censer in our hands, in order to encourage our petitions. He promises to hear and answer our supplications.

Yes, Christ has become the medium of prayer between man and God. He has also become the medium of blessing between God and man. He has united divinity with humanity. Men are to co-operate with Him for the salvation of their own souls, and then make earnest, persevering efforts to save those who are ready to die.—(*Testimonies for the Church,* vol. 8, 178.)

As the high priest sprinkled the warm blood upon the mercy-seat while the fragrant cloud of incense ascended before God, so, while we confess our sins and plead the efficacy of Christ's atoning blood, our prayers are to ascend to heaven, fragrant with the merits of our Saviour's character. Notwithstanding our unworthiness, we are to remember that there is One who can take away sin, and who is willing and anxious to save the sinner. With His own blood He paid the penalty for all wrong-doers. Every sin acknowledged before God with a contrite heart, He will remove. "Though your sins be as scarlet, they shall be as white as snow; though they be red like crimson, they shall be as wool."—(*Review and Herald,* September 29, 1896.)

PRAYERS AMOUNT TO NOTHING IF THERE IS WILLFUL INIQUITY IN THE HEART.—"The grace of God that bringeth salvation hath appeared to all men, teaching us that, denying ungodliness and worldly lusts, we should live soberly, righteously, and godly, in this present world." Christ says: "Be ye therefore perfect, even as your Father which is in heaven is perfect." What do your prayers amount to while you regard iniquity in your hearts? Unless you make a thorough change, you will, not far hence, become weary of reproof, as did the children of Israel; and, like them, you will apostatize from God. Some of you in words acknowledge reproof, but you do not in heart accept it. You go on the same as before, only being less susceptible to the influence of the Spirit of God, becoming more and more blinded, having less wisdom, less self-control, less moral power, and less zeal and relish for religious exercises; and, unless converted, you will finally yield your hold upon God entirely. You have not made decided changes in your life when reproof has come, because you have not seen and realized your defects of character and the great contrast between your life and the life of Christ. It has been your policy to place yourselves in a position where you would not entirely lose the confidence of your brethren.—(*Testimonies for the Church,* vol. 4, 332.)

PRAYER DOES NOT TAKE THE PLACE OF OBEDIENCE.—There are conditions to the fulfillment of God's promises, and prayer can never take the place of duty. "If ye love Me," Christ says, "Keep My commandments." "He that hath My commandments, and keepeth them, he it is that loveth Me; and he that loveth Me shall be loved of My Father, and I will love him, and will manifest Myself to him." John 14:15, 21. Those who bring their petitions to God, claiming His promise while they do not comply with the conditions, insult Jehovah. They bring the name of Christ as their authority for the fulfillment of the promise, but they do not those things that would show faith in Christ and love for Him.

Many are forfeiting the condition of acceptance with the Father. We need to examine closely the deed of trust wherewith we approach God. If we are disobedient, we bring to the Lord a note to be cashed when we have not fulfilled the conditions that would make it payable to us. We present to God His promises, and ask Him to fulfill them, when by so doing He would dishonor His own name.

The promise is "If ye abide in Me, and My words abide in you, ye shall ask what ye will, and it shall be done unto you." John 15:7. And John declares: "Hereby we do know that we know Him, if we keep His commandments. He that saith, I know Him, and keepeth not His commandments, is a liar, and the truth is not in him. But whoso keepeth His word, in him verily is the love of God perfected." 1 John 2:3-5.—(*Christ's Object Lessons,* 143, 144.)

WE ARE TO BELIEVE GOD HEARS AND THEN LIVE OUT OUR PRAYERS.—Children and youth may come to Jesus with their burdens and perplexities, and know that He will respect their appeals to Him, and give them the very things they need. Be earnest; be resolute. Present the promise of God, and then believe without a doubt. Do not wait to feel special emotions before you think the Lord answers. Do not mark out some particular way that the Lord must work for you before you believe you receive the things you ask of Him; but trust His word, and leave the whole matter in the hands of the Lord, with full faith that your prayer will be honored, and the answer will come at the very time and in the very way your heavenly Father sees is for your good; and then live out your prayers. Walk humbly and keep moving forward.—(*Messages to Young People,* 123.)

PRAY FOR GRACE TO RESIST TEMPTATION.—In the daily life you will meet with sudden surprises, disappointments, and temptations. What saith the word? "Resist the devil," by firm reliance upon God, "and he will flee from you. Draw nigh to God, and He will draw nigh to you." "Let him take hold of My strength, that he may make peace with Me; and he shall make peace with Me." Look unto Jesus at all times and in all places, offering a silent prayer from a sincere heart that you may know how to do His will. Then when the enemy comes in like a flood, the Spirit of the Lord will lift up a standard for you against the enemy. When you are almost ready to yield, to lose patience and self-control, to be hard and denunciatory, to find fault and accuse—this is the time for you to send to heaven the prayer, "Help me, O God, to resist temptation, to put all bitterness and wrath and evilspeaking out of my heart. Give me Thy meekness, Thy lowliness, Thy long-suffering, and Thy love. Leave me not to dishonor my Redeemer, to misinterpret the words and motives of my wife, my children, and my brethren and sisters in the faith. Help me that I may be kind, pitiful, tenderhearted, forgiving. Help me to be a real house-band in my home and to represent the character of Christ to others."—(*Adventist Home,* 214, 215.)

We know the dangers and temptations that beset the youth at the present time are not few or small. . . . We live in an age when to resist evil calls for constant watchfulness and prayer. God's precious Word is the standard for youth who would be loyal to the King of heaven. Let them study the Scriptures. Let them commit text after text to memory, and acquire a knowledge of what the Lord has said. . . . And in trial let the youth spread out the Word of God before them, and with humble hearts, and in faith, seek the Lord for wisdom to find out His way, and for strength to walk in it. —(*The Youth's Instructor,* August 3, 1887.)

Let our young men institute a warfare against every habit that has the least danger of leading the soul from duty and devotion. Let them have stated seasons for prayer, never neglecting them if it can possibly be avoided. If they go out to battle with their vicious habits indulged as before they professed fellowship with Christ, they will soon fall an easy prey to Satan's devices. But armed with the Word of God, having it treasured in heart and mind, they will come forth unharmed by all the assaults of the foes of God or man—(*My Life Today,* 315.)

8

Prevailing
Prayer

DO NOT LET GO OF GOD'S PROMISES.—Every saint who comes to God with a true heart, and sends his honest petitions to Him in faith, will have his prayers answered. Your faith must not let go of the promises of God, if you do not see or feel the immediate answer to your prayers. Be not afraid to trust God. Rely upon His sure promise: "Ask, and ye shall receive." God is too wise to err, and too good to withhold any good thing from His saints that walk uprightly. Man is erring, and although his petitions are sent up from an honest heart, he does not always ask for the things that are good for himself, or that will glorify God. When this is so, our wise and good Father hears our prayers, and will answer, sometimes immediately; but He gives us the things that are for our best good and His own glory. God gives us blessings; if we could look into His plan, we would clearly see that He knows what is best for us and that our prayers are answered. Nothing hurtful is given, but the blessing we need, in the place of something we asked for that would not be good for us, but to our hurt.

I saw that if we do not feel immediate answers to our prayers, we should hold fast our faith, not allowing distrust to come in, for that will separate us from God. If our faith wavers, we shall receive nothing from Him. Our confidence in God should be strong; and when we need it most, the blessing will fall upon us like a shower of rain.—(*Testimonies for the Church,* vol. 1, 120, 121.)

OUR PRAYERS ARE TO BE EARNEST AND PERSISTENT.—God does not say, Ask once, and you shall receive. He bids us ask. Unwearyingly persist in prayer. The persistent asking brings the petitioner into a more earnest attitude, and gives him an increased desire to receive the things for which he asks. Christ said to Martha at the grave of Lazarus, "If thou wouldest believe, thou shouldest see the glory of God." John 11:40.

But many have not a living faith. This is why they do not see more of the power of God. Their weakness is the result of their unbelief. They have more faith in their own working than in the working of God for them. They take themselves into their own keeping. They plan and devise, but pray little, and have little real trust in God. They think they have faith, but it is only the impulse of the moment. Failing to realize their own need, or God's willingness to give, they do not persevere in keeping their requests before the Lord.

Our prayers are to be as earnest and persistent as was the petition of the needy friend who asked for the loaves at midnight. The more earnestly and steadfastly we ask, the closer will be our spiritual union with Christ. We shall receive increased blessings because we have increased faith.

Our part is to pray and believe. Watch unto prayer. Watch, and co-operate with the prayer-hearing God. Bear in mind that "we are labourers together with God." 1 Cor. 3:9. Speak and act in harmony with your prayers. It will make an infinite difference with you whether trial shall prove your faith to be genuine, or show that your prayers are only a form.—(*Christ's Object Lessons,* 145, 146.)

EARNEST PRAYER AVAILS MUCH.—That prayer which comes forth from an earnest, believing heart is the effectual, fervent prayer that availeth much. God does not always answer our prayers as we expect, for we may not ask what would be for our highest good;

but in His infinite love and wisdom He will give us those things which we most need.—(*Testimonies for the Church,* vol. 4, 531.)

Do NOT LET GO OF GOD'S ARM TOO SOON.—I asked the angel why there was no more faith and power in Israel. He said, "Ye let go of the arm of the Lord too soon. Press your petitions to the throne, and hold on by strong faith. The promises are sure. Believe ye receive the things ye ask for, and ye shall have them." I was then pointed to Elijah. He was subject to like passions as we are, and he prayed earnestly. His faith endured the trial. Seven times he prayed before the Lord, and at last the cloud was seen. I saw that we had doubted the sure promises, and wounded the Saviour by our lack of faith. Said the angel, "Gird the armor about thee, and above all take the shield of faith; for that will guard the heart, the very life, from the fiery darts of the wicked." If the enemy can lead the desponding to take their eyes off from Jesus, and look to themselves, and dwell upon their own unworthiness, instead of dwelling upon the worthiness of Jesus, His love, His merits, and His great mercy, he will get away their shield of faith and gain his object; they will be exposed to his fiery temptations. The weak should therefore look to Jesus, and believe in Him; they then exercise faith.—(*Early Writings,* 73.)

PERSIST UNWEARYINGLY IN PRAYER.—When a man breathes an intensely earnest prayer to God (Jesus Christ is the only name given under heaven whereby we can be saved), there is in that intensity and earnestness a pledge from God that He is about to answer that prayer exceeding abundantly, above all that we can ask or think. We must not only pray in the name of Jesus, but by the inspiration and kindling of the Holy Spirit. This explains what is meant when it is said, "the Spirit itself maketh intercession for us with groanings which can not be uttered." The petitions must be offered in earnest faith. Then they will reach the mercy-seat. Unwearyingly persist in prayer. God does not say, Pray once, and I will answer you. His word is pray, be instant in prayer, believing ye have the things ye ask, and ye shall receive them; I will answer you.—(*The Gospel Herald,* May 28, 1902.)

EARNEST, FERVENT PRAYER IS NEEDED, NOT FEEBLE, HEARTLESS PRAYERS.—There is need of prayer,—most earnest, fervent, agonizing prayer,—such prayer as David offered when he exclaimed: "As the hart panteth after the water brooks, so panteth my soul after Thee, O God." "I have longed after Thy precepts;" "I have longed for Thy salvation." "My soul longeth, yea, even fainteth for the courts of the Lord: my heart and my flesh crieth out for the living God." "My soul breaketh for the longing that it hath unto Thy judgments." This is the spirit of wrestling prayer, such as was possessed by the royal psalmist.

Daniel prayed to God, not exalting himself or claiming any goodness: "O Lord, hear; O Lord, forgive; O Lord, hearken and do; defer not, for Thine own sake, O my God." This is what James calls the effectual, fervent prayer. Of Christ it is said: "And being in an agony He prayed more earnestly." In what contrast to this intercession by the Majesty of heaven are the feeble, heartless prayers that are offered to God. Many are content with lip service, and but few have a sincere, earnest, affectionate longing after God.—(*Testimonies for the Church,* vol. 4, 534.)

PREVAILING PRAYER DOES NOT HAVE TO INCLUDE TEARS AND STRUGGLES.—There are many souls who wrestle for special victories and special blessings that they may do some great thing. To this end they are always feeling that they must make an agonizing struggle in prayer and tears. When these persons search the Scriptures with prayer to know the expressed will of God, and then do His will from the heart without one reservation or self-indulgence, they will find rest. All the agonizing, all the tears and struggles, will not bring them the blessing they long for. Self must be entirely surrendered. They must do the work that presents itself, appropriating the abundance of the grace of God which is promised to all who ask in faith.— (*Testimonies for the Church,* vol. 9, 165.)

FERVENT, CONSTANT PRAYER IS A NECESSITY.—If the Saviour of men, the Son of God, felt the need of prayer, how much more should feeble, sinful mortals feel the necessity of fervent, constant prayer.

Our heavenly Father waits to bestow upon us the fullness of His blessing. It is our privilege to drink largely at the fountain of boundless love. What a wonder it is that we pray so little! God is ready and willing to hear the sincere prayer of the humblest of His children, and yet there is much manifest reluctance on our part to make known our wants to God. What can the angels of heaven think of poor helpless human beings, who are subject to temptation, when God's heart of infinite love yearns toward them, ready to give them more than they can ask or think, and yet they pray so little and have so little faith? The angels love to bow before God; they love to be near Him. They regard communion with God as their highest joy; and yet the children of earth, who need so much the help that God only can give, seem satisfied to walk without the light of His Spirit, the companionship of His presence.

The darkness of the evil one encloses those who neglect to pray. The whispered temptations of the enemy entice them to sin; and it is all because they do not make use of the privileges that God has given them in the divine appointment of prayer. Why should the sons and daughters of God be reluctant to pray, when prayer is the key in the hand of faith to unlock heaven's storehouse, where are treasured the boundless resources of Omnipotence? Without unceasing prayer and diligent watching we are in danger of growing careless and of deviating from the right path. The adversary seeks continually to obstruct the way to the mercy seat, that we may not by earnest supplication and faith obtain grace and power to resist temptation. (*Steps to Christ*, 93-95.)

LIKE JACOB, WRESTLE IN PRAYER.—Be in earnest, be sincere. Fervent prayer availeth much. Jacoblike, wrestle in prayer. Agonize. Jesus, in the garden, sweat great drops of blood; you must make an effort. Do not leave your closet until you feel strong in God; then watch, and just as long as you watch and pray you can keep these evil besetments under, and the grace of God can and will appear in you.—(*Testimonies for the Church*, vol. 1, 158.)

Jacob prevailed because he was persevering and determined. His experience testifies to the power of importunate prayer. It is now that we are to learn this lesson of prevailing prayer, of unyielding faith. The greatest victories to the church of Christ or to the individual Christian are not those that are gained by talent or education, by wealth or the favor of men. They are those victories that are gained in the audience chamber with God, when earnest, agonizing faith lays hold upon the mighty arm of power.

Those who are unwilling to forsake every sin and to seek earnestly for God's blessing, will not obtain it. But all who will lay hold of God's promises as did Jacob, and be as earnest and persevering as he was, will succeed as he succeeded.—(*Patriarchs and Prophets,* 203.)

WRESTLE IN PRAYER UNTIL VICTORY COMES.—God will be to us everything we will let Him be. Our languid, half-hearted prayers will not bring us returns from heaven. Oh, we need to press our petitions! Ask in faith, wait in faith, receive in faith, rejoice in hope, for everyone that seeketh findeth. Be in earnest in the matter. Seek God with all the heart. People put soul and earnestness into everything they undertake in temporal things, until their efforts are crowned with success. With intense earnestness learn the trade of seeking the rich blessings that God has promised, and with persevering, determined effort you shall have His light and His truth and His rich grace.

In sincerity, in soul hunger, cry after God. Wrestle with the heavenly agencies until you have the victory. Put your whole being into the Lord's hands, soul, body, and spirit, and resolve to be His loving, consecrated agency, moved by His will, controlled by His mind, infused by His Spirit.

Tell Jesus your wants in the sincerity of your soul. You are not required to hold a long controversy with, or preach a sermon to, God, but with a heart of sorrow for your sins, say, "Save me, Lord, or I perish." There is hope for such souls. They will seek, they will ask, they will knock, and they will find. When Jesus has taken away the burden of sin that is crushing the soul, you will experience the blessedness of the peace of Christ.—(*Our High Calling,* 131.)

PRAY WITHOUT CEASING.—In the work of heart-keeping we must be instant in prayer, unwearied in petitioning the throne of grace for assistance. Those who take the name of Christian should come to God in earnestness and humility, pleading for help. The Saviour has told us to pray without ceasing. The Christian can not always be in the position of prayer, but his thoughts and desires can always be upward. Our self-confidence would vanish, did we talk less and pray more.—(*Sons and Daughters of God,* 99.)

EVERY BREATH SHOULD BE A PRAYER.—The reason why so many are left to themselves in places of temptation is that they do not set the Lord always before them. When we permit our communion with God to be broken, our defense is departed from us. Not all your good purposes and good intentions will enable you to withstand evil. You must be men and women of prayer. Your petitions must not be faint, occasional, and fitful, but earnest, persevering, and constant. It is not always necessary to bow upon your knees in order to pray. Cultivate the habit of talking with the Saviour when you are alone, when you are walking, and when you are busy with your daily labor. Let the heart be continually uplifted in silent petition for help, for light, for strength, for knowledge. Let every breath be a prayer.—(*Ministry of Healing,* 510, 511.)

PRAY WITH UNSHAKEN FAITH.—Pray, yes, pray with unshaken faith and trust. The Angel of the covenant, even our Lord Jesus Christ, is the Mediator who secures the acceptance of the prayers of His believing ones.—(*Testimonies for the Church,* vol. 8, 179.)

COME BOLDLY IN PRAYER.—Why not pray as if you had a conscience void of offense, and could come to the throne of grace in humility, yet with holy boldness, lifting up holy hands without wrath and doubting? Do not bow down and cover up your faces as if there were something that you desired to conceal; but lift up your eyes toward the heavenly sanctuary, where Christ your Mediator stands before the Father to present your prayers, mingled with His own merit and spotless righteousness, as fragrant incense.

You are invited to come, to ask, to seek, to knock; and you are assured that you will not come in vain. Jesus says, "Ask, and it shall be given you; seek, and ye shall find; knock, and it shall be opened unto you: for everyone that asketh receiveth; and he that seeketh findeth; and to him that knocketh it shall be opened." Matthew 7:7, 8.—(*Counsels to Parents, Teachers, and Students*, 241, 242.)

FERVENT PRAYER ASCENDS AS A FRAGRANT INFLUENCE.—They have willingly endured hardship and privation, and have watched and prayed for the success of the cause. Their gifts and sacrifices express the fervent gratitude and praise of their hearts to Him who has called them out of darkness into His marvelous light. No more fragrant influence can ascend to heaven. Their prayers and their alms come up as a memorial before God.—(*Selected Messages,* bk. 2, 212.)

Two lovely cherubs, one on each end of the ark, stood with their wings outstretched above it, and touching each other above the head of Jesus as He stood before the mercy seat. Their faces were turned toward each other, and they looked downward to the ark, representing all the angelic host looking with interest at the law of God. Between the cherubim was a golden censer, and as the prayers of the saints, offered in faith, came up to Jesus, and He presented them to His Father, a cloud of fragrance arose from the incense, looking like smoke of most beautiful colors. Above the place where Jesus stood, before the ark, was exceedingly bright glory that I could not look upon; it appeared like the throne of God. As the incense ascended to the Father, the excellent glory came from the throne to Jesus, and from Him it was shed upon those whose prayers had come up like sweet incense. Light poured upon Jesus in rich abundance and overshadowed the mercy seat, and the train of glory filled the temple. I could not long look upon the surpassing brightness. No language can describe it. I was overwhelmed and turned from the majesty and glory of the scene.—(*Early Writings,* 252.)

WE ARE TO IMITATE CHRIST'S EXAMPLE OF IMPORTUNATE PRAYER.—
The strength of Christ was in prayer. He had taken humanity, and
He bore our infirmities and became sin for us. Christ retired to the
groves or mountains with the world and everything else shut out.
He was alone with His Father. With intense earnestness, He poured
out His supplications, and put forth all the strength of His soul in
grasping the hand of the Infinite. When new and great trials were
before Him, He would steal away to the solitude of the mountains,
and pass the entire night in prayer to His Heavenly Father.

As Christ is our example in all things, if we imitate His example in earnest, importunate prayer to God that we may have
strength in His name who never yielded to the temptations of
Satan to resist the devices of the wily foe, we shall not be overcome by him.—(*The Youth's Instructor,* April 1, 1873.)

PERSEVERING EFFORT AND PRAYER PREPARE US FOR DAILY DUTIES.—
Those who seek God in secret telling the Lord their needs and
pleading for help, will not plead in vain. "Thy Father which seeth
in secret Himself shall reward thee openly." As we make Christ
our daily companion we shall feel that the powers of an unseen
world are all around us; and by looking unto Jesus we shall become assimilated to His image. By beholding we become changed.
The character is softened, refined, and ennobled for the heavenly
kingdom. The sure result of our intercourse and fellowship with
our Lord will be to increase piety, purity, and fervor. There will be
a growing intelligence in prayer. We are receiving a divine education, and this is illustrated in a life of diligence and zeal.

The soul that turns to God for its help, its support, its power, by
daily, earnest prayer, will have noble aspirations, clear perceptions of
truth and duty, lofty purposes of action, and a continual hungering
and thirsting after righteousness. By maintaining a connection with
God, we shall be enabled to diffuse to others, through our association
with them, the light, the peace, the serenity, that rule in our hearts.
The strength acquired in prayer to God, united with persevering effort in training the mind in thoughtfulness and care-taking, prepares

one for daily duties and keeps the spirit in peace under all circumstances.—(*Thoughts From the Mount of Blessing,* 85.)

NOTHING TO DIVERT US FROM BIBLE STUDY AND EARNEST PRAYER.—Let nothing, however dear, however loved, absorb your mind and affections, diverting you from the study of God's word or from earnest prayer. Watch unto prayer. Live your own requests.—(*Testimonies for the Church,* vol. 8, 53.)

PREVAILING PRAYER INCLUDES FAITH.—Another element of prevailing prayer is faith. "He that cometh to God must believe that He is, and that He is a rewarder of them that diligently seek Him." Hebrews 11:6. Jesus said to His disciples, "What things soever ye desire, when ye pray, believe that ye receive them, and ye shall have them." Mark 11:24.—(*Steps to Christ,* 96.)

Faith is an essential element of prevailing prayer. "He that cometh to God must believe that He is, and that He is a rewarder of them that diligently seek Him." "If we ask anything according to His will, He heareth us: and if we know that He hear us, whatsoever we ask, we know that we have the petitions that we desired of Him." Hebrews 11:6, 1 John 5:14, 15. With the persevering faith of Jacob, with the unyielding persistence of Elijah, we may present our petitions to the Father, claiming all that He has promised. The honor of His throne is staked for the fulfillment of His word.—(*Prophets and Kings,* 157, 158.)

PRAYER GIVES EVIDENCE OF OUR CONFIDENCE IN GOD.—The Lord says, "Call upon Me in the day of trouble." Ps. 50:15. He invites us to present to Him our perplexities and necessities, and our need of divine help. He bids us be instant in prayer. As soon as difficulties arise, we are to offer to Him our sincere, earnest petitions. By our importunate prayers we give evidence of our strong confidence in God. The sense of our need leads us to pray earnestly, and our heavenly Father is moved by our supplications.—(*Christ's Object Lessons,* 172.)

GOD ANSWERS EARNEST PRAYERS.—It is only as we ask in earnest prayer, that God will grant us our heart's desire.—(*Gospel Workers*, 255.)

AFTER PRAYING, CONTINUE TO CLAIM THE PROMISE.—After the prayer is made, if the answer is not realized immediately, do not weary of waiting and become unstable. Waver not. Cling to the promise, "Faithful is He that calleth you, who also will do it." Like the importunate widow, urge your case, being firm in your purpose. Is the object important and of great consequence to you? It certainly is. Then waver not, for your faith may be tried. If the thing you desire is valuable, it is worthy of a strong, earnest effort. You have the promise; watch and pray. Be steadfast and the prayer will be answered; for is it not God who has promised? If it costs you something to obtain it you will prize it the more when obtained. You are plainly told that if you waver you need not think that you shall receive anything of the Lord. A caution is here given not to become weary, but to rest firmly upon the promise. If you ask, He will give you liberally and upbraid not.—(*Testimonies for the Church*, vol. 2, 131.)

GOD WILL NOT TURN US AWAY EMPTY.—When temptations and trials rush in upon us, let us go to God and agonize with Him in prayer. He will not turn us away empty, but will give us grace and strength to overcome, and to break the power of the enemy.—(*Early Writings*, 46.)

PRAYER WITHOUT LIVING FAITH AVAILS NOTHING.—Faith is not feeling. "Faith is the substance of things hoped for, the evidence of things not seen." [Heb. 11:1.] True faith is in no sense allied to presumption. Only he who has true faith is secure against presumption, for presumption is Satan's counterfeit of faith.

Faith claims God's promises and brings forth fruit in obedience. Presumption also claims the promises, but uses them as Satan did, to excuse transgression. Faith would have led our first parents to trust the love of God and to obey His commands. Presumption led them to transgress His law, believing that His great love would save them from the consequences of their sin. It is not faith that claims the favor of Heaven without complying with the conditions on which mercy is to be granted. Genuine faith has its foundation in the promises and provisions of the Scriptures.

To talk of religion in a casual way, to pray without soul-hunger and living faith, avails nothing. A nominal faith in Christ, which accepts Him merely as the Saviour of the world, can never bring healing to the soul. The faith that is unto salvation is not a mere intellectual assent to the truth. He who waits for entire knowledge before he will exercise faith, cannot receive blessing from God.

It is not enough to believe about Christ; we must believe in Him. The only faith that will benefit us is that which embraces Him as a personal Saviour; which appropriates His merits to ourselves. Many hold faith as an opinion. But saving faith is a transaction, by which those who receive Christ join themselves in covenant relation with God. Genuine faith is life. A living faith means an increase of vigor, a confiding trust, by which the soul becomes a conquering power.—(*Gospel Workers,* 260, 261.)

PRAYER WILL PREVAIL AGAINST SATAN.—The prayer of faith is the great strength of the Christian and will assuredly prevail against Satan. This is why he insinuates that we have no need of prayer. The name of Jesus, our Advocate, he detests; and when we earnestly come to Him for help, Satan's host is alarmed. It serves his purpose well if we neglect the exercise of prayer, for then his lying wonders are more readily received.—(*Testimonies for the Church,* vol. 1, 296.)

PRAYER BRINGS THE GREATEST VICTORIES.—The greatest victories gained for the cause of God are not the result of labored argument, ample facilities, wide influence, or abundance of means; they are gained in the audience chamber with God, when with earnest, agonizing faith men lay hold upon the mighty arm of power.—(*Gospel Workers,* 259.)

9

Prayer Power

PRAYER BRINGS INCREASED SPIRITUAL STRENGTH.—Those who seek God in secret telling the Lord their needs and pleading for help, will not plead in vain. "Thy Father which seeth in secret Himself shall reward thee openly." As we make Christ our daily companion we shall feel that the powers of an unseen world are all around us; and by looking unto Jesus we shall become assimilated to His image. By beholding we become changed. The character is softened, refined, and ennobled for the heavenly kingdom. The sure result of our intercourse and fellowship with our Lord will be to increase piety, purity, and fervor. There will be a growing intelligence in prayer. We are receiving a divine education, and this is illustrated in a life of diligence and zeal.

The soul that turns to God for its help, its support, its power, by daily, earnest prayer, will have noble aspirations, clear perceptions of truth and duty, lofty purposes of action, and a continual hungering and thirsting after righteousness. By maintaining a connection with God, we shall be enabled to diffuse to others, through our association with them, the light, the peace, the serenity, that rule in our hearts. The strength acquired in prayer to God, united with persevering effort in training the mind in thoughtfulness and care-taking, prepares one for daily duties and keeps the spirit in peace under all circumstances.—(*Thoughts From the Mount of Blessing,* 85.)

Strength and grace can be found in prayer. Sincere love is to be the ruling principle of the heart.—(*The Adventist Home,* 127.)

Devote your mind to spiritual things. Keep your mind from dwelling upon yourself. Cultivate a contented, cheerful spirit. You talk too much upon unimportant things. You gain no spiritual strength from this. If the strength spent in talking were devoted to prayer, you would receive spiritual strength and would make melody in your heart to God.—(*Testimonies for the Church,* vol. 2, 434, 435.)

The greatest blessing that God can give to man is the spirit of earnest prayer. All heaven is open before the man of prayer. . . . The ambassadors of Christ will have power with the people after they have, with earnest supplication, come before God.—(*Review and Herald,* October 20, 1896.)

We do not value the power of prayer as we should.—We do not value the power and efficacy of prayer as we should. Prayer and faith will do what no power on earth can accomplish. We are seldom, in all respects, placed in the same position twice. We continually have new scenes and new trials to pass through, where past experience cannot be a sufficient guide. We must have the continual light that comes from God.—(*Ministry of Healing,* 509.)

Prayer keeps us in God's power.—The strength acquired in prayer to God will prepare us for our daily duties. The temptations to which we are daily exposed make prayer a necessity. In order that we may be kept by the power of God through faith, the desires of the mind should be continually ascending in silent prayer. When we are surrounded by influences calculated to lead us away from God, our petitions for help and strength must be unwearied. Unless, this is so, we shall never be successful in breaking down pride and overcoming the power of temptation to sinful indulgences which keep us from the Saviour. The light of truth, sanctifying the life, will discover to the receiver the sinful passions of his heart which are striving for the mastery, and which make it necessary for him to stretch every nerve and exert all his powers to resist Satan that he may conquer through the merits of Christ.—(*Messages to Young People,* 248.)

DIVINE POWER AWAITS THOSE WHO WANT IT.—You may have a deep and abiding sense of eternal things and that love for humanity which Christ has shown in His life. A close connection with heaven will give the right tone to your fidelity and will be the ground of your success. Your feeling of dependence will drive you to prayer, and your sense of duty summon you to effort. Prayer and effort, effort and prayer, will be the business of your life. You must pray as though the efficiency and praise were all due to God, and labor as though duty were all your own. If you want power you may have it; it is waiting your draft upon it. Only believe in God, take Him at His word, act by faith, and blessings will come.— (*Testimonies for the Church,* vol. 4, 538, 539.)

EVEN A BRIEF PRAYER CAN BRING SPIRITUAL POWER.—"I prayed," he [Nehemiah] said, "to the God of heaven." In that brief prayer Nehemiah pressed into the presence of the King of kings and won to his side a power that can turn hearts as the rivers of waters are turned.

To pray as Nehemiah prayed in his hour of need is a resource at the command of the Christian under circumstances when other forms of prayer may be impossible.—(*Prophets and Kings,* 631.)

PRAYER IS THE SECRET OF SPIRITUAL POWER.—Prayer is the breath of the soul. It is the secret of spiritual power. No other means of grace can be substituted and the health of the soul be preserved.

Prayer brings the heart into immediate contact with the Wellspring of life, and strengthens the sinew and muscle of the religious experience. Neglect the exercise of prayer, or engage in prayer spasmodically, now and then, as seems convenient, and you lose your hold on God. The spiritual faculties lose their vitality, the religious experience lacks health and vigor.—(*Messages to Young People,* 249, 250.)

PRAYER BRINGS POWER FROM GOD.—Power will come from God to man in answer to the prayer of faith.—(*Testimonies for the Church,* vol. 4, 402.)

PRAYER BRINGS SUCCESS IN CONFLICT WITH SIN.—Prayer is heaven's ordained means of success in the conflict with sin and the development of Christian character. The divine influences that come in answer to the prayer of faith will accomplish in the soul of the suppliant all for which he pleads. For the pardon of sin, for the Holy Spirit, for a Christlike temper, for wisdom and strength to do His work, for any gift He has promised, we may ask; and the promise is, "Ye shall receive."—(*Acts of the Apostles,* 564.)

PRAYER LAYS HOLD UPON INFINITE POWER.—True faith and true prayer—how strong they are! They are as two arms by which the human suppliant lays hold upon the power of Infinite Love.—(*Gospel Workers,* 259.)

PRAYER STRENGTHENS US AGAINST SATAN'S TEMPTATIONS.—Satan presents many temptations to the youth. He is playing the game of life for their souls, and he leaves no means untried to allure and ruin them. But God does not leave them to fight unaided against the tempter. They have an all-powerful Helper.

Stronger far than their foe is He who in this world and in human nature met and conquered Satan, resisting every temptation that comes to the youth today. He is their Elder Brother. He feels for them a deep and tender interest. He keeps over them a constant watch-care, and He rejoices when they try to please Him. As they pray, He mingles with their prayers the incense of His righteousness, and offers them to God as a fragrant sacrifice. In His strength the youth can endure hardness as good soldiers of the cross. Strengthened with His might, they are enabled to reach the high ideals before them. The sacrifice made on Calvary is the pledge of their victory.—(*Messages to Young People,* 95, 96.)

OUR PRAYERS REACH GOD'S THRONE.—By your fervent prayers of faith you can move the arm that moves the world. You can teach your children to pray effectually as they kneel by your side. Let your prayers arise to the throne of God, "Spare thy people, O Lord, and give not thine heritage to reproach, that the heathen should rule over them: wherefore should they say among the people, Where is their God?"

God is at work. He doeth wonders, and although He is high and lifted up, prayer can reach His throne. He that is turning and overturning, He that can do marvelous things, will regard the contrite prayer of faith from the humblest of His children.—(*Review and Herald,* April 23, 1889.)

OUR VOICES REACH GOD'S EAR.—The word that was spoken to Jesus at the Jordan, "This is My beloved Son, in whom I am well pleased," embraces humanity. God spoke to Jesus as our representative. With all our sins and weaknesses, we are not cast aside as worthless. "He hath made us accepted in the Beloved." Eph. 1:6. The glory that rested upon Christ is a pledge of the love of God for us. It tells us of the power of prayer,—how the human voice may reach the ear of God, and our petitions find acceptance in the courts of heaven. By sin, earth was cut off from heaven, and alienated from its communion; but Jesus has connected it again with the sphere of glory. His love has encircled man, and reached the highest heaven. The light which fell from the open portals upon the head of our Saviour will fall upon us as we pray for help to resist temptation. The voice which spoke to Jesus says to every believing soul, This is My beloved child, in whom I am well pleased.—(*The Desire of Ages,* 113.)

WE NEED TO WRESTLE WITH GOD IN PRAYER.—Will we carry forward the work in the Lord's way? Are we willing to be taught of God? Will we wrestle with God in prayer? Will we receive the baptism of the Holy Spirit? This is what we need and may have at this time. Then we shall go forth with a message from the Lord, and the light of truth will shine forth as a lamp that burneth, reaching to all parts of the world. If we will walk humbly with God, God will walk with us. Let us humble our souls, and we shall see of His salvation.— (*Review and Herald,* July 1, 1909.)

THE GREATEST VICTORIES ARE WON THROUGH EARNEST PRAYER.— Jacob prevailed because he was persevering and determined. His experience testifies to the power of importunate prayer. It is now that we are to learn this lesson of prevailing prayer, of unyielding faith. The greatest victories to the church of Christ or to the individual Christian, are not those that are gained by talent or education, by wealth, or the favor of men. They are those victories that are gained in the audience chamber with God, when earnest, agonizing faith lays hold upon the mighty arm of power.

Those who are unwilling to forsake every sin and to seek earnestly for God's blessing, will not obtain it. But all who will lay hold of God's promises as did Jacob, and be as earnest and persevering as he was, will succeed as he succeeded.—(*Patriarchs and Prophets,* 203.)

PRAISE AND THANKSGIVING BRING POWER TO OUR PRAYERS.— Shall all our devotional exercises consist in asking and receiving? Shall we be always thinking of our wants and never of the benefits we receive? Shall we be recipients of His mercies and never express our gratitude to God, never praise Him for what He has done for us? We do not pray any too much, but we are too sparing of giving thanks. If the loving-kindness of God called forth more thanksgiving and praise, we would have far more power in prayer. We would abound more and more in the love of God and have more bestowed to praise Him for. You who complain that God does not hear your prayers, change your present order and mingle praise with your petitions. When you consider His goodness and mercies you will find that He will consider your wants.

Pray, pray earnestly and without ceasing, but do not forget to praise.—(*Testimonies for the Church,* vol. 5, 317.)

THE POWER OF PRAYER BRINGS FRUIT TO OUR WORK FOR GOD.— Those in the darkness of error are the purchase of the blood of Christ. They are the fruit of His suffering, and they are to be labored for. Let our canvassers know that it is for the advancement of Christ's kingdom that they are laboring. He will teach them as they go forth to their God-appointed work, to warn the world of a soon-coming judgment. Accompanied by the power of persuasion, the power of prayer, the power of the love of God, the evangelist's work will not, can not, be without fruit. Think of the interest that the Father and the Son have in this work. As the Father loves the Son, so the Son loves those that are His,—those who work as He worked to save perishing souls. None need feel that they are powerless: for Christ declares, "All power is given unto Me in heaven and in earth." He has promised that He will give this power to His workers. His power is to become their power.—(*Colporteur Ministry,* 108.)

SATAN CANNOT OVERCOME ONE WHO PRAYS.—The enemy cannot overcome the humble learner of Christ, the one who walks prayerfully before the Lord. Christ interposes Himself as a shelter, a retreat, from the assaults of the wicked one. The promise is given, "When the enemy shall come in like a flood, the Spirit of the Lord shall lift up a standard against him." . . . There is no power in the whole satanic force that can disable the soul that trusts, in simple confidence, in the wisdom that comes from God.—(*My Life Today,* 316.)

PRAYER BRINGS POWER TO RESIST TEMPTATION.—Without un-ceasing prayer and diligent watching, we are in danger of growing careless, and of deviating from the right path. The adversary seeks continually to obstruct the way to the mercy-seat, that we may not by earnest supplication and faith obtain grace and power to resist temptation.—(*Steps to Christ*, 95.)

NEGLECT OF PRAYER AND BIBLE STUDY MAKES US VULNERABLE TO TEMPTATION.—Temptations often appear irresistible because, through the neglect of prayer and the study of the Bible, the tempted one can not readily remember God's promises and meet Satan with the Scripture weapons. But angels are round about those who are willing to be taught in divine things; and in the time of great necessity, they will bring to their remembrance the very truths which are needed.—(*The Great Controversy*, 600.)

SATAN DREADS TO HAVE US PRAY.—There is a mighty power in prayer. Our great adversary is constantly seeking to keep the troubled soul away from God. An appeal to Heaven by the hum-blest saint is more to be dreaded by Satan than the decrees of cabinets or the mandates of kings.—(*In Heavenly Places*, 82.)

THE SOURCE OF POWER IN THE REFORMATION WAS PRAYER.—From the secret place of prayer came the power that shook the world in the Great Reformation. There, with holy calmness, the servants of the Lord set their feet upon the rock of His promises. During the struggle at Augsburg, Luther "did not pass a day with-out devoting three hours at least to prayer, and they were hours selected from those the most favorable to study." In the privacy of his chamber he was heard to pour out his soul before God in words "full of adoration, fear, and hope, as when one speaks to a friend."—(*The Great Controversy*, 210.)

CHAPTER

10

Reasons to Pray

ENLIGHTENS THE MIND REGARDING WHAT IS TRUTH.—Why is it that we do not receive more from Him who is the source of light and power? We expect too little. Has God lost His love for man? Is not this love still flowing earthward? Has He lost His desire to show Himself strong in behalf of His people? Christ will give us victory in the conflict. Who can doubt this when we know that He laid aside His royal robe and kingly crown, and came to this world in the garb of humanity, that He might stand as man's substitute and surety?

We do not value as we should the power and efficacy of prayer. "The Spirit also helpeth our infirmities: for we know not what we should pray for as we ought: but the Spirit itself maketh intercession for us with groanings which can not be uttered." God desires us to come to Him in prayer, that He may enlighten our minds. He alone can give clear conceptions of truth. He alone can soften and subdue the heart. He can quicken the understanding to discern truth from error. He can establish the wavering mind, and give it a knowledge and a faith that will endure the test. Pray then; pray without ceasing. The Lord who heard Daniel's prayer, will hear yours if you will approach Him as Daniel did.—(*Review and Herald,* March 24, 1904.)

ACQUAINTS US WITH THE FATHER.—Oh, do we know God as we should? What comfort, what joy, we should have if we were to learn daily the lessons He desires us to learn! We must know Him by an experimental knowledge. It will be profitable for us to spend more time in secret prayer, in becoming personally acquainted with our heavenly Father.—(*Medical Ministry,* 102.)

UNITES US WITH EACH OTHER AND WITH GOD.—Prayer unites us with one another and with God. Prayer brings Jesus to our side, and gives to the fainting, perplexed soul new strength to overcome the world, the flesh, and the devil. Prayer turns aside the attacks of Satan.—(*Christ's Object Lessons,* 250.)

ENABLES US TO RESIST TEMPTATION.—Why should the sons and daughters of God be reluctant to pray, when prayer is the key in the hand of faith to unlock heaven's storehouse, where are treasured the boundless resources of Omnipotence? Without unceasing prayer and diligent watching we are in danger of growing careless and of deviating from the right path. The adversary seeks continually to obstruct the way to the mercy seat, that we may not by earnest supplication and faith obtain grace and power to resist temptation.—(*Steps to Christ,* 94, 95.)

Christ is our only hope. Come to God in the name of Him who gave His life for the life of the world. Rely upon the efficacy of His sacrifice. Show that His love, His joy, is in your soul, and that because of this, your joy is full. In God is our strength. Pray much. Prayer is the life of the soul. The prayer of faith is the weapon by which we may successfully resist every assault of the enemy.—(*Selected Messages,* bk. 1, 88.)

PREPARES US FOR MEMBERSHIP IN THE CHURCH ABOVE.—To the humble, believing soul, the house of God on earth is the gate of heaven. The song of praise, the prayer, the words spoken by Christ's representatives, are God's appointed agencies to prepare a people for the church above, for that loftier worship into which there can enter nothing that defileth.—(*Testimonies for the Church,* vol. 5, 491.)

REINFORCES OUR CONVICTIONS.—Our convictions need daily to be reinforced by humble, sincere prayer and reading of the word. While we each have an individuality, while we each should hold our convictions firmly, we must hold them as God's truth and in the strength which God imparts. If we do not, they will be wrung from our grasp.—(*Testimonies for the Church,* vol. 6, 401.)

SUPPLIES TEMPORAL NECESSITIES.—Every promise in the word of God furnishes us with subject matter for prayer, presenting the pledged word of Jehovah as our assurance. Whatever spiritual blessing we need, it is our privilege to claim through Jesus. We may tell the Lord, with the simplicity of a child, exactly what we need. We may state to Him our temporal matters, asking Him for bread and raiment as well as for the bread of life and the robe of Christ's righteousness. Your heavenly Father knows that you have need of all these things, and you are invited to ask Him concerning them. It is through the name of Jesus that every favor is received. God will honor that name, and will supply your necessities from the riches of His liberality.—(*Thoughts From the Mount of Blessing,* 133.)

Every soul has the privilege of stating to the Lord his own special necessities and to offer his individual thanksgiving for the blessings that he daily receives.—(*Testimonies for the Church,* vol. 9, 278, 279.)

DOES NOT PROVIDE NEW INFORMATION TO GOD.—Prayer is not understood as it should be. Our prayers are not to inform God of something He does not know. The Lord is acquainted with the secrets of every soul. Our prayers need not be long and loud. God reads the hidden thoughts. We may pray in secret, and He who sees in secret will hear, and will reward us openly.—(*Messages to Young People,* 247.)

DAILY SUPPLIES OF GRACE GIVEN.—Those who at Pentecost were endued with power from on high, were not thereby freed from further temptation and trial. As they witnessed for truth and righteousness they were repeatedly assailed by the enemy of all truth, who sought to rob them of their Christian experience. They were compelled to strive with all their God-given powers to reach the measure of the stature of men and women in Christ Jesus. Daily they prayed for fresh supplies of grace, that they might reach higher and still higher toward perfection. Under the Holy Spirit's working even the weakest, by exercising faith in God, learned to improve their entrusted powers and to become sanctified, refined, and ennobled. As in humility they submitted to the molding influence of the Holy Spirit, they received of the fullness of the Godhead and were fashioned in the likeness of the divine.—(*Acts of the Apostles,* 49, 50.)

Wisdom supplied.—We must seek wisdom from on high that we may stand in this day of error and delusion.—(*Early Writings,* 87, 88.)

Pray most earnestly for an understanding of the times in which we live, for a fuller conception of His purpose, and for increased efficiency in soulsaving.—(*Selected Messages,* bk. 2, 399.)

The baptism of the Holy Spirit given.—God's faithful messengers are to seek to carry forward the Lord's work in His appointed way. They are to place themselves in close connection with the Great Teacher, that they may be daily taught of God. They are to wrestle with God in earnest prayer for a baptism of the Holy Spirit that they may meet the needs of a world perishing in sin. All power is promised those who go forth in faith to proclaim the everlasting gospel. As the servants of God bear to the world a living message fresh from the throne of glory, the light of truth will shine forth as a lamp that burneth, reaching to all parts of the world. Thus the darkness of error and unbelief will be dispelled from the minds of the honest in heart in all lands, who are now seeking after God, "If haply they might feel after Him, and find Him."—(*Testimonies to Ministers,* 459, 460.)

Today's needs provided for.—The truth of God received into the heart is able to make you wise unto salvation. In believing and obeying it you will receive grace sufficient for the duties and trials of today. Grace for tomorrow you do not need. You should feel that you have only to do with today. Overcome for today; deny self for today; watch and pray for today; obtain victories in God for today.—(*Testimonies for the Church,* vol. 3, 333.)

THE NEEDS OF GOD'S WORK CARED FOR.—The varied interests of the cause furnish us with food for reflection and inspiration for our prayers.—(*Testimonies for the Church,* vol. 4, 459.)

ANSWERED PRAYERS ARE CAUSE FOR PRAISE AND THANKSGIVING.— In the second chapter of I Samuel is recorded the prayer of a consecrated woman who served and glorified God. She prayed: "My heart rejoiceth in the Lord, mine horn is exalted in the Lord: my mouth is enlarged over mine enemies; because I rejoice in thy salvation. There is none holy as the Lord: for there is none beside thee: neither is there any rock like our God." Hannah's offering of thanksgiving for the answer to her prayer is a lesson to those who today receive answers to their requests. Do we not neglect to return praise and thanksgiving to God for His loving-kindness?

David declares, "I love the Lord, because he hath heard my voice and my supplications. Because he hath inclined his ear unto me, therefore will I call upon him as long as I live." God's goodness in hearing and answering prayer places us under heavy obligation to express our thanksgiving for the favors bestowed upon us. We should praise God much more than we do. The blessings received in answer to prayer should be promptly acknowledged. The record of them should be placed in our diary, that when we take the book in hand, we may remember the goodness of the Lord, and praise His holy name.—(*Review and Herald,* May 7, 1908.)

OUR CHARACTERS MAY BE TRANSFORMED.—The change we need is a change of heart, and can only be obtained by seeking God individually for His blessing, by pleading with Him for His power, by fervently praying that His grace may come upon us, and that our characters may be transformed. This is the change we need today, and for the attainment of this experience we should exercise persevering energy and manifest heartfelt earnestness. We should ask with true sincerity, "What shall I do to be saved?" We should know just what steps we are taking heavenward.—(*Selected Messages,* bk. 1, 187.)

OUR UNDERSTANDING OF GOD'S WORD EXPANDED.—No man is safe for a day or an hour without prayer. Especially should we entreat the Lord for wisdom to understand His word. Here are revealed the wiles of the tempter and the means by which he may be successfully resisted. Satan is an expert in quoting Scripture, placing his own interpretation upon passages, by which he hopes to cause us to stumble. We should study the Bible with humility of heart, never losing sight of our dependence upon God. While we must constantly guard against the devices of Satan, we should pray in faith continually: "Lead us not into temptation."—(*The Great Controversy,* 530.)

The Bible should never be studied without prayer. The Holy Spirit alone can cause us to feel the importance of those things easy to be understood, or prevent us from wresting truths difficult of comprehension. It is the office of heavenly angels to prepare the heart so to comprehend God's word that we shall be charmed with its beauty, admonished by its warnings, or animated and strengthened by its promises. We should make the psalmist's petition our own: "Open Thou mine eyes, that I may behold wondrous things out of Thy law." Psalm 119:18. Temptations often appear irresistible because, through neglect of prayer and the study of the Bible, the tempted one cannot readily remember God's promises and meet Satan with the Scripture weapons. But angels are round about those who are willing to be taught in divine things; and in the time of great necessity they will bring to their remembrance the very truths which are needed. Thus "when the enemy shall come in like a flood, the Spirit of the Lord shall lift up a standard against him." Isaiah 59:19—(*The Great Controversy,* 599, 600.)

11

Answered
Prayer

GOD WILL ANSWER, IF WE ASK.—Worldly wisdom teaches that prayer is not essential. Men of science claim that there can be no real answer to prayer; that this would be a violation of law, a miracle, and that miracles have no existence. The universe, say they, is governed by fixed laws, and God Himself does nothing contrary to these laws. Thus they represent God as bound by His own laws— as if the operation of divine laws could exclude divine freedom. Such teaching is opposed to the testimony of the Scriptures. Were not miracles wrought by Christ and His apostles? The same compassionate Saviour lives today, and He is as willing to listen to the prayer of faith as when He walked visibly among men. The natural cooperates with the supernatural. It is a part of God's plan to grant us, in answer to the prayer of faith, that which He would not bestow did we not thus ask.—(*The Great Controversy,* 525.)

When you are privileged to meet with your brethren in the church, tell them of the necessity of keeping open the channel of communication between God and the soul. Tell them that if they will find heart and voice to pray, God will find answers to their prayers. Tell them not to neglect their religious duties. Exhort the brethren to pray. We must seek if we would find, we must ask if we would receive, we must knock if we would have the door opened unto us.—(*Signs of the Times,* February 10, 1890.)

Jesus does not call on us to follow Him, and then forsake us. If we surrender our lives to His service, we can never be placed in a position for which God has not made provision. Whatever may be our situation, we have a Guide to direct our way; whatever our perplexities, we have a sure Counselor; whatever our sorrow, bereavement, or loneliness, we have a sympathizing Friend. If in our ignorance we make missteps, Christ does not leave us. . . .

"All things, whatsoever ye shall ask in prayer, believing, ye shall receive." [Matt 21:22.]—(*Gospel Workers,* 263.)

GOD'S BLESSINGS WILL COME AS A RESULT OF HUMBLE FAITH.—A close connection with heaven will give the right tone to your fidelity and will be the ground of your success. Your feeling of dependence will drive you to prayer, and your sense of duty summon you to effort. Prayer and effort, effort and prayer, will be the business of your life. You must pray as though the efficiency and praise were all due to God, and labor as though duty were all your own. If you want power you may have it; it is waiting your draft upon it. Only believe in God, take Him at His word, act by faith, and blessings will come.

In this matter, genius, logic, and eloquence will not avail. Those who have a humble, trusting, contrite heart, God accepts, and hears their prayer; and when God helps, all obstacles will be overcome. How many men of great natural abilities and high scholarships have failed when placed in positions of responsibility, while those of feebler intellect, with less favorable surroundings, have been wonderfully successful. The secret was: The former trusted to themselves, while the latter united with Him who is wonderful in counsel and mighty in working to accomplish what He will.—(*Testimonies for the Church,* vol. 4, 538, 539.)

The simple prayers indited by the Holy Spirit will ascend through the gates ajar, the open door which Christ has declared: I have opened, and no man can shut. These prayers, mingled with the incense of the perfection of Christ, will ascend as fragrance to the Father, and answers will come.—(*Testimonies for the Church,* vol. 6, 467.)

PRAYERS OF CHILD-LIKE SIMPLICITY AND FAITH WILL BE AN-SWERED.— "If any man thirst, let him come unto Me, and drink." "Whosoever drinketh of the water that I shall give him shall never thirst; but the water that I shall give him shall be in him a well of water springing up into everlasting life." John 7:37; 4:14.

If, with these promises before us, we choose to remain parched and withered for want of the water of life, it is our own fault. If we would come to Christ with the simplicity of a child coming to its earthly parents, and ask for the things that He has promised, believing that we receive them, we should have them.—(*Testimonies for the Church,* vol. 9, 179.)

PRAY AND BELIEVE.—God does not say, Ask once, and you shall receive. He bids us ask. Unwearyingly persist in prayer. The persistent asking brings the petitioner into a more earnest attitude, and gives him an increased desire to receive the things for which he asks. Christ said to Martha at the grave of Lazarus, "If thou wouldest believe, thou shouldest see the glory of God." John 11:40.

But many have not a living faith. This is why they do not see more of the power of God. Their weakness is the result of their unbelief. They have more faith in their own working than in the working of God for them. They take themselves into their own keeping. They plan and devise, but pray little, and have little real trust in God. They think they have faith, but it is only the impulse of the moment. Failing to realize their own need, or God's willingness to give, they do not persevere in keeping their requests before the Lord.

Our prayers are to be as earnest and persistent as was the petition of the needy friend who asked for the loaves at midnight. The more earnestly and steadfastly we ask, the closer will be our spiritual union with Christ. We shall receive increased blessings because we have increased faith.

Our part is to pray and believe. Watch unto prayer. Watch, and co-operate with the prayer-hearing God. Bear in mind that "we are labourers together with God." 1 Cor. 3:9. Speak and act in harmony with your prayers. It will make an infinite difference with you whether trial shall prove your faith to be genuine, or show that your prayers are only a form.—(*Christ's Object Lessons,* 145, 146.)

PRAY IN FAITH AND ANSWERS WILL COME.—The lessons that God sends will always, if well learned, bring help in due time. Put your trust in God. Pray much, and believe. Trusting, hoping, believing, holding fast the hand of Infinite Power, you will be more than conquerors.

True workers walk and work by faith. Sometimes they grow weary with watching the slow advance of the work when the battle wages strong between the powers of good and evil. But if they refuse to fail or be discouraged they will see the clouds breaking away and the promise of deliverance fulfilling. Through the mist with which Satan has surrounded them, they will see the shining of the bright beams of the Sun of Righteousness.

Work in faith, and leave results with God. Pray in faith, and the mystery of His providence will bring its answer. At times it may seem that you cannot succeed. But work and believe, putting into your efforts faith, hope, and courage. After doing what you can, wait for the Lord, declaring His faithfulness, and He will bring His word to pass. Wait, not in fretful anxiety, but in undaunted faith and unshaken trust.—(*Testimonies for the Church,* vol. 7, 245.)

There is strength to be obtained of God. He can help. He can give grace and heavenly wisdom. If you ask in faith, you will receive; but you must watch unto prayer. Watch, pray, work, should be your watchword.—(*Testimonies for the Church,* vol. 2, 427.)

God has sent us to work in His vineyard. It is our duty to do all we can. "In the morning sow thy seed, and in the evening withhold not thine hand: for thou knowest not whether shall prosper, either this or that." We have too little faith. We limit the Holy One of Israel. We should be grateful that He condescends to use any of us as His instruments. For every earnest prayer put up in faith, an answer will be returned. It may not come just as we have expected; but it will come at the very time when we most need it. "If ye abide in me, and my words abide in you, ye shall ask what ye will, and it shall be done unto you."—(*Review and Herald,* March 23, 1897.)

IF WE FIND TIME TO PRAY, GOD WILL FIND TIME TO ANSWER.— Every earnest petition for grace and strength will be answered. . . . Ask God to do for you those things that you cannot do for yourselves. Tell Jesus everything. Lay open before Him the secrets of your heart; for His eye searches the inmost recesses of the soul, and He reads your thoughts as an open book. When you have asked for the things that are necessary for your soul's good, believe that you receive them, and you shall have them. Accept His gifts with your whole heart; for Jesus has died that you might have the precious things of heaven as your own, and at last find a home with the heavenly angels in the kingdom of God.

If you will find voice and time to pray, God will find time and voice to answer.—(*My Life Today,* 16.)

REJOICE THAT GOD HAS ANSWERED YOUR PRAYERS.—Pray in faith. And be sure to bring your lives into harmony with your petitions, that you may receive the blessings for which you pray. Let not your faith weaken, for the blessings received are proportionate to the faith exercised. "According to your faith be it unto you." "All things, whatsoever ye shall ask in prayer, believing, ye shall receive." Matthew 9:29; 21:22. Pray, believe, rejoice. Sing praises to God because He has answered your prayers. Take Him at His word. "He is faithful that promised." Hebrews 10:23. Not one sincere supplication is lost. The channel is open; the stream is flowing. It carries with it healing properties, pouring forth a restoring current of life and health and salvation. —(*Testimonies for the Church,* vol. 7, 274.)

THE VERY INTENSITY OF OUR PRAYERS IS A PLEDGE THAT GOD WILL ANSWER.—When a man breathes an intensely earnest prayer to God (Jesus Christ is the only name given under heaven whereby we can be saved), there is in that intensity and earnestness a pledge from God that He is about to answer that prayer exceeding abundantly, above all that we can ask or think. We must not only pray in the name of Jesus, but by the inspiration and kindling of the Holy Spirit. This explains what is meant when it is said, "the Spirit itself maketh intercession for us with groanings which can not be uttered." The petitions must be offered in earnest faith. Then they will reach the mercy-seat. Unwearyingly persist in prayer. God does not say, Pray once, and I will answer you. His word is pray, be instant in prayer, believing ye have the things ye ask, and ye shall receive them; I will answer you.—(*The Gospel Herald,* May 28, 1902.)

CONDITIONS TO ANSWERED PRAYER.—There are certain conditions upon which we may expect that God will hear and answer our prayers. One of the first of these is that we feel our need of help from Him. He has promised, "I will pour water upon him that is thirsty, and floods upon the dry ground." Isaiah 44:3. Those who hunger and thirst after righteousness, who long after God, may be sure that they will be filled. The heart must be open to the Spirit's influence, or God's blessing cannot be received.

Our great need is itself an argument and pleads most eloquently in our behalf. But the Lord is to be sought unto to do these things for us. He says, "Ask, and it shall be given you." And "He that spared not His own Son, but delivered Him up for us all, how shall He not with Him also freely give us all things?" Matthew 7:7; Romans 8:32.

If we regard iniquity in our hearts, if we cling to any known sin, the Lord will not hear us; but the prayer of the penitent, contrite soul is always accepted. When all known wrongs are righted, we may believe that God will answer our petitions. Our own merit will never commend us to the favor of God; it is the worthiness of Jesus that will save us, His blood that will cleanse us; yet we have a work to do in complying with the conditions of acceptance.

Another element of prevailing prayer is faith. "He that cometh to God must believe that He is, and that He is a rewarder of them that diligently seek Him." Hebrews 11:6. Jesus said to His disciples, "What things soever ye desire, when ye pray, believe that ye receive them, and ye shall have them." Mark 11:24. Do we take Him at His word?

The assurance is broad and unlimited, and He is faithful who has promised. When we do not receive the very things we asked for, at the time we ask, we are still to believe that the Lord hears and that He will answer our prayers. We are so erring and short-sighted that we sometimes ask for things that would not be a blessing to us, and our heavenly Father in love answers our prayers by giving us that which will be for our highest good—that which we ourselves would desire if with vision divinely enlightened we could see all things as they really are. When our prayers seem not to be answered, we are to cling to the promise; for the time of answering will surely come, and we shall receive the blessing we need most. But to claim that prayer will always be answered in the very way and for the particular thing that we desire, is presumption. God is too wise to err, and too good to withhold any good thing from them that walk uprightly. Then do not fear to trust Him, even though you do not see the immediate answer to your prayers. Rely upon His sure promise, "Ask, and it shall be given you."

If we take counsel with our doubts and fears, or try to solve everything that we cannot see clearly, before we have faith, perplexities will only increase and deepen. But if we come to God, feeling helpless and dependent, as we really are, and in humble, trusting faith make known our wants to Him whose knowledge is infinite, who sees everything in creation, and who governs everything by His will and word, He can and will attend to our cry, and will let light shine into our hearts. Through sincere prayer we are brought into connection with the mind of the Infinite. We may have no remarkable evidence at the time that the face of our Redeemer is bending over us in compassion and love, but this is even so. We may not feel His visible touch, but His hand is upon us in love and pitying tenderness.

When we come to ask mercy and blessing from God we should have a spirit of love and forgiveness in our own hearts. How can we pray, "Forgive us our debts, as we forgive our debtors," and yet indulge an unforgiving spirit? Matthew 6:12. If we expect our own prayers to be heard we must forgive others in the same manner and to the same extent as we hope to be forgiven.

Perseverance in prayer has been made a condition of receiving. We must pray always if we would grow in faith and experience. We are to be "instant in prayer," to "continue in prayer, and watch in the same with thanksgiving." Romans 12:12; Colossians 4:2. Peter exhorts believers to be "sober, and watch unto prayer." 1 Peter 4:7. Paul directs, "In everything by prayer and supplication with thanksgiving let your requests be made known unto God." Philippians 4:6. "But ye, beloved," says Jude, "praying in the Holy Ghost, keep yourselves in the love of God." Jude 20, 21.—(*Steps to Christ*, 95-97.)

If we render to Him only a partial, halfhearted obedience, His promises will not be fulfilled to us.—(*Ministry of Healing*, 227.)

WE MUST LIVE OUR PRAYERS IF THEY ARE TO BE ANSWERED.—We are to pray and watch unto prayer, that there may be no inconsistency in our lives. We must not fail to show others that we understand that watching unto prayer means living our prayers before God, that He may answer them.—(*Selected Messages*, bk. 1, 116, 117.)

PRAYER IS OF NO AVAIL IF THE LIFE DOES NOT MATCH THE PRAYER.—"If ye abide in me, and my words abide in you, ye shall ask what ye will, and it shall be done unto you." When you pray, present this promise. It is our privilege to come to Him with holy boldness. As in sincerity we ask Him to let His light shine upon us, He will hear and answer us. But we must live in harmony with our prayers. They are of no avail if we walk contrary to them. I have seen a father who, after reading a portion of scripture and offering prayer, would often, almost as soon as he had risen from his knees, begin to scold his children. How could God answer the prayer he had offered? And if, after scolding his children, a father offers prayer, does that prayer benefit the children? No; not unless it is a prayer of confession to God.—(*Child Guidance,* 499.)

PRAISE NEEDS TO BE INCLUDED IF OUR PRAYERS ARE TO BE AN- SWERED.—Shall all our devotional exercises consist in asking and receiving? Shall we be always thinking of our wants and never of the benefits we receive? Shall we be recipients of His mercies and never express our gratitude to God, never praise Him for what He has done for us? We do not pray any too much, but we are too sparing of giving thanks. If the loving-kindness of God called forth more thanksgiving and praise, we would have far more power in prayer. We would abound more and more in the love of God and have more bestowed to praise Him for. You who complain that God does not hear your prayers, change your present order and mingle praise with your petitions. When you consider His good- ness and mercies you will find that He will consider your wants.

Pray, pray earnestly and without ceasing, but do not forget to praise.—(*Testimonies for the Church,* vol. 5, 317.)

UNFAITHFULNESS IN STEWARDSHIP MAY BE A CAUSE OF UNAN- SWERED PRAYER.—As the Giver of every blessing, God claims a certain portion of all we possess. This is His provision to sustain the preaching of the gospel. And by making this return to God, we are to show our appreciation of His gifts. But if we withhold from Him that which is His own, how can we expect Him to entrust us with the things of heaven? It may be that here is the secret of unanswered prayer.—(*Christ's Object Lessons,* 144.)

WE INSULT GOD BY CLAIMING THE PROMISE WITHOUT MEETING THE CONDITIONS.—There are conditions to the fulfillment of God's promises, and prayer can never take the place of duty. "If ye love Me," Christ says, "Keep My commandments." "He that hath My commandments, and keepeth them, he it is that loveth Me; and he that loveth Me shall be loved of My Father, and I will love him, and will manifest Myself to him." John 14:15, 21. Those who bring their petitions to God, claiming His promise while they do not comply with the conditions, insult Jehovah. They bring the name of Christ as their authority for the fulfillment of the promise, but they do not those things that would show faith in Christ and love for Him.—(*Christ's Object Lessons,* 143.)

IF THE CONDITIONS ARE MET, THE PROMISE OF ANSWERED PRAYER IS UNEQUIVOCAL.—Prayer and faith are closely allied, and they need to be studied together. In the prayer of faith there is a divine science; it is a science that everyone who would make his lifework a success must understand. Christ says, "What things soever ye desire, when ye pray, believe that ye receive them, and ye shall have them." Mark 11:24. He makes it plain that our asking must be according to God's will; we must ask for the things that He has promised, and whatever we receive must be used in doing His will. The conditions met, the promise is unequivocal.

For the pardon of sin, for the Holy Spirit, for a Christlike temper, for wisdom and strength to do His work, for any gift He has promised, we may ask; then we are to believe that we receive, and return thanks to God that we have received.

We need look for no outward evidence of the blessing. The gift is in the promise, and we may go about our work assured that what God has promised He is able to perform, and that the gift, which we already possess, will be realized when we need it most.—(*Education,* 257, 258.)

OUR PRAYERS ARE NOT COMMANDS TO GOD.—We know that He hears us if we ask according to His will. Our petitions must not take the form of a command, but of intercession for Him to do the things we desire of Him.—(*Testimonies for the Church,* vol. 2, 149.)

PRAYERS NOT ALWAYS ANSWERED IMMEDIATELY.—God has a heaven full of blessings for those who will co-operate with Him. All who obey Him may with confidence claim the fulfillment of His promises.

But we must show a firm, undeviating trust in God. Often He delays to answer us in order to try our faith or test the genuineness of our desire. Having asked according to His word, we should believe His promise and press our petitions with a determination that will not be denied.—(*Christ's Object Lessons,* 145.)

When those who know the truth practice the self-denial enjoined in God's word, the message will go with power. The Lord will hear our prayers for the conversion of souls. God's people will let their light shine forth, and unbelievers, seeing their good works, will glorify our heavenly Father.—(*Messages to Young People,* 315.)

Christ's two days' delay after hearing that Lazarus was sick was not a neglect or a denial on His part. It was His purpose to remain where He was till the death of Lazarus took place, that He might give the people an evidence of His divinity, not by restoring a dying man, but by raising to life a man that had been buried.

This should be an encouragement to us. We are sometimes tempted to think that the promise, "Ask, and it shall be given you; seek, and ye shall find; knock, and it shall be opened unto you," is not fulfilled unless the answer comes immediately when the request is made. It is our privilege to ask for special blessings, and to believe that they will be given us. But if the blessings asked for are not immediately granted, we are not to think that our prayers are not heard. We shall receive, even if the answer is delayed for a time. In carrying out the plan of redemption, Christ sees enough in humanity to discourage Him. But He does not become discouraged. In mercy and love He continues to offer us opportunities and privileges. So we are to rest in the Lord, and wait patiently for Him. The answer to our prayers may not come as quickly as we desire, and it may not be just what we have asked; but He who knows what is for the highest good of His children will bestow a much greater good than we have asked, if we do not become faithless and discouraged.—(*The Youth's Instructor,* April 6, 1899.)

We all desire immediate and direct answers to our prayers, and are tempted to become discouraged when the answer is delayed or comes in an unlooked-for form. But God is too wise and good to answer our prayers always at just the time and in just the manner we desire. He will do more and better for us than to accomplish all our wishes. And because we can trust His wisdom and love, we should not ask Him to concede to our will, but should seek to enter into and accomplish His purpose. Our desires and interests should be lost in His will. These experiences that test faith are for our benefit. By them it is made manifest whether our faith is true and sincere, resting on the word of God alone, or whether depending on circumstances, it is uncertain and changeable. Faith is strengthened by exercise. We must let patience have its perfect work, remembering that there are precious promises in the Scriptures for those who wait upon the Lord.—(*Ministry of Healing*, 230, 231.)

I saw that the servants of God and the church were too easily discouraged. When they asked their Father in Heaven for things they thought they needed, and because it did not immediately come, their faith wavered, their courage fled, and a murmuring feeling took possession of them. This I saw displeased God.

Every saint that comes to God with a true heart, in faith, and sends their honest petitions to Him, will have their prayers answered. Their faith must not let go of the promises of God if they do not see or feel the immediate answer of their prayers. Be not afraid to trust God. Rely upon His sure promise, "Ask and ye shall receive." God is too wise to err, and too good to withhold any good thing from His saints that walk uprightly. Man is erring, and although his petitions are sent up from an honest heart, he does not always ask for the things that are good for himself, or that will glorify God. When this is so, our wise and good Father hears our prayers, and will answer; sometimes immediately, but gives us the things that are for our best good and His own glory.

If the children of God could see His plan, they would know that He gives them that which is for their best good. Although they may not receive just the things they expected, or asked for, yet their prayers were answered. Nothing hurtful was given, but the blessing they most needed, in the place of something they had asked for, that would not have been good for them, but to their hurt.

I saw if we did not feel immediate answers to our prayers, we should hold fast our faith, let no distrust come in; for that will separate us from God. If our faith wavers, we shall receive nothing from Him. Our confidence in God should be strong, and when we need it the most, the blessing will drop upon us like a shower of rain.

When the servants of God have prayed for His Spirit and blessing, it sometimes comes immediately, but it is not always then bestowed. At such times faint not. Let thy faith hold fast the promise, that it will come. Let thy trust be fully in God, and often that blessing will come when you need it the most, and unexpectedly you will receive help from God, when you are speaking the truth to unbelievers, and with clearness you can speak the word, and with power.

It was represented to me like children asking a blessing of their earthly parents that love them. They ask something that the parent knows will hurt them; the parent gives them the things that will be good and healthy for them, in the place of that which the child desired. I saw that every prayer that was sent up in faith from an honest heart will be heard of God and answered, and the one that sent up the petition will have the blessing when he needs it the most, and it will often exceed his expectations. Not a prayer of the true saint is lost if sent up from an honest heart in faith.—(*Spiritual Gifts*, bk. 4b, 7-9.)

After the prayer is made, if the answer is not realized immediately, do not weary of waiting and become unstable. Waver not. Cling to the promise, "Faithful is He that calleth you, who also will do it." Like the importunate widow, urge your case, being firm in your purpose. Is the object important and of great consequence to you? It certainly is. Then waver not, for your faith may be tried. If the thing you desire is valuable, it is worthy of a strong, earnest effort. You have the promise; watch and pray. Be steadfast and the prayer will be answered; for is it not God who has promised? If it costs you something to obtain it you will prize it the more when obtained. You are plainly told that if you waver you need not think that you shall receive anything of the Lord. A caution is here given not to become weary, but to rest firmly upon the promise. If you ask, He will give you liberally and upbraid not.—(*Testimonies for the Church,* vol. 2, 131.)

"Ask, and ye shall receive." The assurance is broad and unlimited, and He is faithful who has promised. We sometimes fail in faith because Infinite Wisdom does not come to our terms. When for any reason we do not receive the very things we ask for at the time we ask, we are still to believe that the Lord hears, and that He will give us those things that are best for us. His own glory is a sufficient reason for sometimes withholding what we ask for, and answering our prayers in a manner that we did not expect. But we are to cling to the promise; for the time of answering will come, and we shall receive the blessings we need most.—(*Signs of the Times,* August 21, 1884.)

GOD DOES NOT ALWAYS ANSWER AS WE EXPECT, BUT ALWAYS FOR OUR GOOD.—Ask, then; ask, and ye shall receive. Ask for humility, wisdom, courage, increase of faith. To every sincere prayer an answer will come. It may not come just as you desire, or at the time you look for it; but it will come in the way and at the time that will best meet your need. The prayers you offer in loneliness, in weariness, in trial, God answers, not always according to your expectations, but always for your good.—(*Messages to Young People,* 250.)

While you prayed in your affliction for peace in Christ, a cloud of darkness seemed to blacken across your mind. The rest and peace did not come as you expected. At times your faith seemed to be tested to the utmost. As you looked back to your past life, you saw sorrow and disappointment; as you viewed the future, all was uncertainty. The divine Hand led you wondrously to bring you to the cross and to teach you that God was indeed a rewarder of those who diligently seek Him. Those who ask aright will receive. He that seeketh in faith shall find. The experience gained in the furnace of trial and affliction is worth more than all the inconvenience and painful experience it costs.

The prayers that you offered in your loneliness, in your weariness and trial, God answered, not always according to your expectations, but for your good. You did not have clear and correct views of your brethren, neither did you see yourself in a correct light. But, in the providence of God, He has been at work to answer the prayers you have offered in your distress, in a way to save you and glorify His own name. In your ignorance of yourself you asked for things which were not best for you. God heard your prayers of sincerity, but the blessing granted was something very different from your expectations. God designed, in His providence, to place you more directly in connection with His church, that your confidence might be less in yourself and greater in others whom He is leading out to advance His work.

God hears every sincere prayer.—(*Testimonies for the Church,* vol. 3, 415, 416.)

GOD ANSWERS PRAYER AT HIS OWN APPOINTED TIME.—Throughout his married life, Zacharias had prayed for a son. He and his wife were now old, and as yet their prayer had remained unanswered; but he murmured not. God had not forgotten. He had His appointed time for answering this prayer, and when the case seemed hopeless, Zacharias received his answer.—(*SDA Bible Commentary,* vol. 5, 1114.)

WHY ANSWERS TO PRAYER MAY BE DELAYED.—God does not always answer our prayers the first time we call upon Him; for should He do this, we might take it for granted that we had a right to all the blessings and favors He bestowed upon us. Instead of searching our hearts to see if any evil was entertained by us, any sin indulged, we would become careless, and fail to realize our dependence upon Him, and our need of His help.—(*Review and Herald,* June 9, 1891.)

There are precious promises in the Scriptures to those who wait upon the Lord. We all desire an immediate answer to our prayers and are tempted to become discouraged if our prayer is not immediately answered. Now, my experience has taught me that this is a great mistake. The delay is for our special benefit. We have a chance to see whether our faith is true and sincere or changeable like the waves of the sea. We must bind ourselves upon the altar with the strong cords of faith and love, and let patience have her perfect work. Faith strengthens through continual exercise. This waiting does not mean that because we ask the Lord to heal there is nothing for us to do. On the contrary, we are to make the very best use of the means which the Lord in His goodness has provided for us in our necessities.—(*Counsels on Health*, 380, 381.)

KEEP ASKING, EVEN IF THE ANSWER DOES NOT COME.—Sometimes answers to our prayers come immediately; sometimes we have to wait patiently and continue earnestly to plead for the things that we need, our cases being illustrated by the case of the importunate solicitor for bread. "Which of you shall have a friend, and shall go unto him at midnight," etc. This lesson means more than we can imagine. We are to keep on asking, even if we do not realize the immediate response to our prayers. "I say unto you, Ask, and it shall be given you; seek, and ye shall find; knock, and it shall be opened unto you. For everyone that asketh receiveth; and he that seeketh findeth; and to him that knocketh it shall be opened." Luke 11:9, 10.

We need grace, we need divine enlightenment, that through the Spirit we may know how to ask for such things as we need. If our petitions are indited by the Lord they will be answered.—(*Counsels on Health*, 380.)

ANSWERS DELAYED TO REVEAL OUR SELFISHNESS.—He who blessed the nobleman at Capernaum is just as desirous of blessing us. But like the afflicted father, we are often led to seek Jesus by the desire for some earthly good; and upon the granting of our request we rest our confidence in His love. The Saviour longs to give us a greater blessing than we ask; and He delays the answer to our request that He may show us the evil of our own hearts, and our deep need of His grace. He desires us to renounce the selfishness that leads us to seek Him. Confessing our helplessness and bitter need, we are to trust ourselves wholly to His love.

The nobleman wanted to see the fulfillment of his prayer before he should believe; but he had to accept the word of Jesus that his request was heard and the blessing granted. This lesson we also have to learn. Not because we see or feel that God hears us are we to believe. We are to trust in His promises. When we come to Him in faith, every petition enters the heart of God. When we have asked for His blessing, we should believe that we receive it, and thank Him that we have received it. Then we are to go about our duties, assured that the blessing will be realized when we need it most. When we have learned to do this, we shall know that our prayers are answered. God will do for us "exceeding abundantly," "according to the riches of His glory," and "the working of His mighty power." Eph. 3:20, 16; 1:19.—(*The Desire of Ages,* 200.)

SEEMINGLY UNANSWERED PRAYERS MAY BE AMONG OUR GREATEST BLESSINGS.—In His loving care and interest for us, often He who understands us better than we understand ourselves refuses to permit us selfishly to seek the gratification of our own ambition. He does not permit us to pass by the homely but sacred duties that lie next us. Often these duties afford the very training essential to prepare us for a higher work. Often our plans fail that God's plans for us may succeed.

We are never called upon to make a real sacrifice for God. Many things He asks us to yield to Him, but in doing this we are but giving up that which hinders us in the heavenward way. Even when called upon to surrender those things which in themselves are good, we may be sure that God is thus working out for us some higher good.

In the future life the mysteries that here have annoyed and disappointed us will be made plain. We shall see that our seemingly unanswered prayers and disappointed hopes have been among our greatest blessings.

We are to look upon every duty, however humble, as sacred because it is a part of God's service. Our daily prayer should be, "Lord, help me to do my best. Teach me how to do better work.

Give me energy and cheerfulness. Help me to bring into my service the loving ministry of the Saviour."—(*Ministry of Healing*, 473, 474.)

SOMETIMES GOD DOES NOT GIVE US WHAT WE PRAY FOR BECAUSE HE HAS SOMETHING BETTER FOR US.—When we come to Him we should pray that we may enter into and accomplish His purpose, and that our desires and interests may be lost in His. We should acknowledge our acceptance of His will, not praying Him to concede to ours. It is better for us that God does not always answer our prayers just when we desire, and in just the manner we wish. He will do more and better for us than to accomplish all our wishes, for our wisdom is folly.—(*Testimonies for the Church*, vol. 2, 148.)

That prayer which comes forth from an earnest, believing heart is the effectual, fervent prayer that availeth much. God does not always answer our prayers as we expect, for we may not ask what would be for our highest good; but in His infinite love and wisdom He will give us those things which we most need.—(*Testimonies for the Church*, vol. 4, 531.)

WE ARE TO COOPERATE WITH GOD IN ANSWERING OUR PRAYERS.—In the Word of God are represented two contending parties that influence and control human agencies in our world. Constantly these parties are working with every human being. Those who are under God's control and who are influenced by the heavenly angels, will be able to discern the crafty workings of the unseen powers of darkness. Those who desire to be in harmony with the heavenly agencies should be intensely in earnest to do God's will. They must give no place whatever to Satan and his angels.

But unless we are constantly on guard, we shall be overcome by the enemy. Although a solemn revelation of God's will concerning us has been revealed to all, yet a knowledge of His will does not set aside the necessity of offering earnest supplications to Him for help, and of diligently seeking to cooperate with Him in answering the prayers offered. He accomplishes His purposes through human instrumentalities.—(*SDA Bible Commentary*, vol. 6, 1119.)

HALF-HEARTED PRAYERS WILL NOT BRING ANSWERS.—God will be to us everything we will let Him be. Our languid, half-hearted prayers will not bring us returns from heaven. Oh, we need to press our petitions! Ask in faith, wait in faith, receive in faith, rejoice in hope, for everyone that seeketh findeth. Be in earnest in the matter. Seek God with all the heart. People put soul and earnestness into everything they undertake in temporal things, until their efforts are crowned with success. With intense earnestness learn the trade of seeking the rich blessings that God has promised, and with persevering, determined effort you shall have His light and His truth and His rich grace.

In sincerity, in soul hunger, cry after God. Wrestle with the heavenly agencies until you have the victory. Put your whole being into the Lord's hands, soul, body, and spirit, and resolve to be His loving, consecrated agency, moved by His will, controlled by His mind, infused by His Spirit.

Tell Jesus your wants in the sincerity of your soul. You are not required to hold a long controversy with, or preach a sermon to, God, but with a heart of sorrow for your sins, say, "Save me, Lord, or I perish." There is hope for such souls. They will seek, they will ask, they will knock, and they will find. When Jesus has taken away the burden of sin that is crushing the soul, you will experience the blessedness of the peace of Christ.—(*Our High Calling,* 131.)

THE PRAYER FOR FORGIVENESS IS ALWAYS ANSWERED AT ONCE.— In some instances of healing, Jesus did not at once grant the blessing sought. But in the case of leprosy, no sooner was the appeal made than it was granted. When we pray for earthly blessings, the answer to our prayer may be delayed, or God may give us something other than we ask, but not so when we ask for deliverance from sin. It is His will to cleanse us from sin, to make us His children, and to enable us to live a holy life. Christ "gave Himself for our sins, that He might deliver us from this present evil world, according to the will of God and our Father." Gal. 1:4. And "this is the confidence that we have in Him, that, if we ask anything according to His will, He heareth us: and if we know that He hear us, whatsoever we ask, we know that we have the petitions that we desired of Him." 1 John 5:14, 15. "If we confess our sins, He is faithful and just to forgive us our sins, and to cleanse us from all unrighteousness." 1 John 1:9.—(*The Desire of Ages*, 266.)

CHRIST PRESENTS OUR PRAYERS BEFORE THE FATHER AS HIS OWN REQUEST.—No sooner does the child of God approach the mercy seat than he becomes the client of the great Advocate. At his first utterance of penitence and appeal for pardon Christ espouses his case and makes it His own, presenting the supplication before His Father as His own request.—(*Testimonies for the Church*, vol. 6, 364.)

PRAY TO THANK AND PRAISE GOD FOR ANSWERED PRAYERS.—In the second chapter of I Samuel is recorded the prayer of a consecrated woman who served and glorified God. She prayed: "My heart rejoiceth in the Lord, mine horn is exalted in the Lord: my mouth is enlarged over mine enemies; because I rejoice in thy salvation. There is none holy as the Lord: for there is none beside thee: neither is there any rock like our God." Hannah's offering of thanksgiving for the answer to her prayer is a lesson to those who today receive answers to their requests. Do we not neglect to return praise and thanksgiving to God for His loving-kindness?

David declares, "I love the Lord, because He hath heard my voice and my supplications. Because He hath inclined His ear unto me, therefore will I call upon Him as long as I live." God's goodness in hearing and answering prayer places us under heavy obligation to express our thanksgiving for the favors bestowed upon us. We should praise God much more than we do. The blessings received in answer to prayer should be promptly acknowledged. The record of them should be placed in our diary, that when we take the book in hand, we may remember the goodness of the Lord, and praise His holy name.—(*Review and Herald*, May 7, 1908.)

12

Prayer and Revival

REVIVAL WILL COME ONLY IN ANSWER TO PRAYER.—A revival of true godliness among us is the greatest and most urgent of all our needs. To seek this should be our first work. There must be earnest effort to obtain the blessing of the Lord, not because God is not willing to bestow His blessing upon us, but because we are unprepared to receive it. Our Heavenly Father is more willing to give His Holy Spirit to them that ask Him, than are earthly parents to give good gifts to their children. But it is our work, by confession, humiliation, repentance, and earnest prayer, to fulfill the conditions upon which God has promised to grant us His blessing. A revival need be expected only in answer to prayer.— (*Selected Messages*, bk. 1, 121.)

There is need today of such a revival of true heart-religion as was experienced by ancient Israel. We need, like them, to bring forth fruit meet for repentance,—to put away our sins, cleansing the defiled temple of the heart that Jesus may reign within. There is need of prayer—earnest, prevailing prayer. Our Saviour has left precious promises for the truly penitent petitioner. Such shall not seek His face in vain. He has also by His own example taught us the necessity of prayer. Himself the Majesty of Heaven, He often spent all night in communion with His Father. If the world's Redeemer was not too pure, too wise, or too holy to seek help from God, surely weak, erring mortals have every need of that divine assistance. With penitence and faith, every true Christian will often seek "the throne of grace, that he may obtain mercy, and find grace to help in time of need."—(*Signs of the Times,* January 26, 1882.)

PRAYER BRINGS US INTO CONNECTION WITH GOD.—If we come to God, feeling helpless and dependent, as we really are, and in humble, trusting faith make known our wants to Him whose knowledge is infinite, who sees everything in creation, and who governs everything by His will and word, He can and will attend to our cry, and will let light shine into our hearts. Through sincere prayer we are brought into connection with the mind of the Infinite. We may have no remarkable evidence at the time that the face of our Redeemer is bending over us in compassion and love, but this is even so. We may not feel His visible touch, but His hand is upon us in love and pitying tenderness.—(*Steps to Christ,* 97.)

OUR PRAYERS ASCEND TO HEAVEN MOIST WITH CHRIST'S CLEANSING BLOOD.—The religious services, the prayers, the praise, the penitent confession of sin ascend from true believers as incense to the heavenly sanctuary, but passing through the corrupt channels of humanity, they are so defiled that unless purified by blood, they can never be of value with God. They ascend not in spotless purity, and unless the Intercessor, who is at God's right hand, presents and purifies all by His righteousness, it is not acceptable to God. All incense from earthly tabernacles must be moist with the cleansing drops of the blood of Christ. He holds before the Father the censer of His own merits, in which there is no taint of earthly corruption. He gathers into this censer the prayers, the praise, and the confessions of His people, and with these He puts His own spotless righteousness. Then, perfumed with the merits of Christ's propitiation, the incense comes up before God wholly and entirely acceptable. Then gracious answers are returned.—(*Selected Messages,* bk. 1, 344.)

IN PRAYER WE SENSE THE PRESENCE OF JESUS.—If we keep the Lord ever before us, allowing our hearts to go out in thanksgiving and praise to Him, we shall have a continual freshness in our religious life. Our prayers will take the form of a conversation with God as we would talk with a friend. He will speak His mysteries to us personally. Often there will come to us a sweet joyful sense of the presence of Jesus.—(*Christ's Object Lessons,* 129.)

THE HOLY SPIRIT CAME AT PENTECOST IN ANSWER TO PRAYER.—The Spirit came upon the waiting, praying disciples with a fullness that reached every heart. The Infinite One revealed Himself in power to His church. It was as if for ages this influence had been held in restraint, and now Heaven rejoiced in being able to pour out upon the church the riches of the Spirit's grace. And under the influence of the Spirit, words of penitence and confession mingled with songs of praise for sins forgiven. Words of thanksgiving and of prophecy were heard. All heaven bent low to behold and to adore the wisdom of matchless, incomprehensible love. Lost in wonder, the apostles exclaimed, "Herein is love." They grasped the imparted gift. And what followed? The sword of the Spirit, newly edged with power and bathed in the lightnings of heaven, cut its way through unbelief. Thousands were converted in a day.—(*Acts of the Apostles,* 38.)

WE SHOULD PRAY FOR THE HOLY SPIRIT AS DID THE DISCIPLES AT PENTECOST.—The heart must be emptied of every defilement and cleansed for the indwelling of the Spirit. It was by the confession and forsaking of sin, by earnest prayer and consecration of themselves to God, that the early disciples prepared for the outpouring of the Holy Spirit on the Day of Pentecost. The same work, only in greater degree, must be done now. . . .

Unless we are daily advancing in the exemplification of the active Christian virtues, we shall not recognize the manifestations of the Holy Spirit in the latter rain. It may be falling on hearts all around us, but we shall not discern or receive it. . . .

Divine grace is needed at the beginning, divine grace at every step of advance, and divine grace alone can complete the work. There is no place for us to rest in a careless attitude. We must never forget the warnings of Christ, "Watch unto prayer," "Watch, . . . and pray always." A connection with the divine agency every moment is essential to our progress. We may have had a measure of the Spirit of God, but by prayer and faith we are continually to seek more of the Spirit.—(*Testimonies to Ministers,* 507, 508.)

We should pray as earnestly for the descent of the Holy Spirit as the disciples prayed on the day of Pentecost. If they needed it at that time, we need it more today.

Without the Spirit and power of God, it will be in vain that we labor to present the truth.—(*Australasian Union Conference Record,* April 1, 1898.)

Claim the promise of the Spirit by faith.—Only to those who wait humbly upon God, who watch for His guidance and grace, is the Spirit given. The power of God awaits their demand and reception. This promised blessing, claimed by faith, brings all other blessings in its train. It is given according to the riches of the grace of Christ, and He is ready to supply every soul according to the capacity to receive.—(*The Desire of Ages,* 672.)

Pray for the latter rain.—We must pray that God will unseal the fountain of the water of life. And we must ourselves receive of the living water. Let us, with contrite hearts, pray most earnestly that now, in the time of the latter rain, the showers of grace may fall upon us. At every meeting we attend our prayers should ascend, that at this very time God will impart warmth and moisture to our souls. As we seek God for the Holy Spirit, it will work in us meekness, humbleness of mind, a conscious dependence upon God for the perfecting latter rain. If we pray for the blessing in faith, we shall receive it as God has promised.—(*Testimonies to Ministers,* 508.)

BE FERVENT IN PRAYER AND IN THE POWER OF THE HOLY SPIRIT.— What we need is the quickening influence of the Holy Spirit of God. "Not by might, nor by power, but by My Spirit, saith the Lord of hosts." Pray without ceasing, and watch by working in accordance with your prayers. As you pray, believe, trust in God. It is the time of the latter rain, when the Lord will give largely of His Spirit. Be fervent in prayer, and watch in the Spirit.—(*Testimonies to Ministers,* 512.)

SATAN FEARS GOD'S PEOPLE PRAYING FOR THE HOLY SPIRIT.— There is nothing that Satan fears so much as that the people of God shall clear the way by removing every hindrance, so that the Lord can pour out His Spirit upon a languishing church and an impenitent congregation. If Satan had his way, there would never be another awakening, great or small, to the end of time. But we are not ignorant of his devices. It is possible to resist his power. When the way is prepared for the Spirit of God, the blessing will come. Satan can no more hinder a shower of blessing from descending upon God's people than he can close the windows of heaven that rain cannot come upon the earth. Wicked men and devils cannot hinder the work of God, or shut out His presence from the assemblies of His people, if they will, with subdued, contrite hearts, confess and put away their sins, and in faith claim His promises.—(*Selected Messages,* bk. 1, 124.)

THE SPIRIT ACCOMPANIES EVERY SINCERE PRAYER.—The religion that comes from God is the only religion that will lead to God. In order to serve Him aright, we must be born of the divine Spirit. This will purify the heart and renew the mind, giving us a new capacity for knowing and loving God. It will give us a willing obedience to all His requirements. This is true worship. It is the fruit of the working of the Holy Spirit. By the Spirit every sincere prayer is indited, and such prayer is acceptable to God. Wherever a soul reaches out after God, there the Spirit's working is manifest, and God will reveal Himself to that soul. For such worshipers He is seeking. He waits to receive them, and to make them His sons and daughters.—(*The Desire of Ages,* 189.)

PRAYER WITHOUT EARNEST ACTIVITY FOR OTHERS LEADS TO FORMALISM.—God does not mean that any of us shall become hermits or monks, and retire from the world to devote ourselves to acts of worship. The life must be like Christ's life,—between the mountain and the multitude. He who does nothing but pray will soon cease to pray, or his prayers will become a formal routine. When men take themselves out of social life, away from the sphere of Christian duty and cross-bearing; when they cease to work earnestly for the Master, who worked earnestly for them, they lose the subject matter of prayer, and have no incentive to devotion. Their prayers become personal and selfish. They cannot pray in regard to the wants of humanity or the upbuilding of Christ's kingdom, pleading for strength wherewith to work.—(*Steps to Christ,* 101.)

SPIRITUAL PROGRESS DEPENDS UPON PRAYER.—We must be much in prayer if we would make progress in the divine life. When the message of truth was first proclaimed, how much we prayed. How often was the voice of intercession heard in the chamber, in the barn, in the orchard, or the grove. Frequently we spent hours in earnest prayer, two or three together claiming the promise; often the sound of weeping was heard and then the voice of thanksgiving and the song of praise. Now the day of God is nearer than when we first believed, and we should be more earnest, more zealous, and fervent than in those early days. Our perils are greater now than then.—(*Testimonies for the Church,* vol. 5, 161, 162.)

13

Men and Women of Prayer

ENOCH

PRAYER WAS THE BREATH OF HIS SOUL.—Communing thus with God, Enoch came more and more to reflect the divine image. His face was radiant with a holy light, even the light that shineth in the face of Jesus. As he came forth from these divine communings, even the ungodly beheld with awe the impress of heaven upon his countenance.

His faith waxed stronger, his love became more ardent, with the lapse of centuries. To him prayer was as the breath of the soul. He lived in the atmosphere of heaven.—(*Gospel Workers,* 52.)

Distressed by the increasing wickedness of the ungodly, and fearing that their infidelity might lessen his reverence for God, Enoch avoided constant association with them, and spent much time in solitude, giving himself to meditation and prayer. Thus he waited before the Lord, seeking a clearer knowledge of His will, that he might perform it. To him prayer was as the breath of the soul; he lived in the very atmosphere of heaven.—(*Patriarchs and Prophets,* 85.)

ENOCH WALKED WITH GOD THROUGH PRAYER.—I wish I could impress upon every worker in God's cause, the great need of continual, earnest prayer. They cannot be constantly upon their knees, but they can be uplifting their hearts to God. This is the way that Enoch walked with God.—(*Review and Herald,* November 10, 1885.)

While engaged in our daily work, we should lift the soul to heaven in prayer. These silent petitions rise like incense before the throne of grace; and the enemy is baffled. The Christian whose heart is thus stayed upon God cannot be overcome. No evil arts can destroy his peace. All the promises of God's word, all the power of divine grace, all the resources of Jehovah, are pledged to secure his deliverance. It was thus that Enoch walked with God. And God was with him, a present help in every time of need.—(*Messages to Young People,* 249.)

INDIVIDUALS SOUGHT OUT ENOCH FOR PRAYER.—Enoch became a preacher of righteousness, making known to the people what God had revealed to him. Those who feared the Lord sought out this holy man, to share his instruction and his prayers.—(*Patriarchs and Prophets,* 86.)

THE GREATER ENOCH'S LABORS, THE MORE EARNEST HIS PRAYERS.— In the midst of a life of active labor, Enoch steadfastly maintained his communion with God. The greater and more pressing his labors, the more constant and earnest were his prayers. He continued to exclude himself, at certain periods, from all society. After remaining for a time among the people, laboring to benefit them by instruction and example, he would withdraw, to spend a season in solitude, hungering and thirsting for that divine knowledge which God alone can impart.—(*Patriarchs and Prophets,* 86, 87.)

ABRAHAM

DAILY PRAYER TO ASCEND TO GOD AS SWEET INCENSE.—The life of Abraham, the friend of God, was a life of prayer. Wherever he pitched his tent, close beside it was built an altar, upon which were offered the morning and the evening sacrifice. When his tent was removed, the altar remained. And the roving Canaanite, as he came to that altar, knew who had been there. When he had pitched his tent he repaired the altar and worshiped the living God.

So the homes of Christians should be lights in the world. From them, morning and evening, prayer should ascend to God as sweet incense. And as the morning dew, His mercies and blessings will descend upon the suppliants.

Fathers and mothers, each morning and evening gather your children around you, and in humble supplication lift the heart to God for help. Your dear ones are exposed to temptation. Daily annoyances beset the path of young and old. Those who would live patient, loving, cheerful lives must pray. Only by receiving constant help from God can we gain the victory over self.

Each morning consecrate yourselves and your children to God for that day. Make no calculation for months or years; these are not yours. One brief day is given you. As if it were your last on earth, work during its hours for the Master. Lay all your plans before God, to be carried out or given up, as His providence shall indicate. Accept His plans instead of your own, even though their acceptance requires the abandonment of cherished projects. Thus the life will be molded more and more after the divine example; "and the peace of God, which passeth all understanding, shall keep your hearts and minds through Christ Jesus." Philippians 4:7.—(*Testimonies for the Church,* vol. 7, 44.)

ABRAHAM PRAYED IN FAITH IN SPITE OF DIFFICULT CIRCUMSTANCES.—Abraham could not explain the leadings of Providence; he had not realized his expectations; but he held fast the promise, "I will bless thee, and make thy name great; and thou shalt be a blessing." With earnest prayer he considered how to preserve the life of his people and his flocks, but he would not allow circumstances to shake his faith in God's word.—(*Conflict and Courage,* 45.)

ABRAHAM PRAYED TO GOD WITH THE CONFIDENCE OF A CHILD PLEADING WITH HIS FATHER.—Two of the heavenly messengers departed, leaving Abraham alone with Him whom he now knew to be the Son of God. And the man of faith pleaded for the inhabitants of Sodom. Once he had saved them by his sword, now he endeavored to save them by prayer. Lot and his household were still dwellers there; and the unselfish love that prompted Abraham to their rescue from the Elamites, now sought to save them, if it were God's will, from the storm of divine judgment.

With deep reverence and humility he urged his plea: "I have taken upon me to speak unto the Lord, which am but dust and ashes." There was no self-confidence, no boasting of his own righteousness. He did not claim favor on the ground of his obedience, or of the sacrifices he had made in doing God's will. Himself a sinner, he pleaded in the sinner's behalf. Such a spirit all who approach God should possess. Yet Abraham manifested the confidence of a child pleading with a loved father. He came close to the heavenly Messenger, and fervently urged his petition. . . .

Love for perishing souls inspired Abraham's prayer. While he loathed the sins of that corrupt city, he desired that the sinners might be saved. His deep interest for Sodom shows the anxiety that we should feel for the impenitent. We should cherish hatred of sin, but pity and love for the sinner.—(*Patriarchs and Prophets,* 139, 140.)

JACOB

JACOB'S EXPERIENCE TEACHES THE IMPORTANCE OF PREVAILING PRAYER.—Jacob prevailed because he was persevering and determined. His experience testifies to the power of importunate prayer. It is now that we are to learn this lesson of prevailing prayer, of unyielding faith. The greatest victories to the church of Christ or to the individual Christian are not those that are gained by talent or education, by wealth or the favor of men. They are those victories that are gained in the audience chamber with God, when earnest, agonizing faith lays hold upon the mighty arm of power.

Those who are unwilling to forsake every sin and to seek earnestly for God's blessing, will not obtain it. But all who will lay hold of God's promises as did Jacob, and be as earnest and persevering as he was, will succeed as he succeeded.—(*Patriarchs and Prophets,* 203.)

MOSES

FOLLOW MOSES' EXAMPLE IN PRAYER.—Talk less; much precious time is lost in talk that brings no light. Let brethren unite in fasting and prayer for the wisdom that God has promised to supply liberally. Make known your troubles to God. Tell Him, as did Moses, "I cannot lead this people unless Thy presence shall go with me." And then ask still more; pray with Moses, "Show me Thy glory." [Ex. 33:18.] What is this glory? —The character of God. This is what He proclaimed to Moses.—(*Gospel Workers,* 417.)

MOSES INTERCEDED SUCCESSFULLY FOR ISRAEL.—God's covenant with His people had been disannulled, and He declared to Moses, "Let Me alone, that My wrath may wax hot against them, and that I may consume them: and I will make of thee a great nation." The people of Israel, especially the mixed multitude, would be constantly disposed to rebel against God. They would also murmur against their leader, and would grieve him by their unbelief and stubbornness, and it would be a laborious and soul-trying work to lead them through to the Promised Land. Their sins had already forfeited the favor of God, and justice called for their destruction. The Lord therefore proposed to destroy them, and make of Moses a mighty nation.

"Let Me alone, . . . that I may consume them," were the words of God. If God had purposed to destroy Israel, who could plead for them? How few but would have left the sinners to their fate! How few but would have gladly exchanged a lot of toil and burden and sacrifice, repaid with ingratitude and murmuring, for a position of ease and honor, when it was God Himself that offered the release.

But Moses discerned ground for hope where there appeared only discouragement and wrath. The words of God, "Let Me alone," he understood not to forbid but to encourage intercession, implying that nothing but the prayers of Moses could save

Israel, but that if thus entreated, God would spare His people. . . .

As Moses interceded for Israel, his timidity was lost in his deep interest and love for those for whom he had, in the hands of God, been the means of doing so much. The Lord listened to his pleadings, and granted his unselfish prayer. God had proved His servant; He had tested his faithfulness and his love for that erring, ungrateful people, and nobly had Moses endured the trial. His interest in Israel sprang from no selfish motive. The prosperity of God's chosen people was dearer to him than personal honor, dearer than the privilege of becoming the father of a mighty nation. God was pleased with his faithfulness, his simplicity of heart, and his integrity, and He committed to him, as a faithful shepherd, the great charge of leading Israel to the Promised Land.—(*Patriarchs and Prophets,* 318, 319.)

MOSES CONTINUED TO PRESS HIS PETITIONS TO GOD.—Moses knew well the perversity and blindness of those who were placed under his care; he knew the difficulties with which he must contend. But he had learned that in order to prevail with the people, he must have help from God. He pleaded for a clearer revelation of God's will and for an assurance of His presence: "See, Thou sayest unto me, Bring up this people: and Thou hast not let me know whom Thou wilt send with me. Yet Thou hast said, I know thee by name, and thou hast also found grace in My sight. Now therefore, I pray Thee, if I have found grace in Thy sight, show me now Thy way, that I may know Thee, that I may find grace in Thy sight: and consider that this nation is Thy people."

The answer was, "My presence shall go with thee, and I will give thee rest." But Moses was not yet satisfied. There pressed upon his soul a sense of the terrible results should God leave Israel to hardness and impenitence. He could not endure that his interests should be separated from those of his brethren, and he prayed that the favor of God might be restored to His people, and that the token of His presence might continue to direct their journeyings: "If Thy presence go not with me, carry us not up hence. For wherein shall it be known here that I and Thy people have found grace in Thy sight? is it not in that Thou goest with us? So shall we be separated, I and Thy people, from all the people that are upon the face of the earth."

And the Lord said, "I will do this thing also that thou hast spoken: for thou hast found grace in My sight, and I know thee by name." Still the prophet did not cease pleading. Every prayer had been answered, but he thirsted for greater tokens of God's favor. He now made a request that no human being had ever made before: "I beseech Thee, show me Thy glory."

God did not rebuke his request as presumptuous; but the gracious words were spoken, "I will make all My goodness pass before thee." The unveiled glory of God, no man in this mortal state can look upon and live; but Moses was assured that he should behold as much of the divine glory as he could endure. Again he was summoned to the mountain summit; then the hand that made the world, that hand that "removeth the mountains, and they know not" (Job 9:5), took this creature of the dust, this mighty man of faith, and placed him in a cleft of the rock, while the glory of God and all His goodness passed before him.

This experience—above all else the promise that the divine Presence would attend him—was to Moses an assurance of success in the work before him; and he counted it of infinitely greater worth than all the learning of Egypt or all his attainments as a statesman or a military leader. No earthly power or skill or learning can supply the place of God's abiding presence.—(*Patriarchs and Prophets*, 327, 328.)

UNDER STRESS, MOSES' PRAYER WAS ALMOST A COMPLAINT.— The heart of Moses sank. He had pleaded that Israel should not be destroyed, even though his own posterity might then become a great nation. In his love for them he had prayed that his name might be blotted from the book of life rather than that they should be left to perish. He had imperiled all for them, and this was their response. All their hardships, even their imaginary sufferings, they charged upon him; and their wicked murmurings made doubly heavy the burden of care and responsibility under which he staggered. In his distress he was tempted even to distrust God. His prayer was almost a complaint. "Wherefore hast Thou afflicted Thy servant? and wherefore have I not found favor in Thy sight, that Thou layest the burden of all this people upon me? . . . Whence should I have flesh to give unto all this people? for they weep unto me, saying, Give us flesh, that we may eat. I am not able to bear all this people alone, because it is too heavy for me."

The Lord hearkened to his prayer, and directed him to summon seventy men of the elders of Israel—men not only advanced in years, but possessing dignity, sound judgment, and experience. "And bring them unto the tabernacle of the congregation," He said, "that they may stand there with thee. And I will come down and talk with thee there: and I will take of the spirit which is upon thee, and will put it upon them; and they shall bear the burden of the people with thee, that thou bear it not thyself alone."—(*Patriarchs and Prophets,* 379, 380.)

MOSES PRAYED FOR MERCY FOR ISRAEL.—Moses now arose and entered the tabernacle. The Lord declared to him, "I will smite them with the pestilence, and disinherit them, and will make of thee a greater nation." But again Moses pleaded for his people. He could not consent to have them destroyed, and he himself made a mightier nation. Appealing to the mercy of God, he said: "I beseech Thee, let the power of my Lord be great according as Thou hast spoken, saying, The Lord is long-suffering, and of great mercy. . . . Pardon, I beseech Thee, the iniquity of this people according to the greatness of Thy mercy, and as Thou hast forgiven this people, from Egypt even until now."

The Lord promised to spare Israel from immediate destruction; but because of their unbelief and cowardice He could not manifest His power to subdue their enemies. Therefore in His mercy He bade them, as the only safe course, to turn back toward the Red Sea.—(*Patriarchs and Prophets,* 390, 391.)

MOSES' PRAYERS SPARED THE ISRAELITES FROM GOD'S JUDGMENTS.—As the people gazed upon the aged man, so soon to be taken from them, they recalled, with a new and deeper appreciation, his parental tenderness, his wise counsels, and his untiring labors. How often, when their sins had invited the just judgments of God, the prayers of Moses had prevailed with Him to spare them! Their grief was heightened by remorse. They bitterly remembered that their own perversity had provoked Moses to the sin for which he must die.—(*Patriarchs and Prophets,* 470.)

MOSES' FINAL PRAYER FULFILLED AT THE MOUNT OF TRANSFIGURATION.—Never, till exemplified in the sacrifice of Christ, were the justice and the love of God more strikingly displayed than in His dealings with Moses. God shut Moses out of Canaan, to teach a lesson which should never be forgotten—that He requires exact obedience, and that men are to beware of taking to themselves the glory which is due to their Maker. He could not grant the prayer of Moses that he might share the inheritance of Israel, but He did not forget or forsake His servant. The God of heaven understood the suffering that Moses had endured; He had noted every act of faithful service through those long years of conflict and trial. On the top of Pisgah, God called Moses to an inheritance infinitely more glorious than the earthly Canaan.

Upon the mount of transfiguration Moses was present with Elijah, who had been translated. They were sent as bearers of light and glory from the Father to His Son. And thus the prayer of Moses, uttered so many centuries before, was at last fulfilled. He stood upon the "goodly mountain," within the heritage of his people, bearing witness to Him in whom all the promises to Israel centered. Such is the last scene revealed to mortal vision in the history of that man so highly honored of Heaven.—(*Patriarchs and Prophets,* 479.)

HANNAH

HANNAH'S EXAMPLE AN ENCOURAGEMENT TO EVERY MOTHER.—From Shiloh, Hannah quietly returned to her home at Ramah, leaving the child Samuel to be trained for service in the house of God, under the instruction of the high priest. From the earliest dawn of intellect she had taught her son to love and reverence God and to regard himself as the Lord's. By every familiar object surrounding him she had sought to lead his thoughts up to the Creator. When separated from her child, the faithful mother's solicitude did not cease. Every day he was the subject of her prayers. Every year she made, with her own hands, a robe of service for him; and as she went up with her husband to worship at Shiloh, she gave the child this reminder of her love. Every fiber of the little garment had been woven with a prayer that he might be pure, noble, and true. She did not ask for her son worldly greatness, but she earnestly pleaded that he might attain that greatness which Heaven values—that he might honor God and bless his fellow men.

What a reward was Hannah's! and what an encouragement to faithfulness is her example! There are opportunities of inestimable worth, interests infinitely precious, committed to every mother. The humble round of duties which women have come to regard as a wearisome task should be looked upon as a grand and noble work. It is the mother's privilege to bless the world by her influence, and in doing this she will bring joy to her own heart. She may make straight paths for the feet of her children, through sunshine and shadow, to the glorious heights above. But it is only when she seeks, in her own life, to follow the teachings of Christ that the mother can hope to form the character of her children after the divine pattern. The world teems with corrupting influences. Fashion and custom exert a strong power over the young. If the mother fails in her duty to instruct, guide, and restrain, her children will naturally accept the evil, and turn from the good. Let every mother go often to her Saviour with the prayer, "Teach us, how shall we order the child, and what shall we do unto him?" Let her heed the instruction which God has given in His word, and wisdom will be given her as she shall have need.—(*Patriarchs and Prophets,* 572, 573.)

HANNAH WAS A WOMAN OF PRAYER.—Hannah brought no reproach against her husband for his unwise marriage. The grief which she could share with no earthly friend, she carried to her Heavenly Father, and sought consolation from Him alone who hath said, "Call upon me in the day of trouble, and I will deliver thee." There is a mighty power in prayer. Our great adversary is constantly seeking to keep the troubled soul away from God. An appeal to Heaven by the humblest saint is more to be dreaded by Satan than the decrees of cabinets or the mandates of kings.

Hannah's prayer was unheard by mortal ear, but entered the ear of the Lord of hosts. Earnestly she pleaded that God would take away her reproach, and grant her the boon most highly prized by women of that age,—the blessing of motherhood. As she wrestled in prayer, her voice uttered no sound, but her lips moved and her countenance gave evidence of deep emotion. And now another trial awaited the humble suppliant. As the eye of Eli the high priest fell upon her, he hastily decided that she was intoxicated. Feasting revelry had well-nigh supplanted true godliness among the people of Israel. Instances of intemperance, even among women, were of frequent occurrence, and now Eli determined to administer what he considered a deserved rebuke. "How long wilt thou be drunken? Put away thy wine from thee."

Hannah had been communing with God. She believed that her prayer had been heard, and the peace of Christ filled her heart. Hers was a gentle, sensitive nature, yet she yielded neither to grief nor to indignation at the unjust charge of drunkenness in the house of God. With due reverence for the anointed of the Lord, she calmly repelled the accusation and stated the cause of her emotion. "No my Lord, I am a woman of sorrowful spirit. I have drunk neither wine nor strong drink, but have poured out my soul before the Lord. Count not thine handmaid for a daughter of Belial, for out of the abundance of my complaint and grief have I spoken hitherto." Convinced that his reproof had been unjust, Eli replied, "Go in peace, and the God of Israel grant thee thy petition that thou hast asked of him."

In her prayer, Hannah had made a vow that if her request were granted, she would dedicate her child to the service of God. This vow she made known to her husband, and he confirmed it in a solemn act of worship, before leaving Shiloh.

Hannah's prayer was answered, and she received the gift for which she had so earnestly entreated. As she looked upon the pledge of divine favor she called the child Samuel—Asked of God.— (*Signs of the Times*, October 27, 1881.)

ELIJAH

ELIJAH PRAYED FOR ISRAEL'S REPENTANCE.—Among the mountains of Gilead, east of the Jordan, there dwelt in the days of Ahab a man of faith and prayer whose fearless ministry was destined to check the rapid spread of apostasy in Israel. Far removed from any city of renown, and occupying no high station in life, Elijah the Tishbite nevertheless entered upon his mission confident in God's purpose to prepare the way before him and to give him abundant success. The word of faith and power was upon his lips, and his whole life was devoted to the work of reform. His was the voice of one crying in the wilderness to rebuke sin and press back the tide of evil. And while he came to the people as a reprover of sin, his message offered the balm of Gilead to the sin-sick souls of all who desired to be healed.

As Elijah saw Israel going deeper and deeper into idolatry, his soul was distressed and his indignation aroused. God had done great things for His people. He had delivered them from bondage and given them "the lands of the heathen, . . . that they might observe His statutes, and keep His laws." Psalm 105:44, 45. But the beneficent designs of Jehovah were now well-nigh forgotten. Unbelief was fast separating the chosen nation from the Source of their strength. Viewing this apostasy from his mountain retreat, Elijah was overwhelmed with sorrow. In anguish of soul he besought God to arrest the once-favored people in their wicked course, to visit them with judgments, if need be, that they might be led to see in its true light their departure from Heaven. He longed to see them brought to repentance before they should go to such lengths in evil-doing as to provoke the Lord to destroy them utterly.

Elijah's prayer was answered. Oft-repeated appeals, remonstrances, and warnings had failed to bring Israel to repentance. The time had come when God must speak to them by means of judgments. Inasmuch as the worshipers of Baal claimed that the treasures of heaven, the dew and the rain, came not from Jehovah, but from the ruling forces of nature, and that it was through the creative energy of the sun that the earth was enriched and made to bring forth abundantly, the curse of God was to rest heavily upon the polluted land. The apostate tribes of Israel were to be shown the folly of trusting to the power of Baal for temporal blessings. Until they should turn to God with repentance, and acknowledge Him as the source of all blessing, there should fall upon the land neither dew nor rain.—(*Prophets and Kings*, 119, 120.)

The fear of God was daily growing less in Israel. The blasphemous tokens of their blind idolatry were to be seen among the Israel of God. There were none who dared to expose their lives by openly standing forth in opposition to the prevailing blasphemous idolatry. The altars of Baal, and the priests of Baal who sacrificed to the sun, moon, and stars, were conspicuous everywhere. They had consecrated temples and groves, wherein was placed the work of men's hands to worship. The benefits which God gave to this people called forth from them no gratitude to the Giver. For all the bounties of Heaven, the running brooks, and streams of living waters, the gentle dew, and showers of rain to refresh the earth, and to cause their fields to bring forth abundantly, they ascribed to the favor of their gods.

Elijah's faithful soul was grieved. His indignation was aroused, and he was jealous for the glory of God. He saw that Israel was plunged into fearful apostasy. He was overwhelmed with amazement and grief at the apostasy of the people when he called to mind the great things that God had wrought for them. But all this was forgotten by the majority of the people. He went before God, and with his soul wrung with anguish, pled for Him to save His people if it must be by judgments. He pled with God to withhold from His ungrateful people dew and rain, the treasures of heaven, that apostate Israel might look in vain to their idols of gold, wood, and stone, the sun, moon, and stars, their gods, to water the earth and enrich it, and cause it to bring forth plentifully. God told Elijah He had heard his prayer. He would withhold from His people dew and rain, until they should turn unto Him with repentance.—(*Review and Herald,* September 16, 1873.)

Through the long years of drought and famine, Elijah prayed earnestly that the hearts of Israel might be turned from idolatry to allegiance to God. Patiently the prophet waited, while the hand of the Lord rested heavily on the stricken land. As he saw evidences of suffering and want multiplying on every side, his heart was wrung with sorrow, and he longed for power to bring about a reformation quickly. But God Himself was working out His plan, and all that His servant could do was to pray on in faith and await the time for decided action.—(*Prophets and Kings,* 133.)

ELIJAH AN EXAMPLE OF ONE WHO PREVAILED THROUGH EARNEST PRAYER.—We should be much in secret prayer. Christ is the vine, ye are the branches. And if we would grow and flourish, we must continually draw sap and nourishment from the Living Vine; for separated from the Vine we have no strength.

I asked the angel why there was no more faith and power in Israel. He said, "Ye let go of the arm of the Lord too soon. Press your petitions to the throne, and hold on by strong faith. The promises are sure. Believe ye receive the things ye ask for, and ye shall have them." I was then pointed to Elijah. He was subject to like passions as we are, and he prayed earnestly. His faith endured the trial. Seven times he prayed before the Lord, and at last the cloud was seen. I saw that we had doubted the sure promises, and wounded the Saviour by our lack of faith. Said the angel, "Gird the armor about thee, and above all take the shield of faith; for that will guard the heart, the very life, from the fiery darts of the wicked." If the enemy can lead the desponding to take their eyes off from Jesus, and look to themselves, and dwell upon their own unworthiness, instead of dwelling upon the worthiness of Jesus, His love, His merits, and His great mercy, he will get away their shield of faith and gain his object; they will be exposed to his fiery temptations. The weak should therefore look to Jesus, and believe in Him; they then exercise faith.—(*Early Writings,* 73.)

God's messengers must tarry long with Him, if they would have success in their work. The story is told of an old Lancashire woman who was listening to the reasons that her neighbors gave for their minister's success. They spoke of his gifts, of his style of address, of his manners. "Nay," said the old woman, "I will tell you what it is. Your man is very thick with the Almighty."

When men are as devoted as Elijah was and possess the faith that he had, God will reveal Himself as He did then. When men plead with the Lord as did Jacob, the results that were seen then will again be seen. Power will come from God in answer to the prayer of faith.—(*Gospel Workers,* 255.)

ELIJAH'S PRAYER ON MOUNT CARMEL WAS ANSWERED DRAMATI-CALLY.—Reminding the people of the long-continued apostasy that has awakened the wrath of Jehovah, Elijah calls upon them to humble their hearts and turn to the God of their fathers, that the curse upon the land of Israel may be removed. Then, bowing reverently before the unseen God, he raises his hands toward heaven and offers a simple prayer. Baal's priests have screamed and foamed and leaped, from early morning until late in the afternoon; but as Elijah prays, no senseless shrieks resound over Carmel's height. He prays as if he knows Jehovah is there, a witness to the scene, a listener to his appeal. The prophets of Baal have prayed wildly, incoherently. Elijah prays simply and fervently, asking God to show His superiority over Baal, that Israel may be led to turn to Him.

"Lord God of Abraham, Isaac, and of Israel," the prophet pleads, "let it be known this day that Thou art God in Israel, and that I am Thy servant, and that I have done all these things at Thy word. Hear me, O Lord, hear me, that this people may know that Thou art the Lord God, and that Thou hast turned their heart back again."

A silence, oppressive in its solemnity, rests upon all. The priests of Baal tremble with terror. Conscious of their guilt, they look for swift retribution.

No sooner is the prayer of Elijah ended than flames of fire, like brilliant flashes of lightning, descend from heaven upon the upreared altar, consuming the sacrifice, licking up the water in the trench, and consuming even the stones of the altar. The brilliancy of the blaze illumines the mountain and dazzles the eyes of the multitude. In the valleys below, where many are watching in anxious suspense the movements of those above, the descent of fire is clearly seen, and all are amazed at the sight. It resembles the pillar of fire which at the Red Sea separated the children of Israel from the Egyptian host.—(*Prophets and Kings,* 152, 153.)

ELIJAH'S PRAYERS REACHED OUT IN FAITH TO CLAIM GOD'S PROMISES.—With the slaying of the prophets of Baal, the way was opened for carrying forward a mighty spiritual reformation among the ten tribes of the northern kingdom. Elijah had set before the people their apostasy; he had called upon them to humble their hearts and turn to the Lord. The judgments of Heaven had been executed; the people had confessed their sins, and had acknowledged the God of their fathers as the living God; and now the curse of Heaven was to be withdrawn, and the temporal blessings of life renewed. The land was to be refreshed with rain. "Get thee up, eat and drink," Elijah said to Ahab; "for there is a sound of abundance of rain." Then the prophet went to the top of the mount to pray.

It was not because of any outward evidence that the showers were about to fall, that Elijah could so confidently bid Ahab prepare for rain. The prophet saw no clouds in the heavens; he heard no thunder. He simply spoke the word that the Spirit of the Lord had moved him to speak in response to his own strong faith. Throughout the day he had unflinchingly performed the will of God and had revealed his implicit confidence in the prophecies of God's word; and now, having done all that was in his power to do, he knew that Heaven would freely bestow the blessings foretold. The same God who had sent the drought had promised an abundance of rain as the reward of rightdoing; and now Elijah waited for the promised outpouring. In an attitude of humility, "his face between his knees," he interceded with God in behalf of penitent Israel.

Again and again Elijah sent his servant to a point overlooking the Mediterranean, to learn whether there were any visible token that God had heard his prayer. Each time the servant returned with the word, "There is nothing." The prophet did not become impatient or lose faith, but continued his earnest pleading. Six times the servant returned with the word that there was no sign of rain in the brassy heavens. Undaunted, Elijah sent him forth once more; and this time the servant returned with the word, "Behold, there ariseth a little cloud out of the sea like a man's hand."

This was enough. Elijah did not wait for the heavens to gather blackness. In that small cloud he beheld by faith an abundance of rain; and he acted in harmony with his faith, sending his servant quickly to Ahab with the message, "Prepare thy chariot, and get thee down, that the rain stop thee not."

It was because Elijah was a man of large faith that God could use him in this grave crisis in the history of Israel. As he prayed, his faith reached out and grasped the promises of Heaven, and he persevered in prayer until his petitions were answered. He did not wait for the full evidence that God had heard him, but was willing to venture all on the slightest token of divine favor. And yet what he was enabled to do under God, all may do in their sphere of activity in God's service; for of the prophet from the mountains of Gilead it is written: "Elias was a man subject to like passions as we are, and he prayed earnestly that it might not rain: and it rained not on the earth by the space of three years and six months." James 5:17.

Faith such as this is needed in the world today—faith that will lay hold on the promises of God's word and refuse to let go until Heaven hears. Faith such as this connects us closely with Heaven, and brings us strength for coping with the powers of darkness. Through faith God's children have "subdued kingdoms, wrought righteousness, obtained promises, stopped the mouths of lions, quenched the violence of fire, escaped the edge of the sword, out of weakness were made strong, waxed valiant in fight, turned to flight the armies of the aliens." Hebrews 11:33, 34. And through faith we today are to reach the heights of God's purpose for us. "If thou canst believe, all things are possible to him that believeth." Mark 9:23.

Faith is an essential element of prevailing prayer. "He that cometh to God must believe that He is, and that He is a rewarder of them that diligently seek Him." "If we ask anything according to His will, He heareth us: and if we know that He hear us, whatsoever we ask, we know that we have the petitions that we desired of Him." Hebrews 11:6, 1 John 5:14, 15. With the persevering faith of Jacob, with the unyielding persistence of Elijah, we may present our petitions to the Father, claiming all that He has promised. The honor of His throne is staked for the fulfillment of His word.—(*Prophets and Kings*, 155-158.)

ELIJAH PERSEVERED IN PRAYER UNTIL THE ANSWER CAME.—Important lessons are presented to us in the experience of Elijah. When upon Mt. Carmel he offered the prayer for rain, his faith was tested, but he persevered in making known his request unto God. Six times he prayed earnestly, and yet there was no sign that his petition was granted, but with a strong faith he urged his plea to the throne of grace. Had he given up in discouragement at the sixth time, his prayer would not have been answered, but he persevered till the answer came. We have a God whose ear is not closed to our petitions; and if we prove His word, He will honor our faith. He wants us to have all our interests interwoven with His interests, and then He can safely bless us; for we shall not then take glory to self when the blessing is ours, but shall render all the praise to God. God does not always answer our prayers the first time we call upon Him; for should He do this, we might take it for granted that we had a right to all the blessings and favors He bestowed upon us. Instead of searching our hearts to see if any evil was entertained by us, any sin indulged, we should become careless, and fail to realize our dependence upon Him, and our need of His help.

Elijah humbled himself until he was in a condition where he would not take the glory to himself. This is the condition upon which the Lord hears prayer, for then we shall give the praise to Him. The custom of offering praise to men is one that results in great evil. One praises another, and thus men are led to feel that glory and honor belong to them. When you exalt man, you lay a snare for his soul, and do just as Satan would have you. You should praise God with all your heart, soul, might, mind, and strength; for God alone is worthy to be glorified.—(*SDA Bible Commentary,* vol. 2, 1034, 1035.)

The servant watched while Elijah prayed. Six times he returned from the watch, saying, There is nothing, no cloud, no sign of rain. But the prophet did not give up in discouragement. He kept reviewing his life, to see where he had failed to honor God, he confessed his sins, and thus continued to afflict his soul before God, while watching for a token that his prayer was answered. As he searched his heart, he seemed to be less and less, both in his own estimation and in the sight of God. It seemed to him that he was nothing, and that God was everything; and when he reached the point of renouncing self, while he clung to the Saviour as his only strength and righteousness, the answer came.—(*Review and Herald,* May 26, 1891.)

DAVID

DAVID'S FALL A WARNING NOT TO NEGLECT PRAYER.—God intended the history of David's fall to serve as a warning that even those whom He has greatly blessed and favored are not to feel secure and neglect watchfulness and prayer. And thus it has proved to those who in humility have sought to learn the lesson that God designed to teach. From generation to generation thousands have thus been led to realize their own danger from the tempter's power. The fall of David, one so greatly honored by the Lord, has awakened in them distrust of self. They have felt that God alone could keep them by His power through faith. Knowing that in Him was their strength and safety, they have feared to take the first step on Satan's ground.—(*Patriarchs and Prophets,* 724.)

GOD RESPONDED TO DAVID'S PRAYER FOR FORGIVENESS.—One of the most earnest prayers recorded in the Word of God is that of David when he plead, "Create in me a clean heart, O God." God's response to such a prayer is, A new heart will I give you. This is a work that no finite man can do. Men and women are to begin at the beginning, seeking God most earnestly for a true Christian experience. They are to feel the creative power of the Holy Spirit. They are to receive the new heart, that is kept soft and tender by the grace of heaven. The selfish spirit is to be cleansed from the soul. They are to labor earnestly and with humility of heart, each one looking to Jesus for guidance and encouragement. Then the building, fitly framed together, will grow into a holy temple in the Lord.—(*SDA Bible Commentary,* vol. 4, 1165.)

SOLOMON

WE NEED TO LEARN THE LESSON IN SOLMON'S HUMBLE PRAYER.— At the beginning of his reign Solomon prayed: "O Lord my God, Thou hast made Thy servant king instead of David my father: and I am but a little child: I know not how to go out or come in." 1 Kings 3:7.

Solomon had succeeded his father David to the throne of Israel. God greatly honored him, and, as we know, he became in later years the greatest, richest, and wisest king that had ever sat upon an earthly throne. Early in his reign Solomon was impressed by the Holy Spirit with the solemnity of his responsibilities, and, though rich in talents and ability, he realized that without divine aid he was helpless as a little child to perform them. Solomon was never so rich or so wise or so truly great as when he confessed to the Lord: "I am but a little child: I know not how to go out or come in.". . . .

"And the speech pleased the Lord, that Solomon had asked this thing. And God said unto him, Because thou hast asked this thing, and hast not asked for thyself long life; neither hast asked riches for thyself, nor hast asked the life of thine enemies; but hast asked for thyself understanding to discern judgment; behold, I have done according to thy words: lo, I have given thee a wise and an understanding heart; so that there was none like thee before thee, neither after thee shall any arise like unto thee. And I have also given thee that which thou hast not asked, both riches, and honor: so that there shall not be any among the kings like unto thee all thy days." Now the conditions: "And if thou wilt walk in My ways, to keep My statutes and My commandments, as thy father David did walk, then I will lengthen thy days." . . . .

All who occupy responsible positions need to learn the lesson that is taught in Solomon's humble prayer. They are ever to remember that position will never change the character or render man infallible. The higher the position a man occupies, the greater the responsibility he has to bear, the wider will be the influence he exerts and the greater his need to feel his dependence on the wisdom and strength of God and to cultivate the best and most holy character.—(*Testimonies for the Church,* vol. 9, 281, 282).

SOLOMON'S EXAMPLE A LESSON TO WATCH UNTO PRAYER.—How, in Solomon's case, was weak, vacillating character—naturally bold, firm, and determined—shaken like a reed in the wind under the tempter's power! How has an old, gnarled cedar of Lebanon, a sturdy oak of Bashan, bent before the blast of temptation! What a lesson for all who desire to save their souls to watch unto prayer continually. What a warning to keep the grace of Christ ever in their heart, to battle with inward corruptions and outward temptations.—(*Manuscript Releases,* vol. 21, 383.)

HEZEKIAH

HEZEKIAH PRAYED FOR THE REMNANT OF ISRAEL.— "This day is a day of trouble, and of rebuke, and blasphemy," was the word the king sent. "It may be the Lord thy God will hear all the words of

Rabshakeh, whom the king of Assyria his master hath sent to reproach the living God; and will reprove the words which the Lord thy God hath heard: wherefore lift up thy prayer for the remnant that are left." Verses 3, 4.

"For this cause Hezekiah the king, and the prophet Isaiah the son of Amoz, prayed and cried to Heaven." 2 Chronicles 32:20.

God answered the prayers of His servants. To Isaiah was given the message for Hezekiah: "Thus saith the Lord, Be not afraid of the words which thou hast heard, with which the servants of the king of Assyria have blasphemed Me. Behold, I will send a blast upon him, and he shall hear a rumor, and shall return to his own land; and I will cause him to fall by the sword in his own land." 2 Kings 19:6, 7.—(*Prophets and Kings, 354.*)

HEZEKIAH'S PRAYER WAS IN HARMONY WITH THE MIND OF GOD .—
When the king of Judah received the taunting letter, he took it into the temple and "spread it before the Lord" and prayed with strong faith for help from heaven, that the nations of earth might know that the God of the Hebrews still lived and reigned. Verse 14. The honor of Jehovah was at stake; He alone could bring deliverance.

"O Lord God of Israel, which dwellest between the cherubims," Hezekiah pleaded, "Thou art the God, even Thou alone, of all the kingdoms of the earth; Thou hast made heaven and earth. Lord, bow down Thine ear, and hear: open, Lord, Thine eyes, and see: and hear the words of Sennacherib, which hath sent him to reproach the living God. Of a truth, Lord, the kings of Assyria have destroyed the nations and their lands, and have cast their gods into the fire: for they were no gods, but the work of men's hands, wood and stone: therefore they have destroyed them. Now therefore, O Lord our God, I beseech Thee, save Thou us out of his hand, that all the kingdoms of the earth may know that Thou art the Lord God, even Thou only." 2 Kings 19:15-19. . . .

Hezekiah's pleadings in behalf of Judah and of the honor of their Supreme Ruler were in harmony with the mind of God. Solomon, in his benediction at the dedication of the temple, had prayed the Lord to maintain "the cause of His people Israel at all times, as the matter shall require: that all the people of the earth may know that the Lord is God, and that there is none else." 1 Kings 8:59, 60. Especially was the Lord to show favor when, in times of war or of oppression by an army, the chief men of Israel should enter the house of prayer and plead for deliverance. Verses 33, 34.

Hezekiah was not left without hope. Isaiah sent to him, saying, "Thus saith the Lord God of Israel, That which thou hast prayed to Me against Sennacherib king of Assyria I have heard.— (*Prophets and Kings,* 355, 356, 359.)

HEZEKIAH HEALED IN ANSWER TO PRAYER.—Since the days of David, there had reigned no king who had wrought so mightily for the upbuilding of the kingdom of God in a time of apostasy and discouragement as had Hezekiah. The dying ruler had served his God faithfully, and had done much to strengthen the confidence of the people in Jehovah as their Supreme Ruler. And, like David, he could now plead: "Let my prayer come before thee: incline thine ear unto my cry; for my soul is full of troubles: and my life draweth nigh unto the grave." "Thou art my hope, O Lord God: thou art my trust from my youth. By thee have I been holden up. . . . Forsake me not when my strength faileth. . . . O God, be not far from me: O my God, make haste for my help. . . . O God, forsake me not; until I have showed thy strength unto this generation, and thy power to every one that is to come." Ps. 88:2, 3; 71:5-18.

He whose "compassions fail not" (Lam. 3:22) heard the prayer of His servant. "It came to pass, afore Isaiah was gone out into the middle court, that the word of the Lord came to him, saying, Turn again, and tell Hezekiah the captain of my people, Thus saith the Lord, the God of David thy father, I have heard thy prayer, I have seen thy tears: behold, I will heal thee: on the third day thou shalt go up unto the house of the Lord. And I will add unto thy days fifteen years; and I will deliver thee and this city out of the hand of the king of Assyria; and I will defend this city for mine own sake, and for my servant David's sake." 2 Kings 20:4-6.—(*Review and Herald,* May 6, 1915.)

DANIEL

DANIEL'S PRAYER EFFECTUAL AND FERVENT.—Daniel prayed to God, not exalting himself or claiming any goodness: "O Lord, hear; O Lord, forgive; O Lord, hearken and do; defer not, for Thine own sake, O my God." This is what James calls the effectual, fervent prayer. Of Christ it is said: "And being in an agony He prayed more earnestly." In what contrast to this intercession by the Majesty of heaven are the feeble, heartless prayers that are offered to God. Many are content with lip service, and but few have a sincere, earnest, affectionate longing after God.—(*Testimonies for the Church*, vol. 4, 534.)

DANIEL REMAINED FAITHFUL IN PRAYER IN SPITE OF PERSECUTION.— Did Daniel cease to pray because this decree was to go into force!— No, that was just the time when he needed to pray. "When Daniel knew that the writing was signed, he went into his house; and, his window being open in his chamber toward Jerusalem, he kneeled upon his knees three times a day, and prayed, and gave thanks before his God, as he did aforetime." Daniel did not seek to hide his loyalty to God. He did not pray in his heart, but with his voice, aloud, with his window open toward Jerusalem, he offered up his petition to heaven. Then his enemies made their complaint to the king, and Daniel was thrown into the den of lions. But the Son of God was there. The angel of the Lord encamped round about the servant of the Lord, and when the king came in the morning, and called, "O Daniel, servant of the living God, is thy God, whom thou servest continually, able to deliver thee from the lions? Then said Daniel unto the king, O king, live forever. My God hath sent His angel, and hath shut the lions' mouths, that they have not hurt me." No harm had come to him, and he magnified the Lord God of heaven.—(*Review and Herald*, May 3, 1892.)

EARNESTNESS AND FERVOR CHARACTERIZED DANIEL'S PRAYERS.—As the time approached for the close of the seventy years' captivity, Daniel's mind became greatly exercised upon the prophecies of Jeremiah. He saw that the time was at hand when God would give His chosen people another trial; and with fasting, humiliation, and prayer, he importuned the God of heaven in behalf of Israel, in these words: "O Lord, the great and dreadful God, keeping the covenant and mercy to them that love Him, and to them that keep His commandments; we have sinned, and have committed iniquity, and have done wickedly, and have rebelled, even by departing from thy precepts and from thy judgments; neither have we hearkened unto thy servants the prophets, which spake in thy name to our kings, our princes, and our fathers, and to all the people of the land" (Dan. 9:4-6).

Daniel does not proclaim his own fidelity before the Lord. Instead of claiming to be pure and holy, this honored prophet humbly identifies himself with the really sinful of Israel. The wisdom which God had imparted to him was as far superior to the wisdom of the great men of the world as the light of the sun shining in the heavens at noonday is brighter than the feeblest star. Yet ponder the prayer from the lips of this man so highly favored of Heaven. With deep humiliation, with tears and rending of heart, he pleads for himself and for his people. He lays his soul open before God, confessing his own unworthiness and acknowledging the Lord's greatness and majesty.

What earnestness and fervor characterize his supplications! The hand of faith is reached upward to grasp the never-failing promises of the Most High. His soul is wrestling in agony. And he has the evidence that his prayer is heard. He knows that victory is his. If we as a people would pray as Daniel prayed, and wrestle as he wrestled, humbling our souls before God, we should realize as marked answers to our petitions as were granted to Daniel. Hear how he presses his case at the court of heaven:

"O my God, incline thine ear, and hear; open thine eyes, and behold our desolations, and the city which is called by thy name; for we do not present our supplications before thee for our righteousnesses, but for thy great mercies. O Lord, hear; O Lord, forgive; O Lord, hearken and do; defer not; for thine own sake, O my God: for thy city and thy people are called by thy name" (verses 18, 19).

The man of God was praying for the blessing of Heaven upon his people and for a clearer knowledge of the divine will. The burden of his heart was for Israel, who were not, in the strictest sense, keeping the law of God. He acknowledges that all their misfortunes have come upon them in consequence of their transgressions of that holy law. He says, "We have sinned, we have done wickedly. . . . Because for our sins, and for the iniquities of our fathers, Jerusalem and thy people are become a reproach to all that are about us" (verses 15, 16). The Jews had lost their peculiar, holy character as God's chosen people. "Now therefore, O our God, hear the prayer of thy servant, and his supplications, and cause thy face to shine upon thy sanctuary that is desolate" (verse 17). Daniel's heart turns with intense longing to the desolate sanctuary of God. He knows that its prosperity can be restored only as Israel shall repent of their transgressions of God's law, and become humble, faithful, and obedient.

As Daniel's prayer is going forth, the angel Gabriel comes sweeping down from the heavenly courts to tell him that his petitions are heard and answered. This mighty angel has been commissioned to give him skill and understanding—to open before him the mysteries of future ages. Thus, while earnestly seeking to know and understand the truth, Daniel was brought into communion with Heaven's delegated messenger.

In answer to his petition, Daniel received not only the light and truth which he and his people most needed, but a view of the great events of the future, even to the advent of the world's Redeemer. Those who claim to be sanctified, while they have no desire to search the Scriptures or to wrestle with God in prayer for a clearer understanding of Bible truth, know not what true sanctification is.—(*The Sanctified Life,* 46-49.)

NEHEMIAH

NEHEMIAH'S PRAYER IS AN EXAMPLE TO GOD'S PEOPLE TODAY.— The hearts of those who advocate this cause must be filled with the Spirit of Jesus. The Great Physician alone can apply the balm of

Gilead. Let these men read the book of Nehemiah with humble hearts touched by the Holy Spirit, and their false ideas will be modified, and correct principles will be seen, and the present order of things will be changed. Nehemiah prayed to God for help, and God heard his prayer. The Lord moved upon heathen kings to come to his help. When his enemies zealously worked against him, the Lord worked through kings to carry out His purpose, and to answer the many prayers which were ascending to Him for the help which they so much needed.—(*Review and Herald,* March 23, 1911.)

PRAYER MADE NEHEMIAH'S FAITH AND COURAGE STRONGER.— By messengers from Judea the Hebrew patriot learned that days of trial had come to Jerusalem, the chosen city. The returned exiles were suffering affliction and reproach. The temple and portions of the city had been rebuilt; but the work of restoration was hindered, the temple services were disturbed, and the people kept in constant alarm by the fact that the walls of the city were still largely in ruins.

Overwhelmed with sorrow, Nehemiah could neither eat nor drink; he "wept, and mourned certain days, and fasted." In his grief he turned to the divine Helper. "I . . . prayed," he said, "before the God of heaven." Faithfully he made confession of his sins and the sins of his people. He pleaded that God would maintain the cause of Israel, restore their courage and strength, and help them to build up the waste places of Judah.

As Nehemiah prayed, his faith and courage grew strong. His mouth was filled with holy arguments. He pointed to the dishonor that would be cast upon God, if His people, now that they had returned to Him, should be left in weakness and oppression; and he urged the Lord to bring to pass His promise: "If ye turn unto Me, and keep My Commandments, and do them; though there were of you cast out unto the uttermost part of the heaven, yet will I gather them from thence, and will bring them unto the place that I have chosen to set My name there." See Deuteronomy 4:29-31. This promise had been given to Israel through Moses before they had entered Canaan, and during the centuries it had stood unchanged. God's people had now returned to Him in penitence and faith, and His promise would not fail.

Nehemiah had often poured out his soul in behalf of his people. But now as he prayed a holy purpose formed in his mind. He resolved that if he could obtain the consent of the king, and the necessary aid in procuring implements and material, he would himself undertake the task of rebuilding the walls of Jerusalem and restoring Israel's national strength. And he asked the Lord to grant him favor in the sight of the king, that this plan might be carried out. "Prosper, I pray Thee, Thy servant this day," he entreated, "and grant him mercy in the sight of this man."

Four months Nehemiah waited for a favorable opportunity to present his request to the king. During this time, though his heart was heavy with grief, he endeavored to bear himself with cheerfulness in the royal presence. In those halls of luxury and splendor all must appear light-hearted and happy. Distress must not cast its shadow over the countenance of any attendant of royalty. But in Nehemiah's seasons of retirement, concealed from human sight, many were the prayers, the confessions, the tears, heard and witnessed by God and angels.—(*Prophets and Kings,* 628-630.)

NEHEMIAH ACKNOWLEDGED HIS PERSONAL SIN IN HIS PRAYERS.— Not only did Nehemiah say that Israel had sinned. He acknowledged with penitence that he and his father's house had sinned. "We have dealt corruptly against Thee," he says, placing himself among those who had dishonored God by not standing stiffly for the truth. . . .

Nehemiah humbled himself before God, giving Him the glory due unto His name. Thus also did Daniel in Babylon. Let us study the prayers of these men. They teach us that we are to humble ourselves, but that we are never to obliterate the line of demarcation between God's commandment-keeping people and those who have no respect for His law.—(*SDA Bible Commentary,* vol. 3, 1136.)

NEHEMIAH PRAYED, CERTAIN THAT GOD WOULD FULFILL HIS PROMISES.—By faith taking fast hold of the divine promise, Nehemiah laid down at the footstool of heavenly mercy his petition that God would maintain the cause of His penitent people, restore their strength, and build up their waste places. God had been faithful to His threatenings when His people separated from Him; He had scattered them abroad among the nations, according to His Word. And Nehemiah found in this very fact an assurance that He would be equally faithful in fulfilling His promises.—(*SDA Bible Commentary,* vol. 3, 1136.)

NEHEMIAH SHAPED HIS PRAYERS TO THE NEEDS OF THE MOMENT.—The recital of the condition of Jerusalem awakened the sympathy of the monarch without arousing his prejudices. Another question gave the opportunity for which Nehemiah had long waited: "For what dost thou make request?" But the man of God did not venture to reply till he had sought direction from One higher than Artaxerxes. He had a sacred trust to fulfill, in which he required help from the king; and he realized that much depended upon his presenting the matter in such a way as to win his approval and enlist his aid. "I prayed," he said, "to the God of heaven." In that brief prayer Nehemiah pressed into the presence of the King of kings and won to his side a power that can turn hearts as the rivers of waters are turned.—(*Prophets and Kings,* 631.)

NEHEMIAH'S PRAYERS WERE BRACED WITH FIRM PURPOSE.—There is need of Nehemiahs in the church today,—not men who can pray and preach only, but men whose prayers and sermons are braced with firm and eager purpose.—(*Signs of the Times,* December 6, 1883.)

LIKE NEHEMIAH, WE CAN PRAY AT ANY TIME OR PLACE.—To pray as Nehemiah prayed in his hour of need is a resource at the command of the Christian under circumstances when other forms of prayer may be impossible. Toilers in the busy walks of life, crowded and almost overwhelmed with perplexity, can send up a petition to God for divine guidance. Travelers by sea and land, when threatened with some great danger, can thus commit themselves to Heaven's protection. In times of sudden difficulty or peril the heart may send up its cry for help to One who has pledged Himself to come to the aid of His faithful, believing ones whenever they call upon Him. In every circumstance, under every condition, the soul weighed down with grief and care, or fiercely assailed by temptation, may find assurance, support, and succor in the unfailing love and power of a covenant-keeping God.

Nehemiah, in that brief moment of prayer to the King of kings, gathered courage to tell Artaxerxes of his desire to be released for a time from his duties at the court, and he asked for authority to build up the waste places of Jerusalem and to make it once more a strong and defensed city. Momentous results to the Jewish nation hung upon this request. "And," Nehemiah declares, "the king granted me, according to the good hand of my God upon me."— (*Prophets and Kings*, 631-633.)

God in His providence does not permit us to know the end from the beginning; but He gives us the light of His word to guide us as we pass along, and bids us to keep our minds stayed upon Jesus. Wherever we are, whatever our employment, our hearts are to be uplifted to God in prayer. This is being instant in prayer. We need not wait until we can bow upon our knees before we pray. On one occasion, when Nehemiah came in before the king, the king asked why he looked so sad, and what request he had to make. But Nehemiah dared not answer at once. Important interests were at stake. The fate of a nation hung upon the impression that should then be made upon the monarch's mind; and Nehemiah darted up a prayer to the God of Heaven, before he dared to answer the king. The result was that he obtained all that he asked or even desired.—(*Signs of the Times,* October 20, 1887.)

There is no time or place in which it is inappropriate to offer up a petition to God. There is nothing that can prevent us from lifting up our hearts in the spirit of earnest prayer. In the crowds of the street, in the midst of a business engagement, we may send up a petition to God and plead for divine guidance, as did Nehemiah when he made his request before King Artaxerxes. A closet of communion may be found wherever we are. We should have the door of the heart open continually and our invitation going up that Jesus may come and abide as a heavenly guest in the soul.

Although there may be a tainted, corrupted atmosphere around us, we need not breathe its miasma, but may live in the pure air of heaven. We may close every door to impure imaginings and unholy thoughts by lifting the soul into the presence of God through sincere prayer. Those whose hearts are open to receive the support and blessing of God will walk in a holier atmosphere than that of earth and will have constant communion with heaven.—(*Steps to Christ,* 99).

NEHEMIAH PRAYED EARNESTLY ALL NIGHT.—In secrecy and silence, Nehemiah completed his circuit of the walls. He declares, "The rulers knew not whither I went, or what I did; neither had I as yet told it to the Jews, nor to the priests, nor to the nobles, nor to the rulers, nor to the rest that did the work." In this painful survey he did not wish to attract the attention of either friends or foes, lest an excitement should be created, and reports be put in circulation that might defeat, or at least hinder, his work. Nehemiah devoted the remainder of the night to prayer; in the morning there must be earnest effort to arouse and unite his dispirited and divided countrymen.—(*Christian Service,* 174.)

NEHEMIAH'S SUCCESS SHOWS THE POWER OF PRAYER.—In their work, Ezra and Nehemiah humbled themselves before God, confessing their sins and the sins of their people, and entreating pardon as if they themselves were the offenders. Patiently they toiled and prayed and suffered. That which made their work most difficult was not the open hostility of the heathen, but the secret opposition of pretended friends, who, by lending their influence to the service of evil, increased tenfold the burden God's servants. These traitors furnished the Lord's enemies with material to use in their warfare upon His people. Their evil passions and rebellious wills were ever at war with the plain requirements of God.

The success attending Nehemiah's efforts shows what prayer, faith, and wise, energetic action will accomplish. Nehemiah was not a priest; he was not a prophet; he made no pretension to high title. He was a reformer raised up for an important time. It was his aim to set his people right with God. Inspired with a great purpose, he bent every energy of his being to its accomplishment. High, unbending integrity marked his efforts. As he came into contact with evil and opposition to right he took so determined a stand that the people were roused to labor with fresh zeal and courage. They could not but recognize his loyalty, his patriotism, and his deep love for God; and, seeing this, they were willing to follow where he led.—(*Prophets and Kings,* 675, 676.)

JOHN THE BAPTIST

JOHN SPENT TIME IN MEDITATION AND PRAYER TO KNOW GOD'S WILL FOR HIS LIFE.—The life of John was not spent in idleness, in ascetic gloom, or in selfish isolation. From time to time he went forth to mingle with men; and he was ever an interested observer of what was passing in the world. From his quiet retreat he watched the unfolding of events. With vision illuminated by the divine Spirit he studied the characters of men, that he might understand how to reach their hearts with the message of heaven. The burden of his mission was upon him. In solitude, by meditation and prayer, he sought to gird up his soul for the lifework before him.—(*The Desire of Ages,* 102.)

PRAYER EMPOWERED JOHN TO FACE THE KINGS OF EARTH.—John the Baptist in his desert life was taught of God. He studied the revelations of God in nature. Under the guiding of the Divine

Spirit, he studied the scrolls of the prophets. By day and by night, Christ was his study, his meditation, until mind and heart and soul were filled with the glorious vision.

He looked upon the King in His beauty, and self was lost sight of. He beheld the majesty of holiness and knew himself to be inefficient and unworthy. It was God's message that he was to declare. It was in God's power and His righteousness that he was to stand. He was ready to go forth as Heaven's messenger, unawed by the human, because he had looked upon the Divine. He could stand fearless in the presence of earthly monarchs because with trembling he had bowed before the King of kings.—(*Testimonies for the Church,* vol. 8, 331, 332.)

PETER

GOD ANSWERED PETER'S PRAYER TO RAISE DORCAS TO LIFE.— The apostle's heart was touched with sympathy as he beheld their sorrow. Then, directing that the weeping friends be sent from the room, he kneeled down and prayed fervently to God to restore Dorcas to life and health. Turning to the body, he said, "Tabitha, arise. And she opened her eyes: and when she saw Peter, she sat up." Dorcas had been of great service to the church, and God saw fit to bring her back from the land of the enemy, that her skill and energy might still be a blessing to others, and also that by this manifestation of His power the cause of Christ might be strengthened.—(*Acts of the Apostles,* 132.)

14

Daily
Prayer

As essential as our daily food.—If we would develop a character which God can accept, we must form correct habits in our religious life. Daily prayer is as essential to growth in grace, and even to spiritual life itself, as is temporal food to physical well-being. We should accustom ourselves to often lift the thoughts to God in prayer. If the mind wanders, we must bring it back; by persevering effort, habit will finally make it easy. We cannot for one moment separate ourselves from Christ with safety. We may have His presence to attend us at every step, but only by observing the conditions which He has Himself laid down.—(*Messages to Young People,* 114, 115.)

Our need of daily prayer.—All who come to Christ today are to remember that His merit is the incense that mingles with the prayers of those who repent of their sins and receive pardon and mercy and grace. Our need of Christ's intercession is constant. Day by day, morning and evening, the humble heart needs to offer up prayers to which will be returned answers of grace and peace and joy. "By Him therefore let us offer the sacrifice of praise to God continually, that is, the fruit of our lips giving thanks to His name. But to do good and to communicate forget not: for with such sacrifice God is well pleased"—(*SDA Bible Commentary,* vol. 6, 1078.)

BEGIN YOUR DAY WITH PRAYER.— It is our privilege to open our hearts, and let the sunshine of Christ's presence in. My brother, my sister, face the light. Come into actual, personal contact with Christ, that you may exert an influence that is uplifting and reviving. Let your faith be strong and pure and steadfast. Let gratitude to God fill your hearts. When you rise in the morning, kneel at your bedside, and ask God to give you strength to fulfil the duties of the day, and to meet its temptations. Ask Him to help you to bring into your work Christ's sweetness of character. Ask Him to help you to speak words that will inspire those around you with hope and courage, and draw you nearer to the Saviour.—(*Sons and Daughters of God,* 199.)

Every morning take time to begin your work with prayer. Do not think this wasted time; it is time that will live through eternal ages. By this means success and spiritual victory will be brought in. The machinery will respond to the touch of the Master's hand. God's blessing is certainly worth asking for, and the work cannot be done aright unless the beginning is right.—(*Testimonies for the Church,* vol. 7, 194.)

My brethren and sisters, old and young, when you have an hour of leisure, open the Bible and store the mind with its precious truths. When engaged in labor, guard the mind, keep it stayed upon God, talk less, and meditate more. Remember: "Every idle word that men shall speak, they shall give account thereof in the day of judgment." Let your words be select; this will close a door against the adversary of souls. Let your day be entered upon with prayer; work as in God's sight. His angels are ever by your side, making a record of your words, your deportment, and the manner in which your work is done. If you turn from good counsel and choose to associate with those who you have reason to suspect are not religiously inclined, although they profess to be Christians, you will soon become like them. You place yourself in the way of temptation, on Satan's battleground, and will, unless constantly guarded, be overcome by his devices.—(*Testimonies for the Church*, vol. 4, 588, 589.)

Go daily to the Lord for instruction and guidance; depend upon God for light and knowledge. Pray for this instruction and this light, until you get it. It will not avail for you to ask, and then forget the thing for which you prayed. Keep your mind upon your prayer. You can do this while working with your hands. You can say, Lord, I believe; with all my heart I believe. Let the Holy Spirit's power come upon me.—(*Fundamentals of Christian Education*, 531.)

In following Christ, looking unto Him who is the Author and Finisher of your faith, you will feel that you are working under His eye, that you are influenced by His presence, and that He knows your motives. At every step you will humbly inquire: Will this please Jesus? Will it glorify God? Morning and evening your earnest prayers should ascend to God for His blessing and guidance. True prayer takes hold upon Omnipotence and gives us the victory. Upon his knees the Christian obtains strength to resist temptation.—(*Testimonies for the Church*, vol. 4, 615.)

DEVOTE SOME TIME EVERY DAY TO PRAYER.—Those who will put on the whole armor of God and devote some time every day to meditation and prayer and to the study of the Scriptures will be connected with heaven and will have a saving, transforming influence upon those around them. Great thoughts, noble aspirations, clear perceptions of truth and duty to God, will be theirs. They will be yearning for purity, for light, for love, for all the graces of heavenly birth. Their earnest prayers will enter into that within the veil. This class will have a sanctified boldness to come into the presence of the Infinite One. They will feel that heaven's light and glories are for them, and they will become refined, elevated, ennobled by this intimate acquaintance with God. Such is the privilege of true Christians.

Abstract meditation is not enough; busy action is not enough; both are essential to the formation of Christian character. Strength acquired in earnest, secret prayer prepares us to withstand the allurements of society. And yet we should not exclude ourselves from the world, for our Christian experience is to be the light of the world. The society of unbelievers will do us no harm if we mingle with them for the purpose of connecting them with God and are strong enough spiritually to withstand their influence.—(*Testimonies for the Church,* vol. 5, 112, 113.)

THE RESULTS OF DAILY PRAYER.—The soul that turns to God for its help, its support, its power, by daily, earnest prayer, will have noble aspirations, clear perceptions of truth and duty, lofty purposes of action, and a continual hungering and thirsting after righteousness. By maintaining a connection with God, we shall be enabled to diffuse to others, through our association with them, the light, the peace, the serenity, that rule in our hearts. The strength acquired in prayer to God, united with persevering effort in training the mind in thoughtfulness and care-taking, prepares one for daily duties and keeps the spirit in peace under all circumstances.

If we draw near to God, He will put a word in our mouth to speak for Him, even praise unto His name. He will teach us a strain from the song of the angels, even thanksgiving to our heavenly Father. In every act of life, the light and love of an indwelling Saviour will be revealed. Outward troubles cannot reach the life that is lived by faith in the Son of God.—(*Thoughts From the Mount of Blessing,* 85.)

PRAYER NEEDED DAILY TO RESIST SATAN.—Sanctification is not the work of a moment, an hour, or a day. It is a continual growth in grace. We know not one day how strong will be our conflict the next. Satan lives, and is active, and every day we need to cry earnestly to God for help and strength to resist him. As long as Satan reigns we shall have self to subdue, besetments to overcome, and there is no stopping place, there is no point to which we can come and say we have fully attained.—(*Testimonies for the Church,* vol. 1, 340.)

DAILY PRAYER TO INCLUDE BOTH PHYSICAL AND SPIRITUAL NEEDS.— The prayer for daily bread includes not only food to sustain the body, but that spiritual bread which will nourish the soul unto life everlasting. Jesus bids us, "Labor not for the meat which perisheth, but for that meat which endureth unto everlasting life." John 6:27. He says, "I am the living bread which came down from heaven: if any man eat of this bread, he shall live forever." Verse 51. Our Saviour is the bread of life, and it is by beholding His love, by receiving it into the soul, that we feed upon the bread which came down from heaven.

We receive Christ through His word, and the Holy Spirit is given to open the word of God to our understanding, and bring home its truths to our hearts. We are to pray day by day that as we read His word, God will send His Spirit to reveal to us the truth that will strengthen our souls for the day's need.

In teaching us to ask every day for what we need—both temporal and spiritual blessings—God has a purpose to accomplish for our good. He would have us realize our dependence upon His constant care, for He is seeking to draw us into communion with Himself. In this communion with Christ, through prayer and the study of the great and precious truths of His word, we shall as hungry souls be fed; as those that thirst, we shall be refreshed at the fountain of life.—(*Thoughts From the Mount of Blessing,* 112, 113.)

LIKE THE EARLY CHRISTIANS, WE NEED TO PRAY DAILY FOR THE HOLY SPIRIT.—Those who at Pentecost were endued with power from on high, were not thereby freed from further temptation and trial. As they witnessed for truth and righteousness they were repeatedly assailed by the enemy of all truth, who sought to rob them of their Christian experience. They were compelled to strive with all their God-given powers to reach the measure of the stature of men and women in Christ Jesus. Daily they prayed for fresh supplies of grace, that they might reach higher and still higher toward perfection. Under the Holy Spirit's working even the weakest, by exercising faith in God, learned to improve their entrusted powers and to become sanctified, refined, and ennobled. As in humility they submitted to the molding influence of the Holy Spirit, they received of the fullness of the Godhead and were fashioned in the likeness of the divine.

The lapse of time has wrought no change in Christ's parting promise to send the Holy Spirit as His representative. It is not because of any restriction on the part of God that the riches of His grace do not flow earthward to men. If the fulfillment of the promise is not seen as it might be, it is because the promise is not appreciated as it should be. If all were willing, all would be filled with the Spirit. Wherever the need of the Holy Spirit is a matter little thought of, there is seen spiritual drought, spiritual darkness, spiritual declension and death. Whenever minor matters occupy the attention, the divine power which is necessary for the growth and prosperity of the church, and which would bring all other blessings in its train, is lacking, though offered in infinite plenitude.

Since this is the means by which we are to receive power, why do we not hunger and thirst for the gift of the Spirit? Why do we not talk of it, pray for it, and preach concerning it? The Lord is more willing to give the Holy Spirit to those who serve Him than parents are to give good gifts to their children. For the daily baptism of the Spirit every worker should offer his petition to God. Companies of Christian workers should gather to ask for special help, for heavenly wisdom, that they may know how to plan and execute wisely. Especially should they pray that God will baptize His chosen ambassadors in mission fields with a rich measure of His Spirit. The presence of the Spirit with God's workers will give the proclamation of truth a power that not all the honor or glory of the world could give.—(*Acts of the Apostles*, 49-51.)

PRAY FOR GRACE FOR EACH DAY'S NEEDS.—The truth of God received into the heart is able to make you wise unto salvation. In believing and obeying it you will receive grace sufficient for the duties and trials of today. Grace for tomorrow you do not need. You should feel that you have only to do with today. Overcome for today; deny self for today; watch and pray for today; obtain victories in God for today. Our circumstances and surroundings, the changes daily transpiring around us, and the written word of God which discerns and proves all things—these are sufficient to teach us our duty and just what we ought to do, day by day. Instead of suffering your mind to run in a channel of thought from which you will derive no benefit, you should be searching the Scriptures daily and doing those duties in daily life which may now be irksome to you, but which must be done by someone.— (*Testimonies for the Church,* vol. 3, 333.)

PRAY DAILY FOR UNDERSTANDING OF THE BIBLE.—Those who profess to believe in Jesus, should ever press to the light. They should daily pray for the light of the Holy Spirit to shine upon the pages of the sacred book, that they may be enabled to comprehend the things of the Spirit of God.—(*Fundamentals of Christian Education,* 188, 189.)

PRAY DAILY FOR THE BLESSING THE SABBATH BRINGS.—All who regard the Sabbath as a sign between them and God, showing that He is the God who sanctifies them, will represent the principles of His government. They will bring into daily practice the laws of His kingdom. Daily it will be their prayer that the sanctification of the Sabbath may rest upon them. Every day they will have the companionship of Christ and will exemplify the perfection of His character. Every day their light will shine forth to others in good works.—(*Testimonies for the Church,* vol. 6, 353.)

A PARENT'S DAILY PRAYER.— Make your work pleasant with songs of praise. If you would have a clean record in the books of heaven, never fret or scold. Let your daily prayer be, "Lord, teach me to do my best. Teach me how to do better work. Give me energy and cheerfulness." . . . Bring Christ into all that you do. Then your lives will be filled with brightness and thanksgiving. . . . Let us do our best, moving forward cheerfully in the service of the Lord, with our hearts filled with His joy.—(*Child Guidance,* 148.)

YOUTH TO PRAY DAILY FOR WISDOM AND GRACE.—The trials and privations of which so many youth complain, Christ endured without murmuring. And this discipline is the very experience the youth need, which will give firmness to their characters, and make them like Christ, strong in spirit to resist temptation. They will not, if they separate from the influence of those who would lead them astray and corrupt their morals, be overcome by the devices of Satan. Through daily prayer to God, they will have wisdom and grace from Him to bear the conflict and stern realities of life, and come off victorious. Fidelity and serenity of mind can only be retained by watchfulness and prayer. Christ's life was an example of persevering energy, which was not allowed to become weakened by reproach, ridicule, privation or hardships.

Thus should it be with the youth. If trials increase upon them, they may know that God is testing and proving their fidelity. And in just that degree that they maintain their integrity of character under discouragements, will their fortitude, stability, and power of endurance increase, and they wax strong in spirit.—(*Messages to Young People,* 80.)

THE TEACHER'S NEED OF DAILY PRAYER.—Every teacher should daily receive instruction from Christ and should labor constantly under His guidance. It is impossible for him rightly to understand or to perform his work unless he is much with God in prayer. Only by divine aid, combined with earnest, self-denying effort, can he hope to do his work wisely and well.

Unless the teacher realizes the need of prayer and humbles his heart before God, he will lose the very essence of education. He should know how to pray and what language to use in prayer. "I am the vine," Jesus said, "ye are the branches: he that abideth in Me, and I in him, the same bringeth forth much fruit: for without Me ye can do nothing." John 15:5. The teacher should let the fruit of faith be manifest in his prayers. He should learn how to come to the Lord and plead with Him until he receives the assurance that his petitions are heard.—(*Counsels to Parents, Teachers, and Students,* 231.)

IN OLD TESTAMENT TIMES, THE ISRAELITES PRAYED DAILY.—As the priests morning and evening entered the holy place at the time of incense, the daily sacrifice was ready to be offered upon the altar in the court without. This was a time of intense interest to the worshipers who assembled at the tabernacle. Before entering into the presence of God through the ministration of the priest, they were to engage in earnest searching of heart and confession of sin. They united in silent prayer, with their faces toward the holy place. Thus their petitions ascended with the cloud of incense, while faith laid hold upon the merits of the promised Saviour prefigured by the atoning sacrifice. The hours appointed for the morning and the evening sacrifice were regarded as sacred, and they came to be observed as the set time for worship throughout the Jewish nation. And when in later times the Jews were scattered as captives in distant lands, they still at the appointed hour turned their faces toward Jerusalem and offered up their petitions to the God of Israel. In this custom Christians have an example for morning and evening prayer. While God condemns a mere round of ceremonies, without the spirit of worship, He looks with great pleasure upon those who love Him, bowing morning and evening to seek pardon for sins committed and to present their requests for needed blessings.—(*Patriarchs and Prophets,* 353, 354.)

DAILY PRAYER NUTURES OUR RELIGIOUS EXPERIENCE.—Religion must begin with emptying and purifying the heart, and must be nurtured by daily prayer.—(*Testimonies for the Church,* vol. 4, 535.)

A DAILY PRAYER LIFE REQUIRES EARNEST EFFORT.—A life of daily prayer and praise, a life which will shed light upon the path of others, cannot be maintained without earnest effort. But such effort will yield precious fruit, blessing not only the receiver, but the giver. The spirit of unselfish labor for others gives depth, stability, and Christlike loveliness to the character and brings peace and happiness to its possessor. The aspirations are elevated. There is no room for sloth or selfishness. Those who exercise the Christian graces will grow. They will have spiritual sinew and muscle, and will be strong to work for God. They will have clear spiritual perceptions, a steady, increasing faith, and prevailing power in prayer. Those who are watching for souls, who devote themselves most fully to the salvation of the erring, are most surely working out their own salvation.—(*Testimonies for the Church,* vol. 5, 607.)

ANGELS MARK THE MORNING PRAYER.—You all have an influence for good or for evil on the minds and characters of others. And just the influence which you exert is written in the book of records in heaven. An angel is attending you and taking record of your words and actions. When you rise in the morning, do you feel your helplessness and your need of strength from God? and do you humbly, heartily make known your wants to your heavenly Father? If so, angels mark your prayers, and if these prayers have not gone forth out of feigned lips, when you are in danger of unconsciously doing wrong and exerting an influence which will lead others to do wrong, your guardian angel will be by your side, prompting you to a better course, choosing your words for you, and influencing your actions.

If you feel in no danger, and if you offer no prayer for help and strength to resist temptations, you will be sure to go astray; your neglect of duty will be marked in the book of God in heaven, and you will be found wanting in the trying day.—(*Testimonies for the Church,* vol. 3, 363, 364.)

THE PRACTICE OF DAILY PRAYER IS NOT TO BE FOLLOWED HAPHAZARDLY.—Family worship should not be governed by circumstances. You are not to pray occasionally and, when you have a large day's work to do, neglect it. In thus doing you lead your children to look upon prayer as of no special consequence. Prayer means very much to the children of God, and thank offerings should come up before God morning and evening. Says the psalmist, "O come, let us sing unto the Lord: let us make a joyful noise to the rock of our salvation. Let us come before His presence with thanksgiving, and make a joyful noise unto Him with psalms."

Fathers and mothers, however pressing your business, do not fail to gather your family around God's altar. Ask for the guardianship of holy angels in your home. Remember that your dear ones are exposed to temptations.

In our efforts for the comfort and happiness of guests, let us not overlook our obligations to God. The hour of prayer should not be neglected for any consideration. Do not talk and amuse yourselves till all are too weary to enjoy the season of devotion. To do this is to present to God a lame offering. At an early hour of the evening, when we can pray unhurriedly and understandingly, we should present our supplications and raise our voices in happy, grateful praise.

Let all who visit Christians see that the hour of prayer is the most precious, the most sacred, and the happiest hour of the day. These seasons of devotion exert a refining, elevating influence upon all who participate in them. They bring a peace and rest grateful to the spirit.—(*Child Guidance*, 520, 521.)

DAILY PRAYER TO ASCEND TO GOD AS SWEET INCENSE.—The life of Abraham, the friend of God, was a life of prayer. Wherever he pitched his tent, close beside it was built an altar, upon which were offered the morning and the evening sacrifice. When his tent was removed, the altar remained. And the roving Canaanite, as he came to that altar, knew who had been there. When he had pitched his tent he repaired the altar and worshiped the living God.

So the homes of Christians should be lights in the world. From them, morning and evening, prayer should ascend to God as sweet incense. And as the morning dew, His mercies and blessings will descend upon the suppliants.

Fathers and mothers, each morning and evening gather your children around you, and in humble supplication lift the heart to God for help. Your dear ones are exposed to temptation. Daily annoyances beset the path of young and old. Those who would live patient, loving, cheerful lives must pray. Only by receiving constant help from God can we gain the victory over self.

Each morning consecrate yourselves and your children to God for that day. Make no calculation for months or years; these are not yours. One brief day is given you. As if it were your last on earth, work during its hours for the Master. Lay all your plans before God, to be carried out or given up, as His providence shall indicate. Accept His plans instead of your own, even though their acceptance requires the abandonment of cherished projects. Thus the life will be molded more and more after the divine example; "and the peace of God, which passeth all understanding, shall keep your hearts and minds through Christ Jesus." Philippians 4:7.— (*Testimonies for the Church,* vol. 7, 44.)

WHAT TO PRAY FOR DAILY.—We are to look upon every duty, however humble, as sacred because it is a part of God's service. Our daily prayer should be, "Lord, help me to do my best. Teach me how to do better work. Give me energy and cheerfulness. Help me to bring into my service the loving ministry of the Saviour."— (*Ministry of Healing,* 474.)

Consecrate yourself to God in the morning; make this your very first work. Let your prayer be, "Take me, O Lord, as wholly Thine. I lay all my plans at Thy feet. Use me today in Thy service. Abide with me, and let all my work be wrought in Thee." This is a daily matter. Each morning consecrate yourself to God for that day. Surrender all your plans to Him, to be carried out or given up as His providence shall indicate. Thus day by day you may be giving your life into the hands of God, and thus your life will be molded more and more after the life of Christ.—(*Steps to Christ,* 70.)

15

Jesus' Example in Prayer

FOLLOW JESUS' EXAMPLE BY STARTING THE DAY WITH PRAYER.—
It was in hours of solitary prayer that Jesus in His earth life received wisdom and power. Let the youth follow His example in finding at dawn and twilight a quiet season for communion with their Father in heaven. And throughout the day let them lift up their hearts to God. At every step of our way He says, "I the Lord thy God will hold thy right hand, . . . Fear not; I will help thee." Isaiah 41:13. Could our children learn these lessons in the morning of their years, what freshness and power, what joy and sweetness, would be brought into their lives!— (*Education,* 259.)

THE EARNEST PRAYERS OF JESUS CONTRAST WITH OUR FEEBLE PRAYERS.—Of Christ it is said: "And being in an agony He prayed more earnestly." In what contrast to this intercession by the Majesty of heaven are the feeble, heartless prayers that are offered to God. Many are content with lip service, and but few have a sincere, earnest, affectionate longing after God.—(*Testimonies for the Church,* vol. 4, 534.)

IF JESUS NEEDED TO PRAY WHILE ON EARTH, HOW MUCH MORE SHOULD WE.— When Jesus was upon the earth, He taught His disciples how to pray. He directed them to present their daily needs before God, and to cast all their care upon Him. And the assurance He gave them that their petitions should be heard, is assurance also to us.

Jesus Himself, while He dwelt among men, was often in prayer. Our Saviour identified Himself with our needs and weakness, in that He became a suppliant, a petitioner, seeking from His Father fresh supplies of strength, that He might come forth braced for duty and trial. He is our example in all things. He is a brother in our infirmities, "in all points tempted like as we are;" but as the sinless one His nature recoiled from evil; He endured struggles and torture of soul in a world of sin. His humanity made prayer a necessity and a privilege. He found comfort and joy in communion with His Father. And if the Saviour of men, the Son of God, felt the need of prayer, how much more should feeble, sinful mortals feel the necessity of fervent, constant prayer.—(*Steps to Christ,* 93, 94.)

Christ wrestled in earnest prayer; He offered up His supplications to the Father with strong crying and tears in behalf of those for whose salvation He had left heaven, and had come to this earth. Then how proper, yea, how essential that men should pray and not faint!—(*Review and Herald,* April 1, 1890.)

JESUS PRAYED FOR STRENGTH TO ENDURE TRIALS.—Few will follow the example of our Saviour in earnest, frequent prayer to God for strength to endure the trials, and to perform the daily duties, of this life. Christ is the captain of our salvation, and by His own sufferings and sacrifice, has given an example to all His followers, that watchfulness and prayer and persevering effort were necessary on their part if they would rightly represent the love which dwelt in His bosom for the fallen race.—(*Review and Herald,* February 23, 1886.)

JESUS' STRENGTH CAME FROM PRAYER.—The strength of Christ was in prayer. He had taken humanity, and He bore our infirmities and became sin for us. Christ retired to the groves or mountains with the world and everything else shut out. He was alone with His Father. With intense earnestness, He poured out His supplications, and put forth all the strength of His soul in grasping the hand of the Infinite. When new and great trials were before Him, He would steal away to the solitude of the mountains, and pass the entire night in prayer to His Heavenly Father.

As Christ is our example in all things, if we imitate His example in earnest, importunate prayer to God that we may have strength in His name who never yielded to the temptations of Satan to resist the devices of the wily foe, we shall not be overcome by him.—(*The Youth's Instructor,* April 1, 1873.)

In a life wholly devoted to the good of others, the Saviour found it necessary to withdraw from the thoroughfares of travel and from the throng that followed Him day after day. He must turn aside from a life of ceaseless activity and contact with human needs, to seek retirement and unbroken communion with His Father. As one with us, a sharer in our needs and weaknesses, He was wholly dependent upon God, and in the secret place of prayer He sought divine strength, that He might go forth braced for duty and trial. In a world of sin Jesus endured struggles and torture of soul. In communion with God He could unburden the sorrows that were crushing Him. Here He found comfort and joy.

In Christ the cry of humanity reached the Father of infinite pity. As a man He supplicated the throne of God till His humanity was charged with a heavenly current that should connect humanity with divinity. Through continual communion He received life from God, that He might impart life to the world. His experience is to be ours.

"Come ye yourselves apart," He bids us. If we would give heed to His word, we should be stronger and more useful. The disciples sought Jesus, and told Him all things; and He encouraged and instructed them. If today we would take time to go to Jesus and tell Him our needs, we should not be disappointed.—(*The Desire of Ages,* 362, 363.)

The Man of Sorrows pours out His supplications with strong crying and tears. He prays for strength to endure the test in behalf of humanity. He must Himself gain a fresh hold on Omnipotence, for only thus can He contemplate the future. And He pours out His heart longings for His disciples, that in the hour of the power of darkness their faith may not fail. The dew is heavy upon His bowed form, but He heeds it not. The shadows of night gather thickly about Him, but He regards not their gloom.—(*The Desire of Ages,* 419, 420.)

When Jesus entered the wilderness He was shut in by the Father's glory. Absorbed in communion with God, He was lifted above human weakness. But the glory departed, and He was left to battle with temptation. It was pressing upon Him every moment. His human nature shrank from the conflict that awaited Him. For forty days He fasted and prayed. Weak and emaciated from hunger, worn and haggard with mental agony, "his visage was so marred more than any man, and his form more than the sons of men" (Isa. 52:14). Now was Satan's opportunity. Now he supposed that he could overcome Christ.—(*Selected Messages,* bk. 1, 227, 228.)

To the consecrated worker there is wonderful consolation in the knowledge that even Christ during His life on earth sought His Father daily for fresh supplies of needed grace; and from this communion with God He went forth to strengthen and bless others.

Behold the Son of God bowed in prayer to His Father! Though He is the Son of God, He strengthens His faith by prayer, and by communion with Heaven gathers to Himself power to resist evil and to minister to the needs of men. As the Elder Brother of our race, He knows the necessities of those who, compassed with infirmity and living in a world of sin and temptation, still desire to serve Him. He knows that the messengers whom He sees fit to send are weak, erring men; but to all who give themselves wholly to His service He promises divine aid. His own example is an assurance that earnest, persevering supplication to God in faith—faith that leads to entire dependence upon God, and unreserved consecration to His work—will avail to bring to men the Holy Spirit's aid in the battle against sin.

Every worker who follows the example of Christ will be prepared to receive and use the power that God has promised to His church for the ripening of earth's harvest. Morning by morning, as the heralds of the gospel kneel before the Lord and renew their vows of consecration to Him, He will grant them the presence of His Spirit, with its reviving, sanctifying power. As they go forth to the day's duties, they have the assurance that the unseen agency of the Holy Spirit enables them to be "laborers together with God." [1 Cor. 3:9.]—(*Gospel Workers,* 510, 511.)

PRAYER STRENGTHENED JESUS FOR TRIALS.—Christ our Saviour was tempted in all points like as we are, yet He was without sin. He took human nature, being made in fashion as a man, and His necessities were the necessities of a man. He had bodily wants to be supplied, bodily weariness to be relieved. It was by prayer to His Father that He was braced for duty and for trial. Day by day He followed His round of duty, seeking to save souls. . . . And He spent whole nights in prayer in behalf of the tempted ones. . . .

The night seasons of prayer which the Saviour spent in the mountain or in the desert were essential to prepare Him for the trials He must meet in the days to follow. He felt the need of the refreshing and invigorating of soul and body, that He might meet the temptations of Satan; and those who are striving to live His life will feel this same need.—(*Maranatha,* 85.)

While Jerusalem was hushed in silence, and the disciples had returned to their homes to obtain refreshment in sleep,

Jesus slept not. His divine pleadings were ascending to His
Father for His disciples, that they might be kept from the evil
influences which they would daily encounter in the world,
and that His own soul might be strengthened and braced for
the duties and trials of the coming day.—(*Review and Herald,*
August 17, 1886.)

PRAYER REJUVENATED JESUS.—His days were passed in ministry to the crowds that pressed upon Him, and in unveiling the
treacherous sophistry of the rabbis, and this incessant labor often
left Him so utterly wearied that His mother and brothers, and
even His disciples, had feared that His life would be sacrificed.
But as He returned from the hours of prayer that closed the toilsome day, they marked the look of peace upon His face, the sense
of refreshment that seemed to pervade His presence. It was from
hours spent with God that He came forth, morning by morning,
to bring the light of heaven to men.—(*Thoughts From the Mount
of Blessing,* 102.)

PRAYER SUSTAINED JESUS' SPIRITUAL LIFE.—It was not on the
cross only that Christ sacrificed Himself for humanity. As He "went
about doing good" (Acts 10:38), every day's experience was an
outpouring of His life. In one way only could such a life be sustained. Jesus lived in dependence upon God and communion with
Him. To the secret place of the Most High, under the shadow of
the Almighty, men now and then repair; they abide for a season,
and the result is manifest in noble deeds; then their faith fails, the
communion is interrupted, and the lifework marred. But the life
of Jesus was a life of constant trust, sustained by continual communion; and His service for heaven and earth was without failure
or faltering.

As a man He supplicated the throne of God, till His humanity was charged with a heavenly current that connected humanity
with divinity. Receiving life from God, He imparted life to men.—
(*Education,* 80, 81.)

Jesus' prayer life reveals the secret of spiritual power.—The Saviour's life on earth was a life of communion with nature and with God. In this communion He revealed for us the secret of a life of power.—(*Counsels on Health,* 162.)

Jesus prayed in preparation for special tasks.—Jesus, when preparing for some great trial or some important work, would resort to the solitude of the mountains and spend the night in prayer to His Father. A night of prayer preceded the ordination of the apostles and the Sermon on the Mount, the transfiguration, the agony of the judgment hall and the cross, and the resurrection glory.

We, too, must have times set apart for meditation and prayer and for receiving spiritual refreshing. We do not value the power and efficacy of prayer as we should.—(*Ministry of Healing,* 509.)

Jesus' humanity made prayer a necessity.—As the human was upon Him, He felt His need of strength from His Father. He had select places of prayer. He loved to hold communion with His Father in the solitude of the mountain. In this exercise His holy, human soul was strengthened for the duties and trials of the day. Our Saviour identifies Himself with our needs and weaknesses, in that He became a suppliant, a nightly petitioner, seeking from His Father fresh supplies of strength, to come forth invigorated and re-freshed, braced for duty and trial. He is our example in all things. He is a brother in our infirmities, but not in possessing like passions. As the sinless One, His nature recoiled from evil. He endured struggles and torture of soul in a world of sin. His humanity made prayer a necessity and privilege. He required all the stronger divine support and comfort which His Father was ready to impart to Him, to Him who had, for the benefit of man, left the joys of heaven and chosen His home in a cold and thankless world. Christ found comfort and joy in communion with His Father. Here He could unburden His heart of the sorrows that were crushing Him. He was a man of sorrows and acquainted with grief.

Through the day He labored earnestly to do good to others, to save men from destruction. He healed the sick, comforted the mourning, and brought cheerfulness and hope to the despairing. He brought the dead to life. After His work was finished for the day, He went forth, evening after evening, away from the confusion of the city, and His form was bowed in some retired grove in supplication to His Father. At times the bright beams of the moon shone upon His bowed form. And then again the clouds and darkness shut away all light. The dew and frost of night rested upon His head and beard while in the attitude of a suppliant. He frequently continued His petitions through the entire night. He is our example. If we could remember this, and imitate Him, we would be much stronger in God.

If the Saviour of men, with His divine strength, felt the need of prayer, how much more should feeble, sinful mortals feel the necessity of prayer—fervent, constant prayer! When Christ was the most fiercely beset by temptation, He ate nothing. He committed Himself to God and, through earnest prayer and perfect submission to the will of His Father, came off conqueror. Those who profess the truth for these last days, above every other class of professed Christians, should imitate the great Exemplar in prayer.

"It is enough for the disciple that he be as his master, and the servant as his lord." Our tables are frequently spread with luxuries neither healthful nor necessary, because we love these things more than we love self-denial, freedom from disease, and soundness of mind. Jesus sought earnestly for strength from His Father. This the divine Son of God considered of more value, even for Himself, than to sit at the most luxurious table. He has given us evidence that prayer is essential in order to receive strength to contend with the powers of darkness, and to do the work allotted us. Our own strength is weakness, but that which God gives is mighty and will make everyone who obtains it more than conqueror.—(*Testimonies for the Church,* vol. 2, 201-203.)

JESUS TOOK TIME FOR PRAYER NO MATTER HOW BUSY OR WEARY.— Christ gave no stinted service. He did not measure His work by hours. His time, His heart, His soul and strength, were given to labor for the benefit of humanity. Through weary days He toiled, and through long nights He bent in prayer for grace and endurance that He might do a larger work. With strong crying and tears He sent His petitions to heaven, that His human nature might be strengthened, that He might be braced to meet the wily foe in all his deceptive workings, and fortified to fulfill His missions of uplifting humanity. To His workers He says, "I have given you an example, that ye should do as I have done." John 13:15.—(*Ministry of Healing,* 500.)

JESUS PRAYED EARLY IN THE MORNING.—The early morning often found Him in some secluded place, meditating, searching the Scriptures, or in prayer. With the voice of singing He welcomed the morning light. With songs of thanksgiving He cheered His hours and brought heaven's gladness to the toilworn and disheartened.—(*Counsels on Health,* 162.)

JESUS HAD SPECIFIC PLACES FOR PRAYER.—Have a place for secret prayer. Jesus had select places for communion with God, and so should we. We need often to retire to some spot, however humble, where we can be alone with God.—(*Thoughts From the Mount of Blessing,* 84.)

JESUS PRAYED ON OUR ACCOUNT.—Jesus was often weary from incessant toil and self-denial and self-sacrifice to bless the suffering and needy. He spent whole nights in prayer upon the lonely mountains, not because of His weakness and His necessities, but because He saw, He felt, the weakness of your natures to resist the temptations of the enemy upon the very points where you are now overcome. He knew that you would be indifferent in regard to your dangers and would not feel your need of prayer. It was on our account that He poured out His prayers to His Father with strong cries and tears.—(*Testimonies for the Church,* vol. 3, 379.)

Jesus' disciples were impressed by His prayer habits.—"The Son of man came not to be ministered unto, but to minister." Not for Himself, but for others, He lived and thought and prayed. From hours spent with God He came forth morning by morning, to bring the light of heaven to men. Daily He received a fresh baptism of the Holy Spirit. In the early hours of the new day the Lord awakened Him from His slumbers, and His soul and His lips were anointed with grace, that He might impart to others. His words were given Him fresh from the heavenly courts, words that He might speak in season to the weary and oppressed. "The Lord God hath given me," He said, "the tongue of the learned, that I should know how to speak a word in season to him that is weary: he wakeneth morning by morning, he wakeneth mine ear to hear as the learned."

Christ's disciples were much impressed by His prayers and by His habit of communion with God. One day after a short absence from their Lord, they found Him absorbed in supplication. Seemingly unconscious of their presence, He continued praying aloud. The hearts of the disciples were deeply moved. As He ceased praying, they exclaimed, "Lord, teach us to pray."—(*Review and Herald,* August 11, 1910.)

The Lord's Prayer exhibits beauty in simplicty.—Jesus taught His disciples that only that prayer which arises from unfeigned lips, prompted by the actual wants of the soul, is genuine, and will bring heaven's blessing to the petitioner. He gave a brief, comprehensive prayer to His disciples. This prayer, for its beautiful simplicity, is without a parallel. It is a perfect prayer for public and private life; it is dignified and elevated, yet so simple that the child at its mother's knee can understand it. The children of God have repeated this prayer for centuries, and yet its luster has not dimmed. Like a gem of value it continues to be loved and cherished. This prayer is a wonderful production. None will pray in vain if in their prayers are incorporated the principles contained therein. Our prayers in public should be short, and express only the real wants of the soul, asking in simplicity and simple trusting faith for the very things we need. Prayer from the humble, contrite heart is the vital breath of the soul hungering for righteousness.—(*Signs of the Times,* December 3, 1896.)

JESUS KNELT WHEN HE PRAYED.—Both in public and in private worship, it is our privilege to bow on our knees before the Lord when we offer our petitions to Him. Jesus, our example, "kneeled down, and prayed." Of His disciples it is recorded that they, too, "kneeled down, and prayed." Paul declared, "I bow my knees unto the Father of our Lord Jesus Christ." In confessing before God the sins of Israel, Ezra knelt. Daniel "kneeled upon his knees three times a day, and prayed, and gave thanks before his God."—(*Messages to Young People,* 251.)

CAREFULLY CONSIDER JESUS' LESSONS ABOUT PRAYER.—Christ's lessons in regard to prayer should be carefully considered. There is a divine science in prayer, and His illustration brings to view principles that all need to understand. He shows what is the true spirit of prayer, He teaches the necessity of perseverance in presenting our requests to God, and assures us of His willingness to hear and answer prayer.—(*Christ's Object Lessons,* 142.)

CHAPTER 16

Private Prayer

PRIVATE PRAYER IS ESSENTIAL.—It is impossible for the soul to flourish while prayer is not a special exercise of the mind. Family or public prayer alone is not sufficient. Secret prayer is very important; in solitude the soul is laid bare to the inspecting eye of God, and every motive is scrutinized. Secret prayer! How precious! The soul communing with God! Secret prayer is to be heard only by the prayer-hearing God. No curious ear is to receive the burden of such petitions. In secret prayer the soul is free from surrounding influences, free from excitement. Calmly, yet fervently, will it reach out after God. Secret prayer is frequently perverted, and its sweet designs lost, by loud vocal prayer. Instead of the calm, quiet trust and faith in God, the soul drawn out in low, humble tones, the voice is raised to a loud pitch, and excitement is encouraged, and secret prayer loses its softening, sacred influence. There is a storm of feeling, a storm of words, making it impossible to discern the still, small voice that speaks to the soul while engaged in its secret, true, heartfelt devotion. Secret prayer, properly carried out, is productive of great good. But prayer which is made public to the entire family and neighborhood is not secret prayer, even though thought to be, and divine strength is not received from it. Sweet and abiding will be the influence emanating from Him who seeth in secret, whose ear is open to answer the prayer arising from the heart. By calm, simple faith the soul holds communion with God and gathers to itself divine rays of light to strengthen and sustain it to endure the conflicts of Satan. God is our tower of strength.—(*Testimonies for the Church,* vol. 2, 189, 190.)

Private prayer, family prayer, prayer in public gatherings for the worship of God—all are essential. And we are to live our prayers. We are to co-operate with Christ in His work.—(*Testimonies for the Church,* vol. 7, 239.)

ALL NEED TO WATCH AND PRAY CONTINUALLY.—The very beginning of the evil was a neglect of watchfulness and secret prayer, then came a neglect of other religious duties, and thus the way was opened for all the sins that followed. Every Christian will be assailed by the allurements of the world, the clamors of the carnal nature, and the direct temptations of Satan. No one is safe. No matter what our experience has been, no matter how high our station, we need to watch and pray continually. We must be daily controlled by the Spirit of God or we are controlled by Satan.—(*Testimonies for the Church,* vol. 5, 102.)

PRAY AT ALL TIMES.—Cultivate the habit of talking with the Saviour when you are alone, when you are walking, and when you are busy with your daily labor. Let the heart be continually uplifted in silent petition for help, for light, for strength, for knowledge. Let every breath be a prayer.—(*Temperance,* 135.)

The way to the throne of God is always open. You cannot always be on your knees in prayer, but your silent petitions may constantly ascend to God for strength and guidance. When tempted, as you will be, you may flee to the secret place of the Most High. His everlasting arms will be underneath you.—(*Counsels on Health,* 362.)

SECRET PRAYER IS APPROPRIATE ANYWHERE, ANYTIME.—Pray in your closet, and as you go about your daily labor let your heart be often uplifted to God.

It was thus that Enoch walked with God. These silent prayers rise like precious incense before the throne of grace. Satan cannot overcome him whose heart is thus stayed upon God.

There is no time or place in which it is inappropriate to offer up a petition to God. There is nothing that can prevent us from lifting up our hearts in the spirit of earnest prayer. In the crowds of the street, in the midst of a business engagement, we may send up a petition to God and plead for divine guidance, as did Nehemiah when he made his request before King Artaxerxes. A closet of communion may be found wherever we are. We should have the door of the heart open continually and our invitation going up that Jesus may come and abide as a heavenly guest in the soul.—(*Steps to Christ*, 98, 99).

PRAYER BRINGS US INTO THE PRESENCE OF GOD HIMSELF.— Prayer, whether offered in the public assembly, at the family altar, or in secret, places man directly in the presence of God. By constant prayer the youth may obtain principles so firm that the most powerful temptations will not draw them from their allegiance to God.—(*My Life Today*, 18.)

PRAYER KEEPS US CONNECTED WITH CHRIST.—We should be much in secret prayer. Christ is the vine, ye are the branches. And if we would grow and flourish, we must continually draw sap and nourishment from the Living Vine; for separated from the Vine we have no strength.

I asked the angel why there was no more faith and power in Israel. He said, "Ye let go of the arm of the Lord too soon. Press your petitions to the throne, and hold on by strong faith. The promises are sure."—(*Early Writings*, 73.)

PRIVATE PRAYER SUSTAINS THE SOUL.—To live thus by the word of God means the surrender to Him of the whole life. There will be felt a continual sense of need and dependence, a drawing out of the heart after God. Prayer is a necessity; for it is the life of the soul. Family prayer, public prayer, have their place; but it is secret communion with God that sustains the soul life.—(*Education*, 258.)

PRIVATE PRAYER IS NEEDED IN ORDER TO BECOME PERSONALLY ACQUAINTED WITH GOD.—Oh, do we know God as we should? What comfort, what joy, we should have if we were to learn daily the lessons He desires us to learn! We must know Him by an experimental knowledge. It will be profitable for us to spend more time in secret prayer, in becoming personally acquainted with our heavenly Father.—(*Medical Ministry*, 102.)

GOD'S PEOPLE NEGLECT SECRET PRAYER.—I have frequently seen that the children of the Lord neglect prayer, especially secret prayer, altogether too much; that many do not exercise that faith which it is their privilege and duty to exercise, often waiting for that feeling which faith alone can bring. Feeling is not faith; the two are distinct.—(*Early Writings*, 72.)

Our Creator demands our supreme devotion, our first allegiance. Anything which tends to abate our love for God, or to interfere with the service due Him, becomes thereby an idol. With some their lands, their houses, their merchandise, are the idols. Business enterprises are prosecuted with zeal and energy, while the service of God is made a secondary consideration. Family worship is neglected, secret prayer is forgotten.—(*SDA Bible Commentary*, vol. 2, 1011, 1012.)

NEGLECT OF PRAYER IS PROGRESSIVE.—Beware how you neglect secret prayer and a study of God's word. These are your weapons against him who is striving to hinder your progress heavenward. The first neglect of prayer and Bible study makes easier the second neglect. The first resistance to the Spirit's pleading prepares the way for the second resistance. Thus the heart is hardened, and the conscience seared.—(*Messages to Young People,* 96.)

SPORADIC PRAYER WILL CAUSE YOU TO LOSE YOUR HOLD ON GOD.—Prayer is the breath of the soul. It is the secret of spiritual power. No other means of grace can be substituted and the health of the soul be preserved. Prayer brings the heart into immediate contact with the Wellspring of life, and strengthens the sinew and muscle of the religious experience. Neglect the exercise of prayer, or engage in prayer spasmodically, now and then, as seems convenient, and you lose your hold on God. The spiritual faculties lose their vitality, the religious experience lacks health and vigor.—(*Messages to Young People,* 249, 250.)

PRIVATE PRAYER SHOULD BE PRIVATE.—In private prayer all have the privilege of praying as long as they desire and of being as explicit as they please. They can pray for all their relatives and friends. The closet is the place to tell all their private difficulties, and trials, and temptations. A common meeting to worship God is not the place to open the privacies of the heart.—(*Testimonies for the Church,* vol. 2, 578.)

In secret devotion our prayers are to reach the ears of none but the prayer-hearing God. No curious ear is to receive the burden of such petitions.

"When thou prayest, enter into thy closet." Have a place for secret prayer. Jesus had select places for communion with God, and so should we. We need often to retire to some spot, however humble, where we can be alone with God.

"Pray to thy Father which is in secret." In the name of Jesus we may come into God's presence with the confidence of a child. No man is needed to act as a mediator. Through Jesus we may open our hearts to God as to one who knows and loves us.

In the secret place of prayer, where no eye but God's can see, no ear but His can hear, we may pour out our most hidden desires and longings to the Father of infinite pity, and in the hush and silence of the soul that voice which never fails to answer the cry of human need will speak to our hearts.

"The Lord is very pitiful, and of tender mercy." James 5:11. He waits with unwearied love to hear the confessions of the wayward and to accept their penitence. He watches for some return of gratitude from us, as the mother watches for the smile of recognition from her beloved child. He would have us understand how earnestly and tenderly His heart yearns over us. He invites us to take our trials to His sympathy, our sorrows to His love, our wounds to His healing, our weakness to His strength, our emptiness to His fullness. Never has one been disappointed who came unto Him. "They looked unto Him, and were lightened: and their faces were not ashamed." Psalm 34:5.

Those who seek God in secret telling the Lord their needs and pleading for help, will not plead in vain. "Thy Father which seeth in secret Himself shall reward thee openly." As we make Christ our daily companion we shall feel that the powers of an unseen world are all around us; and by looking unto Jesus we shall become assimilated to His image. By beholding we become changed. The character is softened, refined, and ennobled for the heavenly kingdom. The sure result of our intercourse and fellowship with our Lord will be to increase piety, purity, and fervor. There will be a growing intelligence in prayer. We are receiving a divine education, and this is illustrated in a life of diligence and zeal.

The soul that turns to God for its help, its support, its power, by daily, earnest prayer, will have noble aspirations, clear perceptions of truth and duty, lofty purposes of action, and a continual hungering and thirsting after righteousness. By maintaining a connection with God, we shall be enabled to diffuse to others, through our association with them, the light, the peace, the serenity, that rule in our hearts. The strength acquired in prayer to God, united with persevering effort in training the mind in thoughtfulness and care-taking, prepares one for daily duties and keeps the spirit in peace under all circumstances.—(*Thoughts From the Mount of Blessing,* 84, 85.)

There are some, I fear, who do not take their troubles to God in private prayer, but reserve them for the prayer meeting, and there do up their praying for several days. Such may be named conference and prayer meeting killers. They emit no light; they edify no one. Their cold, frozen prayers and long, backslidden testimonies cast a shadow. All are glad when they get through, and it is almost impossible to throw off the chill and darkness which their prayers and exhortations bring into the meeting. From the light which I have received, our meetings should be spiritual and social, and not too long. Reserve, pride, vanity, and fear of man should be left at home. Little differences and prejudices should not be taken with us to these meetings. As in a united family, simplicity, meekness, confidence, and love should exist in the hearts of brethren and sisters who meet to be refreshed and invigorated by bringing their lights together.— (*Testimonies for the Church,* vol. 2, 578, 579.)

SECRET PRAYER PROVIDES A CLEAR PICTURE OF SELF.—Nothing will give such clear views of self as secret prayer. He who seeth in secret and knoweth all things, will enlighten your understanding and answer your petitions. Plain, simple duties that must not be neglected will open before you.—(*Testimonies for the Church,* vol. 5, 163.)

PRIVATE PRAYER CULTIVATES A NOBLE CHARACTER.—Amid the perils of these last days, the only safety of the youth lies in ever-increasing watchfulness and prayer. The youth who finds his joy in reading the word of God, and in the hour of prayer, will be constantly refreshed by drafts from the fountain of life. He will attain a height of moral excellence and a breadth of thought of which others can not conceive. Communion with God encourages good thoughts, noble aspirations, clear perceptions of truth, and lofty purposes of action. Those who thus connect themselves with God are acknowledged by Him as His sons and daughters. They are constantly reaching higher and still higher, obtaining clearer views of God and of eternity, until the Lord makes them channels of light and wisdom to the world.

But prayer is not understood as it should be. Our prayers are not to inform God of something He does not know. The Lord is acquainted with the secrets of every soul. Our prayers need not be long and loud. God reads the hidden thought. We may pray in secret, and He who sees in secret will hear, and will reward us openly.

The prayers that are offered to God to tell Him of all our wretchedness, when we do not feel wretched at all, are the prayers of hypocrisy. It is the contrite prayer that the Lord regards. "For thus saith the high and lofty One that inhabiteth eternity, whose name is Holy; I dwell in the high and holy place, with him also that is of a contrite and humble spirit, to revive the spirit of the humble, and to revive the heart of the contrite ones."—(*The Youth's Instructor,* August 18, 1898.)

SPIRITUAL STRENGTH COMES THROUGH PRIVATE PRAYER.—Those who will put on the whole armor of God and devote some time every day to meditation and prayer and to the study of the Scriptures will be connected with heaven and will have a saving, transforming influence upon those around them. Great thoughts, noble aspirations, clear perceptions of truth and duty to God, will be theirs. They will be yearning for purity, for light, for love, for all the graces of heavenly birth. Their earnest prayers will enter into that within the veil. This class will have a sanctified boldness to come into the presence of the Infinite One. They will feel that heaven's light and glories are for them, and they will become refined, elevated, ennobled by this intimate acquaintance with God. Such is the privilege of true Christians.

Abstract meditation is not enough; busy action is not enough; both are essential to the formation of Christian character. Strength acquired in earnest, secret prayer prepares us to withstand the allurements of society. And yet we should not exclude ourselves from the world, for our Christian experience is to be the light of the world. The society of unbelievers will do us no harm if we mingle with them for the purpose of connecting them with God and are strong enough spiritually to withstand their influence.—(*Testimonies for the Church,* vol. 5, 112, 113.)

GOD ACCEPTS SILENT PRAYER.—The Lord will accept even the silent petition of a burdened heart.—(*The SDA Bible Commentary*, vol. 2, 1014.)

PRAYER MUST PRECEDE WITNESSING.—Personal effort for others should be preceded by much secret prayer; for it requires great wisdom to understand the science of saving souls. Before communicating with men, commune with Christ. At the throne of heavenly grace obtain a preparation for ministering to the people.—(*Christ's Object Lessons*, 149.)

We must receive light and blessing, that we may have something to impart. It is the privilege of every worker first to talk with God in the secret place of prayer and then to talk with the people as God's mouthpiece. Men and women who commune with God, who have an abiding Christ, make the very atmosphere holy, because they are co-operating with holy angels. Such witness is needed for this time.—(*Testimonies for the Church*, vol. 6, 52.)

WORK AND PRAYER MUST BE COMBINED.—We must live a twofold life—a life of thought and action, of silent prayer and earnest work. . . . The soul that turns to God for its strength, its support, its power, by daily, earnest prayer, will have noble aspirations, clear perceptions of truth and duty, lofty purposes of action, and a continual hungering and thirsting after righteousness.—(*Testimonies for the Church*, vol. 4, 459, 460.)

If the rush of work is allowed to drive us from our purpose of seeking the Lord daily, we shall make the greatest mistakes; we shall incur losses, for the Lord is not with us. We have closed the door so that He cannot find access to our souls. But if we pray, even when our hands are employed, the Saviour's ear is open to hear our petitions. . . . God takes care of you in the place where it is your duty to be. But be sure, as often as possible, to go where prayer is wont to be made.—(*Medical Ministry*, 216.)

USE SIMPLE LANGUAGE IN PRAYER.—High-flown language is inappropriate in prayer, whether the petition be offered in the pulpit, in the family circle, or in secret. Especially should the one offering public prayer use simple language, that others may understand what is said and unite with the petition.

It is the heart-felt prayer of faith that is heard in heaven and answered on earth.—(*Gospel Workers,* 177.)

IT IS OUR PRIVILEGE TO KNEEL WHEN IN PRAYER.—Both in public and in private worship it is our privilege to bow on our knees before God when we offer our petitions to Him. Jesus, our example, "kneeled down, and prayed." Luke 22:41. Of His disciples it is recorded that they, too, "kneeled down, and prayed." Acts 9:40. Paul declared, "I bow my knees unto the Father of our Lord Jesus Christ." Ephesians 3:14. In confessing before God the sins of Israel, Ezra knelt. See Ezra 9:5. Daniel "kneeled upon his knees three times a day, and prayed, and gave thanks before his God." Daniel 6:10.—(*Prophets and Kings,* 48.)

ENGAGE IN NO AMUSEMENT THAT DISQUALIFIES YOU FOR PRIVATE PRAYER.—Any amusement in which you can engage asking the blessing of God upon it in faith, will not be dangerous. But any amusement which disqualifies you for secret prayer, for devotion at the altar of prayer, or for taking part in the prayer meeting, is not safe, but dangerous.—(*Messages to Young People,* 386.)

GOD SEES US IN OUR SECRET PRAYER PLACE.—Like Nathanael, we need to study God's word for ourselves, and pray for the enlightenment of the Holy Spirit. He who saw Nathanael under the fig tree will see us in the secret place of prayer. Angels from the world of light are near to those who in humility seek for divine guidance.—(*The Desire of Ages,* 141.)

OUR PRAYERS CANNOT BE LOST.—It is a wonderful thing that we can pray effectually; that unworthy, erring mortals possess the power of offering their requests to God. What higher power can man desire than this,—to be linked with the infinite God? Feeble, sinful man has the privilege of speaking to his Maker. We may utter words that reach the throne of the Monarch of the universe. We may speak with Jesus as we walk by the way, and He says, I am at thy right hand. [See Ps. 16:8.]

We may commune with God in our hearts; we may walk in companionship with Christ. When engaged in our daily labor, we may breathe out our heart's desire, inaudible to any human ear; but that word cannot die away into silence, nor can it be lost. Nothing can drown the soul's desire. It rises above the din of the street, above the noise of machinery. It is God to whom we are speaking, and our prayer is heard.

Ask, then; ask, and ye shall receive. Ask for humility, wisdom, courage, increase of faith. To every sincere prayer an answer will come. It may not come just as you desire, or at the time you look for it; but it will come in the way and at the time that will best meet your need. The prayers you offer in loneliness, in weariness, in trial, God answers, not always according to your expectations, but always for your good.—(*Gospel Workers*, 258.)

Let all who are afflicted or unjustly used, cry to God. Turn away from those whose hearts are as steel, and make your requests known to your Maker. Never is one repulsed who comes to Him with a contrite heart. Not one sincere prayer is lost. Amid the anthems of the celestial choir, God hears the cries of the weakest human being. We pour out our heart's desire in our closets, we breathe a prayer as we walk by the way, and our words reach the throne of the Monarch of the universe. They may be inaudible to any human ear, but they cannot die away into silence, nor can they be lost through the activities of business that are going on. Nothing can drown the soul's desire. It rises above the din of the street, above the confusion of the multitude, to the heavenly courts. It is God to whom we are speaking, and our prayer is heard.— (*Christ's Object Lessons*, 174.)

17

Prayer in the
Home Circle

FAMILIES SHOULD PRAY TOGETHER EVERY MORNING AND
EVENING.—Family worship should not be governed by circumstances. You are not to pray occasionally and, when you have a
large day's work to do, neglect it. In thus doing you lead your
children to look upon prayer as of no special consequence. Prayer
means very much to the children of God, and thank offerings
should come up before God morning and evening. Says the
psalmist, "O come, let us sing unto the Lord: let us make a joyful noise to the rock of our salvation. Let us come before his
presence with thanksgiving, and make a joyful noise unto him
with psalms."

Fathers and mothers, however pressing your business, do not
fail to gather your family around God's altar. Ask for the guardianship of holy angels in your home. Remember that your dear
ones are exposed to temptations.

In our efforts for the comfort and happiness of guests, let us
not overlook our obligations to God. The hour of prayer should
not be neglected for any consideration. Do not talk and amuse
yourselves till all are too weary to enjoy the season of devotion. To

do this is to present to God a lame offering. At an early hour of the evening, when we can pray unhurriedly and understandingly, we should present our supplications and raise our voices in happy, grateful praise.

Let all who visit Christians see that the hour of prayer is the most precious, the most sacred, and the happiest hour of the day. These seasons of devotion exert a refining, elevating influence upon all who participate in them. They bring a peace and rest grateful to the spirit.—(*Child Guidance,* 520, 521.)

The Lord has a special interest in the families of His children here below. Angels offer the smoke of the fragrant incense for the praying saints. Then in every family let prayer ascend to heaven both at morning and at the cool sunset hour, in our behalf presenting before God the Saviour's merits. Morning and evening the heavenly universe takes notice of every praying household.—(*My Life Today,* 29.)

Morning and evening the heavenly universe behold every household that prays, and the angel with the incense, representing the blood of the atonement, finds access to God.—(*SDA Bible Commentary,* vol. 7, 971.)

In the morning the Christian's first thoughts should be upon God. Worldly labor and self-interest should be secondary. Children should be taught to respect and reverence the hour of prayer. . . . It is the duty of Christian parents, morning and evening, by earnest prayer and persevering faith, to make a hedge about their children. They should patiently instruct them—kindly and untiringly teach them how to live in order to please God.—(*Child Guidance,* 519.)

In every Christian home God should be honored by the morning and evening sacrifices of prayer and praise. Children should be taught to respect and reverence the hour of prayer. It is the duty of Christian parents, morning and evening, by earnest prayer and persevering faith, to make a hedge about their children.

In the church at home the children are to learn to pray and to trust in God. Teach them to repeat God's law. Concerning the commandments the Israelites were instructed: "Thou shalt teach them diligently unto thy children, and shalt talk of them when thou sittest in thine house, and when thou walkest by the way, and when thou liest down, and when thou risest up." Deuteronomy 6:7. Come in humility, with a heart full of tenderness, and with a sense of the temptations and dangers before yourselves and your children; by faith bind them to the altar, entreating for them the care of the Lord. Train the children to offer their simple words of prayer. Tell them that God delights to have them call upon Him.—(*Counsels to Parents, Teachers, and Students,* 110.)

Before leaving the house for labor, all the family should be called together; and the father, or the mother in the father's absence, should plead fervently with God to keep them through the day. Come in humility, with a heart full of tenderness, and with a sense of the temptations and dangers before yourselves and your children; by faith bind them upon the altar, entreating for them the care of the Lord. Ministering angels will guard children who are thus dedicated to God.—(*Child Guidance,* 519.)

FAMILIES SHOULD HAVE FIXED TIMES FOR MORNING AND EVENING PRAYER.—In every family there should be a fixed time for morning and evening worship. How appropriate it is for parents to gather their children about them before the fast is broken, to thank the heavenly Father for His protection during the night, and to ask Him for His help and guidance and watch care during the day! How fitting, also, when evening comes, for parents and children to gather once more before Him and thank Him for the blessings of the day that is past!—(*Child Guidance,* 520.)

FAMILY PRAYER IS ESSENTIAL.—Private prayer, family prayer, prayer in public gatherings for the worship of God—all are essential. And we are to live our prayers. We are to co-operate with Christ in His work.—(*Testimonies for the Church,* vol. 7, 239.)

NOTHING SO SAD AS A HOME WITHOUT PRAYER.—I know of nothing that causes me so great sadness as a prayerless home. I do not feel safe in such a house for a single night; and were it not for the hope of helping the parents to realize their necessity and their sad neglect, I would not remain. The children show the result of this neglect, for the fear of God is not before them.—(*Child Guidance,* 518.)

EVERY HOME TO BE A HOUSE OF PRAYER.—If ever there was a time when every house should be a house of prayer it is now.—(*Testimonies for the Church,* vol. 7, 42.)

FAMILY PRAYER PLACES US IN GOD'S DIRECT PRESENCE.—Prayer, whether offered in the public assembly, at the family altar, or in secret, places man directly in the presence of God. By constant prayer the youth may obtain principles so firm that the most powerful temptations will not draw them from their allegiance to God.—(*My Life Today,* 18.)

FAMILY PRAYER BRINGS STRENGTH AND BLESSINGS.—We should pray to God much more than we do. There is great strength and blessing in praying together in our families, with and for our children. When my children have done wrong, and I have talked with them kindly and then prayed with them, I have never found it necessary after that to punish them. Their hearts would melt in tenderness before the Holy Spirit that came in answer to prayer.—(*Child Guidance,* 525.)

SIMPLE LANGUAGE IS THE MOST APPROPRIATE FOR PRAYER.—High-flown language is inappropriate in prayer, whether the petition be offered in the pulpit, in the family circle, or in secret. Especially should the one offering public prayer use simple language, that others may understand what is said and unite with the petition.

It is the heart-felt prayer of faith that is heard in heaven and answered on earth.—(*Gospel Workers,* 177.)

TEACH YOUR CHILDREN TO RESPECT THE TIME FOR PRAYER.—Your children should be educated to be kind, thoughtful of others, gentle, easy to be entreated, and, above everything else, to respect religious things and feel the importance of the claims of God. They should be taught to respect the hour of prayer; they should be required to rise in the morning so as to be present at family worship.—(*Child Guidance,* 521.)

PRAYERS FOR OUR FAMILY ARE BEST PRAYED AT HOME.—We should not come to the house of God to pray for our families unless deep feeling shall lead us while the Spirit of God is convicting them. Generally, the proper place to pray for our families is at the family altar. When the subjects of our prayers are at a distance, the closet is the proper place to plead with God for them. When in the house of God, we should pray for a present blessing and should expect God to hear and answer our prayers. Such meetings will be lively and interesting.—(*Testimonies for the Church,* vol. 1, 145, 146.)

THE LORD DOES NOT ACCEPT FAMILY WORSHIP THAT HAS BECOME A MERE FORM.—In many cases the morning and evening worship is little more than a mere form, a dull, monotonous repetition of set phrases in which the spirit of gratitude or the sense of need finds no expression. The Lord accepts not such service. But the petitions of a humble heart and contrite spirit He will not despise. The opening of our hearts to our heavenly Father, the acknowledgment of our entire dependence, the expression of our wants, the homage of grateful love—this is true prayer.—(*Child Guidance,* 518.)

PARENTS NEED TO PRAY FOR WISDOM TO TRAIN THEIR CHILDREN WISELY.—Every family should rear its altar of prayer, realizing that the fear of the Lord is the beginning of wisdom. If any persons in the world need the strength and encouragement that religion gives, it is those who are responsible for the education and training of children. They cannot do their work in a manner acceptable to God while their daily example teaches those who look to them for guidance that they can live without God. If they educate their children to live for this life only, they will make no preparation for eternity. They will die as they have lived, without God, and parents will be called to account for the loss of their souls. Fathers, mothers, you need to seek God morning and evening at the family altar, that you may learn how to teach your children wisely, tenderly, lovingly.—(*Child Guidance*, 517.)

You have brought children into the world who have had no voice in regard to their existence. You have made yourselves responsible in a great measure for their future happiness, their eternal well-being. The burden is upon you, whether you are sensible of it or not, to train these children for God, to watch with jealous care the first approach of the wily foe and be prepared to raise a standard against him. Build a fortification of prayer and faith about your children, and exercise diligent watching thereunto. You are not secure a moment against the attacks of Satan.—(*Testimonies for the Church*, vol. 2, 397, 398.)

Let parents seek God for guidance in their work. On their knees before Him they will gain a true understanding of their great responsibilities and there they can commit their children to One who will never err in counsel and instruction.—(*Adventist Home*, 321.)

By sincere, earnest prayer parents should make a hedge about their children. They should pray with full faith that God will abide with them, and that holy angels will guard them and their children from Satan's cruel power.—(*Testimonies for the Church,* vol. 7, 42, 43.)

Patiently, lovingly, as faithful stewards of the manifold grace of Christ, parents are to do their appointed work. It is expected of them that they will be found faithful. Everything is to be done in faith. Constantly they must pray that God will impart His grace to their children. Never must they become weary, impatient, or fretful in their work. They must cling closely to their children and to God. If parents work in patience and love, earnestly endeavoring to help their children to reach the highest standard of purity and modesty, they will succeed.—(*Adventist Home,* 208.)

Without human effort divine effort is in vain. God will work with power when in trustful dependence upon Him parents will awake to the sacred responsibility resting upon them, and seek to train their children aright. He will co-operate with those parents who carefully and prayerfully educate their children, working out their own and their children's salvation. He will work in them, to will and to do of His own good pleasure.—(*The Adventist Home,* 206, 207.)

Parents, are you working with unflagging energy in behalf of your children? The God of heaven marks your solicitude, your earnest work, your constant watchfulness. He hears your prayers. With patience and tenderness train your children for the Lord. All heaven is interested in your work. Angels of light will unite with you as you strive to lead your children to heaven. God will unite with you, crowning your efforts with success. Christ delights to honor a Christian family; for such a family is a symbol of the family in heaven.—(*Review and Herald,* January 29, 1901.)

THE GREAT IMPORTANCE OF A MOTHER'S PRAYERS.—Those who keep the law of God look upon their children with indefinable feelings of hope and fear, wondering what part they will act in the great conflict that is just before them. The anxious mother questions, "What stand will they take? What can I do to prepare them to act well their part, so that they will be the recipients of eternal glory?" Great responsibilities rest upon you, mothers. Although you may not stand in national councils, . . . you may do a great work for God and your country. You may educate your children. You may aid them to develop characters that will not be swayed or influenced to do evil, but will sway and influence others to do right. By your fervent prayers of faith you can move the arm that moves the world.—(*Adventist Home,* 264.)

The influence of a praying, God-fearing mother will last through eternity. She may die, but her work will endure.—(*Testimonies for the Church,* vol. 4, 500.)

Did mothers but realize the importance of their mission, they would be much in secret prayer, presenting their children to Jesus, imploring His blessing upon them, and pleading for wisdom to discharge aright their sacred duties. Let the mother improve every opportunity to mold and fashion the disposition and habits of her children. Let her watch carefully the development of character, repressing traits that are too prominent, encouraging those that are deficient. Let her make her own life a pure and noble example to her precious charge.

The mother should enter upon her work with courage and energy, relying constantly upon divine aid in all her efforts. She should never rest satisfied until she sees in her children a gradual elevation of character, until they have a higher object in life than merely to seek their own pleasure.

It is impossible to estimate the power of a praying mother's influence. She acknowledges God in all her ways. She takes her children before the throne of grace and presents them to Jesus, pleading for His blessing upon them. The influence of those prayers is to those children as "a wellspring of life." These prayers, offered in faith, are the support and strength of the Christian mother. To neglect the duty of praying with our children is to lose one of the greatest blessings within our reach, one of the greatest helps amid the perplexities, cares, and burdens of our lifework.

The power of a mother's prayers cannot be too highly estimated. She who kneels beside her son and daughter through the vicissitudes of childhood, through the perils of youth, will never know till the judgment the influence of her prayers upon the life of her children. If she is connected by faith with the Son of God, the mother's tender hand may hold back her son from the power of temptation, may restrain her daughter from indulging in sin. When passion is warring for the mastery, the power of love, the restraining, earnest, determined influence of the mother, may balance the soul on the side of right.—(*Adventist Home,* 265, 266.)

The prayers of Christian mothers are not disregarded by the Father of all, who sent His Son to the earth to ransom a people for Himself. He will not turn away your petitions and leave you and yours to the buffetings of Satan in the great day of final conflict. It is for you to work with simplicity and faithfulness, and God will establish the work of your hands.—(*Child Guidance,* 526.)

FAMILY PRAYER IS IMPORTANT, BUT OTHER TYPES OF PRAYER ARE NEEDED AS WELL.—Family or public prayer alone is not sufficient. Secret prayer is very important; in solitude the soul is laid bare to the inspecting eye of God, and every motive is scrutinized. Secret prayer! How precious! The soul communing with God! Secret prayer is to be heard only by the prayer-hearing God. No curious ear is to receive the burden of such petitions.—(*Testimonies for the Church,* vol. 2, 189, 190.)

18

Prayer and Worship

PRAYER AND WORSHIP ARE ESSENTIAL TO SPIRITUAL GROWTH.—
Seek every opportunity to go where prayer is wont to be made.
Those who are really seeking for communion with God will be
seen in the prayer meeting, faithful to do their duty and earnest
and anxious to reap all the benefits they can gain. They will improve every opportunity of placing themselves where they can receive the rays of light from heaven.—(*Steps to Christ,* 98.)

Private prayer, family prayer, prayer in public gatherings for
the worship of God—all are essential. And we are to live our prayers.
We are to co-operate with Christ in His work.—(*Testimonies for
the Church,* vol. 7, 239.)

In our devotional meetings, our voices should express by prayer
and praise our adoration of the heavenly Father, that all may know
that we worship God in simplicity and truth, and in the beauty of
holiness.—(*Counsels to Parents, Teachers, and Students,* 245.)

Let small companies assemble in the evening, at noon, or in the early morning to study the Bible. Let them have a season of prayer, that they may be strengthened, enlightened, and sanctified by the Holy Spirit. This work Christ wants to have done in the heart of every worker. If you yourselves will open the door to receive it, a great blessing will come to you. Angels of God will be in your assembly. You will feed upon the leaves of the tree of life. What testimonies you may bear of the loving acquaintance made with your fellow workers in these precious seasons when seeking the blessing of God. Let each tell his experience in simple words. This will bring more comfort and joy to the soul than all the pleasant instruments of music that could be brought into the churches. Christ will come into your hearts. It is by this means only that you can maintain your integrity.—(*Testimonies for the Church*, vol. 7, 195.)

Prepare for eternity with such zeal as you have not yet manifested. Educate your mind to love the Bible, to love the prayer meeting, to love the hour of meditation, and, above all, the hour when the soul communes with God. Become heavenly-minded if you would unite with the heavenly choir in the mansions above.— (*Testimonies for the Church*, vol. 2, 267.)

When the Spirit of God shall work upon the heart, cleansing the soul-temple of its defilement of worldliness and pleasure-loving, all will be seen in the prayer meeting, faithful to do their duty and earnest and anxious to reap all the benefit they can gain. The faithful worker for the Master will improve every opportunity to place himself directly under the rays of light from the throne of God, and this light will be reflected upon others.—(*Testimonies for the Church*, vol. 4, 461.)

GOD'S PRESENCE MAKES TIMES OF PRAYER AND PUBLIC WORSHIP SACRED.—True reverence for God is inspired by a sense of His infinite greatness and a realization of His presence. With this sense of the Unseen the heart of every child should be deeply impressed. The hour and place of prayer and the services of public worship the child should be taught to regard as sacred because God is there. And as reverence is manifested in attitude and demeanor, the feeling that inspires it will be deepened.—(*Education,* 242, 243.)

PUBLIC PRAYER BRINGS US INTO GOD'S PRESENCE.—Prayer, whether offered in the public assembly, at the family altar, or in secret, places man directly in the presence of God. By constant prayer the youth may obtain principles so firm that the most powerful temptations will not draw them from their allegiance to God.—(*My Life Today,* 18.)

PUBLIC PRAYERS SHOULD NOT BE LONG AND DRY.—As children of the heavenly King, you should educate yourselves to bear testimony in a clear, distinct voice, and in such a manner that no one may have the impression that you are reluctant to speak of the mercies of the Lord. In social meeting, prayer should be offered so that all may be edified, and those who take part in this exercise should follow the example given us in the Lord's beautiful prayer for the world. The prayer of Jesus is simple, clear, comprehensive, and yet not long and spiritless as are the dry prayers that are often offered in public. These spiritless prayers better not be uttered; for they fail to bless or edify, and are a mere form without vital power.—(*Christian Education,* 129.)

The prayers offered in public should be short and to the point. God does not require us to make the season of worship tedious by lengthy petitions. . . . A few minutes is long enough for any ordinary public petition.—(*Evangelism,* 146.)

Our prayer and social meetings should be seasons of special help and encouragement. Each one has a work to do to make these gatherings as interesting and profitable as possible. This can best be done by having a fresh experience daily in the things of God, and by not hesitating to speak of His love in the assemblies of His people. If you allow no darkness or unbelief to enter your hearts, they will not be manifest in your meetings.

Our meetings should be made intensely interesting. They should be pervaded with the very atmosphere of heaven. Let there be no long, dry speeches and formal prayers, merely for the sake of occupying the time.—(*Christian Service,* 211.)

At family worship let the children take a part. Let all bring their Bibles and each read a verse or two. Then let some familiar hymn be sung, followed by prayer. For this, Christ has given a model. The Lord's Prayer was not intended to be repeated merely as a form, but it is an illustration of what our prayers should be—simple, earnest, and comprehensive. In a simple petition tell the Lord your needs and express gratitude for His mercies. Thus you invite Jesus as a welcome guest into your home and heart. In the family long prayers concerning remote objects are not in place. They make the hour of prayer a weariness, when it should be regarded as a privilege and blessing. Make the season one of interest and joy.—(*Child Guidance,* 524.)

Long, prosy talks and prayers are out of place anywhere, and especially in the social meeting. They weary the angels as well as the people who listen to them. Our prayers should be short, and right to the point. Let the Spirit of God pervade the hearts of the worshipers, and it will sweep away all formality and dullness.— (*Review and Herald,* October 10, 1882.)

One or two minutes is long enough for any ordinary prayer.— (*Testimonies for the Church,* vol. 2, 581.)

LONG PRAYERS MAKE WORSHIP WEARISOME.—In every family there should be a fixed time for morning and evening worship. How appropriate it is for parents to gather their children about them before the fast is broken, to thank the heavenly Father for His protection during the night, and to ask Him for His help and guidance and watchcare during the day! How fitting, also, when evening comes, for parents and children to gather once more before Him and thank Him for the blessings of the day that is past!

The father, or, in his absence, the mother, should conduct the worship, selecting a portion of Scripture that is interesting and easily understood. The service should be short. When a long chapter is read and a long prayer offered, the service is made wearisome, and at its close a sense of relief is felt. God is dishonored when the hour of worship is made dry and irksome, when it is so tedious, so lacking in interest, that the children dread it.

Fathers and mothers, make the hour of worship intensely interesting. There is no reason why this hour should not be the most pleasant and enjoyable of the day. A little thought given to preparation for it will enable you to make it full of interest and profit. From time to time let the service be varied. Questions may be asked on the portion of Scripture read, and a few earnest, timely remarks may be made. A song of praise may be sung. The prayer offered should be short and pointed. In simple, earnest words let the one who leads in prayer praise God for His goodness and ask Him for help. As circumstances permit, let the children join in the reading and the prayer.

Eternity alone will reveal the good with which such seasons of worship are fraught.—(*Testimonies for the Church,* vol. 7, 43, 44.)

Our prayers in public should be short, and express only the real wants of the soul, asking in simplicity and simple trusting faith for the very things we need. Prayer from the humble, contrite heart is the vital breath of the soul hungering for righteousness.—(*Signs of the Times,* December 3, 1896.)

From the light I have had upon the subject I have decided that God does not require us, as we assemble for His worship, to make these seasons tedious and wearisome by remaining bowed quite a length of time, listening to several long prayers. Those in feeble health cannot endure this taxation without extreme weariness and exhaustion. The body becomes weary by remaining bowed down so long; and what is worse still, the mind becomes so wearied by the continuous exercise of prayer that no spiritual refreshment is realized, and the meeting is to them worse than a loss.

They have become wearied mentally and physically, and they have obtained no spiritual strength.

Meetings for conference and prayer should not be made tedious. If possible, all should be prompt to the hour appointed; and if there are dilatory ones, who are half an hour or even fifteen minutes behind the time, there should be no waiting. If there are but two present, they can claim the promise.

The meeting should open at the appointed hour if possible, be there few or many present. Formality and cold stiffness should be laid aside, and all should be prompt to duty. Upon common occasions there should not be prayer of more than ten minutes' duration. After there has been a change of position, and the exercise of singing or exhortation has relieved the sameness, then, if any feel the burden of prayer, let them pray.

All should feel it a Christian duty to pray short. Tell the Lord just what you want, without going all over the world. In private prayer all have the privilege of praying as long as they desire and of being as explicit as they please. They can pray for all their relatives and friends. The closet is the place to tell all their private difficulties, and trials, and temptations. A common meeting to worship God is not the place to open the privacies of the heart.

What is the object of assembling together? Is it to inform God, to instruct Him by telling Him all we know in prayer? We meet together to edify one another by an interchange of thoughts and feelings, to gather strength, and light, and courage by becoming acquainted with one another's hopes and aspirations; and by our earnest, heartfelt prayers, offered up in faith, we receive refreshment and vigor from the Source of our strength. These meetings should be most precious seasons and should be made interesting to all who have any relish for religious things.

There are some, I fear, who do not take their troubles to God in private prayer, but reserve them for the prayer meeting, and there do up their praying for several days. Such may be named conference and prayer meeting killers. They emit no light; they edify no one. Their cold, frozen prayers and long, backslidden testimonies cast a shadow. All are glad when they get through, and it is almost impossible to throw off the chill and darkness which their prayers and exhortations bring into the meeting. From the light which I have received, our meetings should be spiritual and social, and not too long. Reserve, pride, vanity, and fear of man should be left at home. Little differences and prejudices should not be taken with us to these meetings. As in a united family, simplicity, meekness, confidence, and love should exist in the hearts of brethren and sisters who meet to be refreshed and invigorated by bringing their lights together.— (*Testimonies for the Church,* vol. 2, 577-579.)

PUBLIC PRAYERS SHOULD BE SPOKEN DISTINCTLY AND CLEARLY.—Let those who pray and those who speak pronounce their words properly and speak in clear, distinct, even tones. Prayer, if properly offered, is a power for good. It is one of the means used by the Lord to communicate to the people the precious treasures of truth. But prayer is not what it should be, because of the defective voices of those who utter it. Satan rejoices when the prayers offered to God are almost inaudible. Let God's people learn how to speak and pray in a way that will properly represent the great truths they possess. Let the testimonies borne and the prayers offered be clear and distinct. Thus God will be glorified.—(*Testimonies for the Church,* vol. 6, 382.)

USE SIMPLE LANGUAGE WHEN PRAYING PUBLICLY.—High-flown language is inappropriate in prayer, whether the petition be offered in the pulpit, in the family circle, or in secret. Especially should the one offering public prayer use simple language, that others may understand what is said and unite with the petition.

It is the heart-felt prayer of faith that is heard in heaven and answered on earth.—(*Gospel Workers,* 177.)

OUR PRAYERS SHOULD BE ORDERLY.—I have seen that confusion is displeasing to the Lord, and that there should be order in praying and also in singing. We should not come to the house of God to pray for our families unless deep feeling shall lead us while the Spirit of God is convicting them. Generally, the proper place to pray for our families is at the family altar. When the subjects of our prayers are at a distance, the closet is the proper place to plead with God for them. When in the house of God, we should pray for a present blessing and should expect God to hear and answer our prayers. Such meetings will be lively and interesting.—(*Testimonies for the Church,* vol. 1, 145, 146.)

GOD SHOULD BE APPROACHED WITH REVERENCE IN PRAYER.— Some think it a mark of humility to pray to God in a common manner, as if talking with a human being. They profane His name by needlessly and irreverently mingling with their prayers the words, "God Almighty,"—awful, sacred words, which should never pass the lips except in subdued tones and with a feeling of awe.—(*Gospel Workers,* 176.)

IT IS OUR PRIVILEGE TO KNEEL WHEN PRAYING PUBLICLY.—Both in public and private worship it is our duty to bow down upon our knees before God when we offer our petitions to Him. This act shows our dependence upon God.—(*Selected Messages,* bk. 2, 312.)

According to the light that has been given me, it would be pleasing to God for ministers to bow down as soon as they step into the pulpit, and solemnly ask help from God. What impression would that make? There would be solemnity and awe upon the people. Their minister is communing with God; he is committing himself to God before he dares to stand before the people. Solemnity rests upon the people, and angels of God are brought very near. Ministers should look to God the first thing as they come into the desk, thus saying to all: God is the source of my strength.—(*Testimonies for the Church,* vol. 2, 612.)

When the minister enters, it should be with dignified, solemn mien. He should bow down in silent prayer as soon as he steps into the pulpit, and earnestly ask help of God. What an impression this will make! There will be solemnity and awe upon the people. Their minister is communing with God; he is committing himself to God before he dares to stand before the people. Solemnity rests upon all, and angels of God are brought very near. Every one of the congregation, also, who fears God should with bowed head unite in silent prayer with him that God may grace the meeting with His presence and give power to His truth proclaimed from human lips. When the meeting is opened by prayer, every knee should bow in the presence of the Holy One, and every heart should ascend to God in silent devotion. The prayers of faithful worshipers will be heard, and the ministry of the word will prove effectual. The lifeless attitude of the worshipers in the house of God is one great reason why the ministry is not more productive of good. The melody of song, poured forth from many hearts in clear, distinct utterance, is one of God's instrumentalities in the work of saving souls. All the service should be conducted with solemnity and awe, as if in the visible presence of the Master of assemblies.—(*Testimonies for the Church,* vol. 5, 492, 493.)

Both in public and in private worship it is our privilege to bow on our knees before God when we offer our petitions to Him. Jesus, our example, "kneeled down, and prayed." Luke 22:41. Of His disciples it is recorded that they, too, "kneeled down, and prayed." Acts 9:40. Paul declared, "I bow my knees unto the Father of our Lord Jesus Christ." Ephesians 3:14. In confessing before God the sins of Israel, Ezra knelt. See Ezra 9:5. Daniel "kneeled upon his knees three times a day, and prayed, and gave thanks before his God." Daniel 6:10.—(*Prophets and Kings,* 48.)

PUBLIC PRAYER IS IMPORTANT BUT NOT SUFFICIENT BY ITSELF.— Family or public prayer alone is not sufficient. Secret prayer is very important; in solitude the soul is laid bare to the inspecting eye of God, and every motive is scrutinized. Secret prayer! How precious! The soul communing with God! Secret prayer is to be heard only by the prayer-hearing God. No curious ear is to receive the burden of such petitions.—(*Testimonies for the Church,* vol. 2, 189, 190).

CHAPTER

19

Attitudes in Prayer

PROPER ATTITUDES FOR PUBLIC PRAYER.—I have received letters questioning me in regard to the proper attitude to be taken by a person offering prayer to the Sovereign of the universe. Where have our brethren obtained the idea that they should stand upon their feet when praying to God? One who has been educated for about five years in Battle Creek was asked to lead in prayer before Sister White should speak to the people. But as I beheld him standing upright upon his feet while his lips were about to open in prayer to God, my soul was stirred within me to give him an open rebuke. Calling him by name, I said, "Get down upon your knees." This is the proper position always. . . .

To bow down when in prayer to God is the proper attitude to occupy. This act of worship was required of the three Hebrew captives in Babylon. . . . But such an act was homage to be rendered to God alone—the Sovereign of the world, the Ruler of the universe; and these three Hebrews refused to give such honor to any idol even though composed of pure gold. In doing so, they would, to all intents and purposes, be bowing to the king of Babylon. Refusing to do as the king had commanded, they suffered the penalty, and were cast into the burning fiery furnace.

But Christ came in person and walked with them through the fire, and they received no harm.

Both in public and private worship it is our duty to bow down upon our knees before God when we offer our petitions to Him. This act shows our dependence upon God. . . .

"Where did Brother H obtain his education?"—At Battle Creek. Is it possible that with all the light that God has given to His people on the subject of reverence, that ministers, principals, and teachers in our schools, by precept and example, teach young men to stand erect in devotion as did the Pharisees? Shall we look upon this as significant of their self-sufficiency and self-importance? Are these traits to become conspicuous?. . . .

We hope that our brethren will not manifest less reverence and awe as they approach the only true and living God than the heathen manifest for their idol deities, or these people will be our judges in the day of final decision. I would speak to all who occupy the place of teachers in our schools. Men and women, do not dishonor God by your irreverence and pomposity. Do not stand up in your Pharisaism and offer your prayers to God. Mistrust your own strength. Depend not in it; but often bow down on your knees before God, and worship Him.

And when you assemble to worship God, be sure and bow your knees before Him. Let this act testify that the whole soul, body, and spirit are in subjection to the Spirit of truth. Who have searched the Word closely for examples and direction in this respect? Whom can we trust as teachers in our schools in America and foreign countries? After years of study shall students return to their own country with perverted ideas of the respect and honor and reverence that should be given to God, and feel under no obligation to honor the men of gray hairs, the men of experience, the chosen servants of God who have been connected with the work of God through almost all the years of their life? I advise all who attend the schools in America or in any other place, do not catch the spirit of irreverence. Be sure you understand for yourself what kind of education you need, that you may educate others to obtain a fitness of character that will stand the test that is soon to be brought upon all who live upon the earth. Keep company with the soundest Christians. Choose not the pretentious instructors or pupils, but those who show the deepest piety, those who have a spirit of intelligence in the things of God.

We are living in perilous times. Seventh-day Adventists are professedly the commandment-keeping people of God; but they are losing their devotional spirit. This spirit of reverence for God teaches men how to approach their Maker—with sacredness and awe through faith, not in themselves, but in a Mediator. Thus man is kept fast, under whatever circumstances he is placed. Man must come on bended knee, as a subject of grace, a suppliant at the footstool of mercy. And as he receives daily mercies at the hand of God, he is ever to cherish gratitude in his heart, and give expression to it in the words of thanksgiving and praise for these unmerited favors. Angels have been guarding his pathway through all his life, and many of the snares he has been delivered from he has not seen. And for this guardianship and watchcare by eyes that never slumber and never sleep, he is to recognize in every prayer the service of God for him.—(*Selected Messages,* bk. 2, 311-315.)

KNEELING IN PRAYER TEACHES REVERENCE AND AWE FOR GOD.— May God teach His people how to pray. Let the teachers in our schools and the ministers in our churches, learn daily in the school of Christ. Then they will pray with earnestness, and their requests will be heard and answered. Then the word will be proclaimed with power.

Both in public and in private worship, it is our privilege to bow on our knees before the Lord when we offer our petitions to Him. Jesus, our example, "kneeled down, and prayed." Of His disciples it is recorded that they, too, "kneeled down, and prayed." Paul declared, "I bow my knees unto the Father of our Lord Jesus Christ." In confessing before God the sins of Israel, Ezra knelt. Daniel "kneeled upon his knees three times a day, and prayed, and gave thanks before his God."

True reverence for God is inspired by a sense of His infinite greatness and a realization of His presence. With this sense of the Unseen, every heart should be deeply impressed. The hour and place of prayer are sacred, because God is there; and as reverence is manifested in attitude and demeanor, the feeling that inspires it will be deepened. "Holy and reverend is His name," the psalmist declares. Angels, when they speak that name, veil their faces. With what reverence, then, should we, who are fallen and sinful, take it upon our lips!

Well would it be for old and young to ponder those words of Scripture that show how the place marked by God's special presence should be regarded. "Put off thy shoes from off thy feet," He commanded Moses at the burning bush, "for the place whereon thou standest is holy ground." Jacob, after beholding the vision of the angels, exclaimed, "The Lord is in this place; and I knew it not. . . . This is none other but the house of God, and this is the gate of heaven."—(*Gospel Workers,* 178, 179.)

The humility of Solomon at the time he began to bear the burdens of state, when he acknowledged before God, "I am but a little child" (1 Kings 3:7), his marked love of God, his profound reverence for things divine, his distrust of self, and his exaltation of the infinite Creator of all—all these traits of character, so worthy of emulation, were revealed during the services connected with the completion of the temple, when during his dedicatory prayer he knelt in the humble position of a petitioner. Christ's followers today should guard against the tendency to lose the spirit of reverence and godly fear. The Scriptures teach men how they should approach their Maker—with humility and awe, through faith in a divine Mediator.—(*Prophets and Kings,* 47, 48.)

"In the midst of the court" of the temple had been erected "a brazen scaffold," or platform, "five cubits long, and five cubits broad, and three cubits high." Upon this Solomon stood and with uplifted hands blessed the vast multitude before him. "And all the congregation of Israel stood." 2 Chronicles 6:13, 3.

"Blessed be the Lord God of Israel," Solomon exclaimed, "who hath with His hands fulfilled that which He spake with His mouth to my father David, saying, . . . I have chosen Jerusalem, that My name might be there." Verses 4-6.

Solomon then knelt upon the platform, and in the hearing of all the people offered the dedicatory prayer. Lifting his hands toward heaven, while the congregation were bowed with their faces to the ground, the king pleaded: "Lord God of Israel, there is no God like Thee in the heaven, nor in the earth; which keepest covenant, and showest mercy unto Thy servants, that walk before Thee with all their heart."—(*Prophets and Kings,* 39, 40.)

King Solomon stood upon a brazen scaffold before the altar and blessed the people. He then knelt down and, with his hands raised upward, poured forth earnest and solemn prayer to God while the congregation were bowed with their faces to the ground. After Solomon had ended his prayer, a miraculous fire came from heaven and consumed the sacrifice.—(*The Story of Redemption,* 194.)

Your mind was given that you might understand how to work. Your eyes were given that you might be keen to discern your God-given opportunities. Your ears are to listen for the commands of God. Your knees are to bow three times a day in heartfelt prayer. Your feet are to run in the way of God's commandments.—(*Testimonies for the Church,* vol. 6, 297.)

MINISTERS TO BOW IN PRAYER BEFORE PREACHING.—According to the light that has been given me, it would be pleasing to God for ministers to bow down as soon as they step into the pulpit, and solemnly ask help from God. What impression would that make? There would be solemnity and awe upon the people. Their minister is communing with God; he is committing himself to God before he dares to stand before the people. Solemnity rests upon the people, and angels of God are brought very near. Ministers should look to God the first thing as they come into the desk, thus saying to all: God is the source of my strength.—(*Testimonies for the Church,* vol. 2, 612.)

When the minister enters, it should be with dignified, solemn mien. He should bow down in silent prayer as soon as he steps into the pulpit, and earnestly ask help of God. What an impression this will make! There will be solemnity and awe upon the people. Their minister is communing with God; he is committing himself to God before he dares to stand before the people. Solemnity rests upon all, and angels of God are brought very near. Every one of the congregation, also, who fears God should with bowed head unite in silent prayer with him that God may grace the meeting with His presence and give power to His truth proclaimed from human lips. When the meeting is opened by prayer, every knee should bow in the presence of the Holy One, and every heart should ascend to God in silent devotion. The prayers of faithful worshipers will be heard, and the ministry of the word will prove effectual. The lifeless attitude of the worshipers in the house of God is one great reason why the ministry is not more productive of good. The melody of song, poured forth from many hearts in clear, distinct utterance, is one of God's instrumentalities in the work of saving souls. All the service should be conducted with solemnity and awe, as if in the visible presence of the Master of assemblies.—(*Testimonies for the Church,* vol. 5, 492, 493.)

KNEELING NOT ALWAYS REQUIRED WHILE PRAYING.—We cannot always be on our knees in prayer, but the way to the mercy seat is always open. While engaged in active labor, we may ask for help; and we are promised by One who will not deceive us, "Ye shall receive." The Christian can and will find time to pray. Daniel was a statesman; heavy responsibilities rested upon him; yet three times a day he sought God, and the Lord gave him the Holy Spirit. So today men may resort to the sacred pavilion of the Most High and feel the assurance of His promise, "My people shall dwell in a peaceable habitation, and in sure dwellings, and in quiet resting places." Isaiah 32:18. All who really desire it can find a place for communion with God, where no ear can hear but the one open to the cries of the helpless, distressed, and needy—the One who notices even the fall of the little sparrow. He says, "Ye are of more value than many sparrows." Matthew 10:31.—(*Counsels on Health,* 423, 424.)

The reason why so many are left to themselves in places of temptation is that they do not set the Lord always before them. When we permit our communion with God to be broken, our defense is departed from us. Not all your good purposes and good intentions will enable you to withstand evil. You must be men and women of prayer. Your petitions must not be faint, occasional, and fitful, but earnest, persevering, and constant. It is not always necessary to bow upon your knees in order to pray. Cultivate the habit of talking with the Saviour when you are alone, when you are walking, and when you are busy with your daily labor. Let the heart be continually uplifted in silent petition for help, for light, for strength, for knowledge. Let every breath be a prayer.—(*Ministry of Healing,* 510, 511.)

In the work of heart-keeping we must be instant in prayer, unwearied in petitioning the throne of grace for assistance. Those who take the name of Christian should come to God in earnestness and humility, pleading for help. The Saviour has told us to pray without ceasing. The Christian can not always be in the position of prayer, but his thoughts and desires can always be upward. Our self-confidence would vanish, did we talk less and pray more.—(*Sons and Daughters of God,* 99.)

The way to the throne of God is always open. You cannot always be on your knees in prayer, but your silent petitions may constantly ascend to God for strength and guidance. When tempted, as you will be, you may flee to the secret place of the Most High. His everlasting arms will be underneath you. Let these words cheer you, "Thou hast a few names even in Sardis which have not defiled their garments; and they shall walk with Me in white: for they are worthy." Revelation 3:4.—(*Counsels on Health,* 362.)

If all our workers were so situated that they could spend a few hours each day in outdoor labor, and felt free to do this, it would be a blessing to them; they would be able to discharge more successfully the duties of their calling. If they have not time for complete relaxation, they could be planning and praying while at work with their hands, and could return to their labor refreshed in body and spirit.—(*Gospel Workers,* 240.)

GENUINE PRAYER DOES NOT DEPEND UPON TIME OR PLACE OR CIRCUMSTANCES.—Pray in your closet, and as you go about your daily labor let your heart be often uplifted to God.

It was thus that Enoch walked with God. These silent prayers rise like precious incense before the throne of grace. Satan cannot overcome him whose heart is thus stayed upon God.

There is no time or place in which it is inappropriate to offer up a petition to God. There is nothing that can prevent us from lifting up our hearts in the spirit of earnest prayer. In the crowds of the street, in the midst of a business engagement, we may send up a petition to God and plead for divine guidance, as did Nehemiah when he made his request before King Artaxerxes. A closet of communion may be found wherever we are. We should have the door of the heart open continually and our invitation going up that Jesus may come and abide as a heavenly guest in the soul.—(*Steps to Christ,* 98, 99).

Wherever we are, whatever our employment, our hearts are to be uplifted to God in prayer. This is being instant in prayer. We need not wait until we can bow upon our knees before we pray. On one occasion, when Nehemiah came in before the king, the king asked why he looked so sad, and what request he had to make. But Nehemiah dared not answer at once. Important interests were at stake. The fate of a nation hung upon the impression that should then be made upon the monarch's mind; and Nehemiah darted up a prayer to the God of Heaven, before he dared to answer the king. The result was that he obtained all that he asked or even desired.—(*Signs of the Times,* October 20, 1887.)

All your good purposes and good intentions will not enable you to withstand the test of temptation. You must be men of prayer. Your petitions must be not faint, occasional, and fitful, but earnest, persevering, and constant. It is not necessary to be alone, or to bow upon your knees, to pray; but in the midst of your labor your souls may be often uplifted to God, taking hold upon His strength; then you will be men of high and holy purpose, of noble integrity, who will not for any consideration be swayed from truth, right, and justice.—(*Testimonies for the Church,* 542, 543.)

We must pray constantly, with a humble mind and a meek and lowly spirit. We need not wait for an opportunity to kneel before God. We can pray and talk with the Lord wherever we may be.—(*Selected Messages,* bk. 3, 266.)

PRAYERS IN PUBIC SHOULD BE SHORT AND CHARACTERIZED BY A NATURAL TONE OF VOICE.—The long prayers made by some ministers have been a great failure. Praying to great length, as some do, is all out of place. They injure the throat and vocal organs, and then they talk of breaking down by their hard labor. They injure themselves when it is not called for. Many feel that praying injures their vocal organs more than talking. This is in consequence of the unnatural position of the body, and the manner of holding the head. They can stand and talk, and not feel injured. The position in prayer should be perfectly natural. Long praying wearies, and is not in accordance with the gospel of Christ. Half or even quarter of an hour is altogether too long. A few minutes' time is long enough to bring your case before God and tell Him what you want; and you can take the people with you and not weary them out and lessen their interest in devotion and prayer. They may be refreshed and strengthened, instead of exhausted.

A mistake has been made by many in their religious exercises in long praying and long preaching, upon a high key, with a forced voice, in an unnatural strain and an unnatural tone.—(*Testimonies for the Church,* vol. 2, 617.)

SPEAK CLEARLY AND DISTINCTLY IN PRAYER.—By your own example teach your children to pray with clear, distinct voice. Teach them to lift their heads from the chair and never to cover their faces with their hands. Thus they can offer their simple prayers, repeating the Lord's prayer in concert.—(*Child Guidance,* 522, 523.)

DISCIPLINE THE MIND TO PAY ATTENTION DURING PRAYER.—Daily prayer is as essential to growth in grace, and even to spiritual life itself, as is temporal food to physical well-being. We should accustom ourselves to often lift the thoughts to God in prayer. If the mind wanders, we must bring it back; by persevering effort, habit will finally make it easy.—(*The Sanctified Life*, 93.)

PRAYER NEED NOT BE LONG OR LOUD.—Prayer is not understood as it should be. Our prayers are not to inform God of something He does not know. The Lord is acquainted with the secrets of every soul. Our prayers need not be long and loud. God reads the hidden thoughts. We may pray in secret, and He who sees in secret will hear, and will reward us openly.—(*Messages to Young People*, 247.)

WE ARE NOT TO TRY TO COMMAND GOD IN PRAYER.—Our petitions must not take the form of a command, but of intercession for Him to do the things we desire of Him.—(*Counsels on Health*, 379.)

PRAY IN FAITH.—Pray in faith. And be sure to bring your lives into harmony with your petitions, that you may receive the blessings for which you pray. Let not your faith weaken, for the blessings received are proportionate to the faith exercised. "According to your faith be it unto you." "All things, whatsoever ye shall ask in prayer, believing, ye shall receive." Matthew 9:29; 21:22. Pray, believe, rejoice. Sing praises to God because He has answered your prayers. Take Him at His word. "He is faithful that promised." Hebrews 10:23. Not one sincere supplication is lost. The channel is open; the stream is flowing. It carries with it healing properties, pouring forth a restoring current of life and health and salvation. —(*Testimonies for the Church*, vol. 7, 274.)

Let sincerity and faith characterize your prayers. The Lord is willing to do for us "exceeding abundantly above all that we ask or think." Ephesians 3:20. Talk it; pray it. Do not talk unbelief. We cannot afford to let Satan see that he has power to darken our countenances and sadden our lives.—(*Testimonies for the Church*, vol. 7, 273.)

20

Praying in the
Name of Jesus

JESUS' NAME IS THE CONNECTING LINK IN PRAYER BETWEEN HU-
MANITY AND GOD.—In Christ's name our petitions ascend to the
Father. He intercedes in our behalf, and the Father lays open all
the treasures of His grace for our appropriation, for us to enjoy
and impart to others. "Ask in My name," Christ says. "I do not say
that I will pray the Father for you; for the Father Himself loveth
you. Make use of My name. This will give your prayers efficiency,
and the Father will give you the riches of His grace. Wherefore
ask, and ye shall receive, that your joy may be full."

Christ is the connecting link between God and man. He has
promised His personal intercession. He places the whole virtue of His
righteousness on the side of the suppliant. He pleads for man, and
man, in need of divine help, pleads for himself in the presence of
God, using the influence of the One who gave His life for the life of
the world. As we acknowledge before God our appreciation of Christ's
merits, fragrance is given to our intercessions. As we approach God
through the virtue of the Redeemer's merits, Christ places us close by
His side, encircling us with His human arm, while with His divine
arm He grasps the throne of the Infinite. He puts His merits, as sweet

incense, in the censer in our hands, in order to encourage our petitions. He promises to hear and answer our supplications.

Yes, Christ has become the medium of prayer between man and God. He has also become the medium of blessing between God and man. He has united divinity with humanity. Men are to co-operate with Him for the salvation of their own souls, and then make earnest, persevering efforts to save those who are ready to die.—(*Testimonies for the Church,* vol. 8, 178.)

As yet the disciples were unacquainted with the Saviour's unlimited resources and power. He said to them, "Hitherto have ye asked nothing in My name." John 16:24. He explained that the secret of their success would be in asking for strength and grace in His name. He would be present before the Father to make request for them. The prayer of the humble suppliant He presents as His own desire in that soul's behalf. Every sincere prayer is heard in heaven. It may not be fluently expressed; but if the heart is in it, it will ascend to the sanctuary where Jesus ministers, and He will present it to the Father without one awkward, stammering word, beautiful and fragrant with the incense of His own perfection.—(*The Desire of Ages,* 667.)

The disciples were to carry their work forward in Christ's name. Their every word and act was to fasten attention on His name, as possessing that vital power by which sinners may be saved. Their faith was to center in Him who is the source of mercy and power. In His name they were to present their petitions to the Father, and they would receive answer. They were to baptize in the name of the Father, the Son, and the Holy Spirit. Christ's name was to be their watchword, their badge of distinction, their bond of union, the authority for their course of action, and the source of their success.—(*Acts of the Apostles,* 28.)

In the holiest I saw an ark; on the top and sides of it was purest gold. On each end of the ark was a lovely cherub, with its wings spread out over it. Their faces were turned toward each other, and they looked downward. Between the angels was a golden censer. Above the ark, where the angels stood, was an exceeding bright glory, that appeared like a throne where God dwelt. Jesus stood by the ark, and as the saints' prayers came up to Him, the incense in the censer would smoke, and He would offer up their prayers with the smoke of the incense to His Father.—(*Early Writings,* 32.)

WHAT IT MEANS TO PRAY IN JESUS' NAME.—To pray in Christ's name means much. It means that we are to accept His character, manifest His spirit, and work His works. The Saviour's promise is given on condition. "If ye love Me," He says, "keep My commandments." He saves men, not in sin, but from sin; and those who love Him will show their love by obedience.—(*The Desire of Ages,* 668.)

Jesus said, "Ye shall ask in My name: and I say not unto you, that I will pray the Father for you: for the Father Himself loveth you." "I have chosen you: . . . that whatsoever ye shall ask of the Father in My name, He may give it you." John 16:26, 27; 15:16. But to pray in the name of Jesus is something more than a mere mention of that name at the beginning and the ending of a prayer. It is to pray in the mind and spirit of Jesus, while we believe His promises, rely upon His grace, and work His works.—(*Steps to Christ,* 100, 101.)

GOD INVITES US TO COME TO HIM IN THE NAME OF JESUS.—You are invited to come, to ask, to seek, to knock; and you are assured that you will not come in vain. Jesus says, "Ask, and it shall be given you; seek, and ye shall find; knock, and it shall be opened unto you: for everyone that asketh receiveth; and he that seeketh findeth; and to him that knocketh it shall be opened." Matthew 7:7, 8.

Christ illustrates the willingness of God to bless by the willingness of a father to grant the request of his child. He says, "If a son shall ask bread of any of you that is a father, will he give him a stone? or if he ask a fish, will he for a fish give him a serpent? or if he shall ask an egg, will he offer him a scorpion? If ye then, being evil, know how to give good gifts unto your children: how much more shall your heavenly

Father give the Holy Spirit to them that ask Him? Luke 11:11-13.

We come to God in the name of Jesus by special invitation, and He welcomes us to His audience chamber. He imparts to the humble, contrite soul that faith in Christ by which he is justified. Jesus blots out as a thick cloud his transgression, and the comforted heart exclaims, "O Lord, I will praise Thee: though Thou wast angry with me, Thine anger is turned away, and Thou comfortedst me." Isaiah 12:1.—(*Counsels to Parents, Teachers, and Students,* 242.)

PRAY BOTH IN JESUS' NAME AND BY THE INSPIRATION OF THE HOLY SPIRIT.—When a man breathes an intensely earnest prayer to God (Jesus Christ is the only name given under heaven whereby we can be saved), there is in that intensity and earnestness a pledge from God that He is about to answer that prayer exceeding abundantly, above all that we can ask or think. We must not only pray in the name of Jesus, but by the inspiration and kindling of the Holy Spirit. This explains what is meant when it is said, "the Spirit itself maketh intercession for us with groanings which can not be uttered." The petitions must be offered in earnest faith. Then they will reach the mercy-seat. Unwearyingly persist in prayer. God does not say, Pray once, and I will answer you. His word is pray, be instant in prayer, believing ye have the things ye ask, and ye shall receive them; I will answer you.—(*The Gospel Herald,* May 28, 1902.)

WE MAY APPROACH GOD IN CONFIDENCE THROUGH JESUS' NAME.— Humility and reverence should characterize the deportment of all who come into the presence of God. In the name of Jesus we may come before Him with confidence, but we must not approach Him with the boldness of presumption, as though He were on a level with ourselves. There are those who address the great and all-powerful and holy God, who dwelleth in light unapproachable, as they would address an equal, or even an inferior. There are those who conduct themselves in His house as they would not presume to do in the audience chamber of an earthly ruler. These should remember that they are in His sight whom seraphim adore, before whom angels veil their faces.—(*Patriarchs and Prophets,* 252.)

In the name of Jesus we may come into God's presence with the confidence of a child. No man is needed to act as a mediator. Through Jesus we may open our hearts to God as to one who knows and loves us.—(*Thoughts From the Mount of Blessing,* 84.)

GOD WILL HONOR JESUS' NAME IN OUR PRAYERS.—Every promise in the word of God furnishes us with subject matter for prayer, presenting the pledged word of Jehovah as our assurance. Whatever spiritual blessing we need, it is our privilege to claim through Jesus. We may tell the Lord, with the simplicity of a child, exactly what we need. We may state to Him our temporal matters, asking Him for bread and raiment as well as for the bread of life and the robe of Christ's righteousness. Your heavenly Father knows that you have need of all these things, and you are invited to ask Him concerning them. It is through the name of Jesus that every favor is received. God will honor that name, and will supply your necessities from the riches of His liberality.—(*Thoughts From the Mount of Blessing,* 133.)

We must not only pray in Christ's name, but by the inspiration of the Holy Spirit. This explains what is meant when it is said that the Spirit "maketh intercession for us, with groanings which cannot be uttered." Rom. 8:26. Such prayer God delights to answer. When with earnestness and intensity we breathe a prayer in the name of Christ, there is in that very intensity a pledge from God that He is about to answer our prayer "exceeding abundantly above all that we ask or think." Eph. 3:20.

Christ has said, "What things soever ye desire, when ye pray, believe that ye receive them, and ye shall have them." Mark 11:24. "Whatsoever ye shall ask in My name, that will I do, that the Father may be glorified in the Son." John 14:13. And the beloved John, under the inspiration of the Holy Spirit, speaks with great plainness and assurance: "If we ask anything according to His will, He heareth us: and if we know that He hear us, whatsoever we ask, we know that we have the petitions that we desired of Him." 1 John 5:14, 15. Then press your petition to the Father in the name of Jesus. God will honor that name.—(*Christ's Object Lessons,* 147, 148.)

CHAPTER

21

Divine Guidance
Through Prayer

WE MAY LEARN GOD'S WILL FOR US THROUGH PRAYER.—The Lord works in no haphazard way. Seek Him most earnestly in prayer. He will impress the mind, and will give tongue and utterance. The people of God are to be educated not to trust in human inventions and uncertain tests as a means of learning God's will concerning them. Satan and his agencies are always ready to step into any opening to be found that will lead souls away from the pure principles of the Word of God. The people who are led and taught of God will give no place to devisings for which there is not a "Thus saith the Lord."—(*Selected Messages,* bk. 2, 326.)

PRAY FOR GOD'S GUIDANCE.—You must educate your judgment so that it shall not be feeble and inefficient. You must pray for guidance, and commit your way unto the Lord. You must close your heart against all foolishness and sin, and open it to every heavenly influence. You must make the most of your time and opportunities, in order to develop a symmetrical character.—(*Fundamentals of Christian Education,* 302.)

In every family there should be a fixed time for morning and evening worship. How appropriate it is for parents to gather their children about them before the fast is broken, to thank the heavenly Father for His protection during the night, and to ask Him for His help and guidance and watchcare during the day! How fitting, also, when evening comes, for parents and children to gather once more before Him and thank Him for the blessings of the day that is past!—(*Testimonies for the Church,* vol. 7, 43.)

Consecrate yourself to God in the morning; make this your very first work. Let your prayer be, "Take me, O Lord, as wholly Thine. I lay all my plans at Thy feet. Use me today in Thy service. Abide with me, and let all my work be wrought in Thee." This is a daily matter. Each morning consecrate yourself to God for that day. Surrender all your plans to Him, to be carried out or given up as His providence shall indicate. Thus day by day you may be giving your life into the hands of God, and thus your life will be molded more and more after the life of Christ.—(*Steps to Christ,* 70).

You must learn to see with your brain as well as your eyes. You must educate your judgment so that it shall not be feeble and inefficient. You must pray for guidance, and commit your way unto the Lord. You must close your heart against all foolishness and sin, and open it to every heavenly influence. You must make the most of your time and opportunities, in order to develop a symmetrical character.—(*Sons and Daughters of God,* 283.)

PRAYER FOR GOD'S GUIDANCE MAY BE OFFERED ANYTIME, ANY-WHERE.—There is no time or place in which it is inappropriate to offer up a petition to God. There is nothing that can prevent us from lifting up our hearts in the spirit of earnest prayer. In the crowds of the street, in the midst of a business engagement, we may send up a petition to God and plead for divine guidance, as did Nehemiah when he made his request before King Artaxerxes. A closet of communion may be found wherever we are. We should have the door of the heart open continually and our invitation going up that Jesus may come and abide as a heavenly guest in the soul.—(*Steps to Christ*, 99.)

To pray as Nehemiah prayed in his hour of need is a resource at the command of the Christian under circumstances when other forms of prayer may be impossible. Toilers in the busy walks of life, crowded and almost overwhelmed with perplexity, can send up a petition to God for divine guidance. Travelers by sea and land, when threatened with some great danger, can thus commit themselves to Heaven's protection. In times of sudden difficulty or peril the heart may send up its cry for help to One who has pledged Himself to come to the aid of His faithful, believing ones whenever they call upon Him. In every circumstance, under every condition, the soul weighed down with grief and care, or fiercely assailed by temptation, may find assurance, support, and succor in the unfailing love and power of a covenant-keeping God.—(*Prophets and Kings*, 631, 632.)

ANGELS ARE NEAR TO HELP AS WE PRAY FOR GOD'S GUIDANCE.— Like Nathanael, we need to study God's word for ourselves, and pray for the enlightenment of the Holy Spirit. He who saw Nathanael under the fig tree will see us in the secret place of prayer. Angels from the world of light are near to those who in humility seek for divine guidance.—(*The Desire of Ages*, 141.)

The visible and the invisible world are in close contact. Could the veil be lifted, we would see evil angels pressing their darkness around us and working with all their power to deceive and destroy. Wicked men are surrounded, influenced, and aided by evil spirits. The man of faith and prayer has yielded his soul to divine guidance, and angels of God bring to him light and strength from heaven.—(*Testimonies for the Church*, vol. 5, 199.)

A knowledge of the truth depends not so much upon strength of intellect as upon pureness of purpose, the simplicity of an earnest, dependent faith. To those who in humility of heart seek for divine guidance, angels of God draw near. The Holy Spirit is given to open to them the rich treasures of the truth.—(*Christ's Object Lessons,* 59.)

WHATEVER WE NEED, WE MAY CLAIM IN PRAYER.—Every promise in the word of God furnishes us with subject matter for prayer, presenting the pledged word of Jehovah as our assurance. Whatever spiritual blessing we need, it is our privilege to claim through Jesus. We may tell the Lord, with the simplicity of a child, exactly what we need. We may state to Him our temporal matters, asking Him for bread and raiment as well as for the bread of life and the robe of Christ's righteousness. Your heavenly Father knows that you have need of all these things, and you are invited to ask Him concerning them. It is through the name of Jesus that every favor is received. God will honor that name, and will supply your necessities from the riches of His liberality.—(*Thoughts From the Mount of Blessing,* 133.)

PARENTS TO PRAY FOR GOD'S GUIDANCE.—Parents, humble your hearts before God. Begin a thorough work with your children. Plead with the Lord to forgive your disregard of His Word in neglecting to train your children in the way they should go. Ask for light and guidance, for a tender conscience, and for clear discernment that you may see your mistakes and failures. God will hear such prayers from a humble and contrite heart.—(*Child Guidance,* 557.)

THOSE WILLING TO BE GUIDED MAY KNOW GOD'S WILL.—The Lord reveals His will to those who are earnest and anxious to be guided. The reason for your inefficiency is that you have given up the idea of knowing and doing the will of God, therefore you do not know anything positively.—(*Testimonies for the Church,* vol. 3, 466.)

SEARCH THE SCRIPTURES WITH PRAYER FOR DIVINE GUIDANCE.—
Those who are unwilling to accept the plain, cutting truths of the
Bible are continually seeking for pleasing fables that will quiet the
conscience. The less spiritual, self-denying, and humiliating the
doctrines presented, the greater the favor with which they are received. These persons degrade the intellectual powers to serve their
carnal desires. Too wise in their own conceit to search the Scriptures with contrition of soul and earnest prayer for divine guidance, they have no shield from delusion. Satan is ready to supply
the heart's desire, and he palms off his deceptions in the place of
truth.—(*The Great Controversy,* 523.)

TRUST GOD AND HE WILL DIRECT YOUR WAY.—Many are un-
able to make definite plans for the future. Their life is unsettled.
They cannot discern the outcome of affairs, and this often fills
them with anxiety and unrest. Let us remember that the life of
God's children in this world is a pilgrim life. We have not wisdom
to plan our own lives. It is not for us to shape our future. "By faith
Abraham, when he was called to go out into a place which he
should after receive for an inheritance, obeyed; and he went out,
not knowing whither he went." Hebrews 11:8.

Christ in His life on earth made no plans for Himself. He
accepted God's plans for Him, and day by day the Father un-
folded His plans. So should we depend upon God, that our lives
may be the simple outworking of His will. As we commit our
ways to Him, He will direct our steps.

Too many, in planning for a brilliant future, make an utter
failure. Let God plan for you. As a little child, trust to the guidance of Him who will "keep the feet of His saints." 1 Samuel 2:9.
God never leads His children otherwise than they would choose
to be led, if they could see the end from the beginning and discern
the glory of the purpose which they are fulfilling as co-workers
with Him.—(*Ministry of Healing,* 478, 479.)

If you have given yourself to God, to do His work, you have

no need to be anxious for tomorrow. He whose servant you are, knows the end from the beginning. The events of tomorrow, which are hidden from your view, are open to the eyes of Him who is omnipotent.

When we take into our hands the management of things with which we have to do, and depend upon our own wisdom for success, we are taking a burden which God has not given us, and are trying to bear it without His aid. We are taking upon ourselves the responsibility that belongs to God, and thus are really putting ourselves in His place. We may well have anxiety and anticipate danger and loss, for it is certain to befall us. But when we really believe that God loves us and means to do us good we shall cease to worry about the future. We shall trust God as a child trusts a loving parent. Then our troubles and torments will disappear, for our will is swallowed up in the will of God.—(*Thoughts From the Mount of Blessing,* 100, 101.)

ELIEZER PRAYED FOR—AND RECEIVED—GOD'S GUIDANCE.— Remembering the words of Abraham, that God would send His angel with him, he prayed earnestly for positive guidance. In the family of his master he was accustomed to the constant exercise of kindness and hospitality, and he now asked that an act of courtesy might indicate the maiden whom God had chosen.

Hardly was the prayer uttered before the answer was given. Among the women who were gathered at the well, the courteous manners of one attracted his attention. As she came from the well, the stranger went to meet her, asking for some water from the pitcher upon her shoulder. The request received a kindly answer, with an offer to draw water for the camels also, a service which it was customary even for the daughters of princes to perform for their fathers' flocks and herds. Thus the desired sign was given.— (*Patriarchs and Prophets,* 172.)

22

Prayer for the Sick

PRAYER SHOULD BE OFFERED FOR THE SICK WITH CALM FAITH.—
I was shown that in case of sickness, where the way is clear for the
offering up of prayer for the sick, the case should be committed to
the Lord in calm faith, not with a storm of excitement. He alone is
acquainted with the past life of the individual and knows what his
future will be. He who is acquainted with the hearts of all men
knows whether the person, if raised up, would glorify His name or
dishonor Him by backsliding and apostasy. All that we are required to do is to ask God to raise the sick up if in accordance
with His will, believing that He hears the reasons which we present
and the fervent prayers offered. If the Lord sees it will best honor
Him, He will answer our prayers. But to urge recovery without
submission to His will is not right.—(*Testimonies for the Church,*
vol. 2, 147, 148.)

With all our treatments given to the sick, simple fervent prayer
should be offered for the blessing of healing. We are to point the
sick to the compassionate Saviour, and His power to forgive and
to heal.—(*Selected Messages,* bk. 3, 296).

Those who engage in house-to-house labor will find opportunities for ministry in many lines. They should pray for the sick and should do all in their power to relieve them from suffering.—(*Testimonies for the Church,* vol. 6, 83, 84).

The Saviour would have us encourage the sick, the hopeless, the afflicted, to take hold upon His strength. Through faith and prayer the sickroom may be transformed into a Bethel.—(*Ministry of Healing,* 226.)

If we are under infirmities of body, it is certainly consistent to trust the Lord, making supplications to our God in our own case, and if we feel inclined to ask others in whom we have confidence to unite with us in prayer to Jesus who is the Mighty Healer, help will surely come if we ask in faith.—(*Medical Ministry,* 16.)

We sent up our humble petitions for the sick and afflicted one, who was losing his hold on this life. As we presented this case before the Lord, we felt the assurance of the love of God even in this affliction.—(*Review and Herald,* October 11, 1887.)

We anointed the child and prayed over it, believing that the Lord would give both mother and child peace. It was done. The cries of the child ceased, and we left them doing well.—(*Spiritual Gifts,* bk. 2, 110, 111.)

The sick will be led to Christ by the patient attention of nurses who anticipate their wants, and who bow in prayer and ask the great Medical Missionary to look with compassion upon the sufferer and to let the soothing influence of His grace be felt and His restoring power be exercised.—(*Medical Ministry,* 191, 192.)

As missionary nurses care for the sick and relieve the distress of the poor, they will find many opportunities to pray with them, to read to them from God's word, to speak of the Saviour. . . .

They can bring a ray of hope into the lives of the defeated and disheartened.—(*Medical Ministry,* 246, 247.)

If more prayer were offered in our sanitariums for the healing of the sick, the mighty power of the Healer would be seen. Many more would be strengthened and blessed, and many more acute sicknesses would be healed.—(*Selected Messages,* bk. 3, 295.)

I would come before the Lord with this petition: "Lord, we cannot read the heart of this sick one, but thou knowest whether it is for the good of his soul and for the glory of thy name to raise him to health. In thy great goodness, compassionate this case, and let healthy action take place in the system. The work must be entirely thine own."—(*Healthful Living,* 239).

Let the voice of prayer be heard in our institutions in behalf of the sick that they may place themselves where they can cooperate with Him who can save both soul and body.—(*Manuscript Releases,* vol. 6, 379).

Before we were blessed with institutions where the sick could get help from suffering, by diligent treatment and earnest prayer in faith to God, we carried the most seemingly hopeless cases through successfully. Today the Lord invites the suffering ones to have faith in Him. Man's necessity is God's opportunity.—(*Selected Messages,* bk. 3, 295, 296).

All that can be done in praying for the sick is to earnestly importune God in their behalf, and in perfect confidence rest the matter in His hands. If we regard iniquity in our hearts the Lord will not hear us. He can do what He will with His own.—(*Testimonies for the Church,* vol. 2, 148.)

It has often been my privilege to pray with the sick. We should do this much more often than we do.—(*Selected Messages,* bk. 3, 295.)

It is our work to present the sick and suffering to Christ in the arms of our faith. . . . We should lay hold on His promise, and pray for the manifestation of His power. The very essence of the gospel is restoration, and the Saviour would have us bid the sick, the hopeless, and the afflicted take hold upon His strength.—(*The Desire of Ages,* 824, 825.)

PRAYER FOR THE SICK IS TOO IMPORTANT TO BE HANDLED CARELESSLY.—As to praying for the sick, it is too important a matter to be handled carelessly. I believe we should take everything to the Lord, and make known to God all our weaknesses and specify all our perplexities.—(*Medical Ministry,* 16.)

PRAYER FOR THE SICK IS AS EFFECTIVE TODAY AS IN BIBLE TIMES.— The divine Healer is present in the sick-room; He hears every word of the prayers offered to Him in the simplicity of true faith. His disciples today are to pray for the sick, as verily as did the disciples of old. And there will be recoveries; for "the prayer of faith shall save the sick."—(*Gospel Workers,* 215.)

God is just as willing to restore the sick to health now as when the Holy Spirit spoke these words through the psalmist. And Christ is the same compassionate physician now that He was during His earthly ministry. In Him there is healing balm for every disease, restoring power for every infirmity. His disciples in this time are to pray for the sick as verily as the disciples of old prayed. And recoveries will follow; for "the prayer of faith shall save the sick." We have the Holy Spirit's power, the calm assurance of faith, that can claim God's promises. The Lord's promise, "They shall lay hands on the sick, and they shall recover" (Mark 16:18), is just as trustworthy now as in the days of the apostles. It presents the privilege of God's children, and our faith should lay hold of all that it embraces. Christ's servants are the channel of His working, and through them He desires to exercise His healing power. It is our work to present the sick and suffering to God in the arms of our faith. We should teach them to believe in the Great Healer.—(*Ministry of Healing,* 226.)

PRAYER FOR THE SICK SHOULD TAKE INTO ACCOUNT GOD'S
WILL.—In prayer for the sick it should be remembered that "we
know not what we should pray for as we ought." Romans 8:26.
We do not know whether the blessing we desire will be best or
not. Therefore our prayers should include this thought: "Lord,
thou knowest every secret of the soul. Thou art acquainted with
these persons. Jesus, their Advocate, gave His life for them. His
love for them is greater than ours can possibly be. If, therefore, it
is for Thy glory and the good of the afflicted ones, we ask, in the
name of Jesus, that they may be restored to health. If it be not Thy
will that they may be restored, we ask that Thy grace may comfort
and Thy presence sustain them in their sufferings."

God knows the end from the beginning. He is acquainted with
the hearts of all men. He reads every secret of the soul. He knows
whether those for whom prayer is offered would or would not be able
to endure the trials that would come upon them should they live. He
knows whether their lives would be a blessing or a curse to themselves
and to the world. This is one reason why, while presenting our petitions with earnestness, we should say, "Nevertheless not my will, but
Thine, be done." Luke 22:42.—(*Ministry of Healing*, 229, 230.)

In praying for the sick, we are to pray that if it is God's will
that they may be raised to health; but if not that He will give them
His grace to comfort, His presence to sustain them in their suffering. Many who should set their house in order, neglect to do it
when they have hope that they will be raised to health in answer
to prayer. Buoyed up by a false hope, they do not feel the need of
giving words of exhortation and counsel to their children, parents, or friends, and it is a great misfortune. Accepting the assurance that they would be healed when prayed for, they dare not
make a reference as to how their property shall be disposed of,
how their family is to be cared for, or express any wish concerning
matters of which they would speak if they thought they would be
removed by death. In this way disasters are brought upon the family and friends; for many things that should be understood, are

left unmentioned, because they fear expression on these points would be a denial of their faith. Believing they will be raised to health by prayer, they fail to use hygienic measures which are within their power to use, fearing it would be a denial of their faith.— (*General Conference Daily Bulletin,* February 26, 1897.)

We have united in earnest prayer around the sickbed of men, women, and children, and have felt that they were given back to us from the dead in answer to our earnest prayers. In these prayers we thought we must be positive, and if we exercised faith, that we must ask for nothing less than life. We dared not say, "If it will glorify God," fearing it would admit a semblance of doubt. We have anxiously watched those who have been given back, as it were, from the dead. We have seen some of these, especially youth, raised to health, and they have forgotten God, become dissolute in life, causing sorrow and anguish to parents and friends, and have become a shame to those who feared to pray. They lived not to honor and glorify God, but to curse Him with their lives of vice.

We no longer mark out a way, nor seek to bring the Lord to our wishes. If the life of the sick can glorify Him, we pray that they may live, nevertheless, not as we will but as He will. Our faith can be just as firm, and more reliable, by committing the desire to the all-wise God and, without feverish anxiety, in perfect confidence trusting all to Him. We have the promise. We know that He hears us if we ask according to His will.—(*Counsels on Health,* 378, 379.)

GOD ANSWERS PRAYERS FOR THE SICK.—No human power can save the sick, but, through the prayer of faith, the Mighty Healer has fulfilled His promise to those who have called upon His name.—(*Selected Messages,* bk. 3, 36).

Let us do as Christ's apostles did; let us offer prayer for the sick, for there are many who cannot have the advantages of our sanitariums. The Lord will remove infirmities in answer to prayer.—(*Medical Ministry,* 242.)

PERSISTENCE IN PRAYER IS NECESSARY WHEN PRAYING FOR THE SICK.—
In praying for the sick, it is essential to have faith; for it is in accordance with the word of God. "The effectual fervent prayer of a righteous man availeth much." James 5:16. So we cannot discard praying for the sick, and we should feel very sad if we could not have the privilege of approaching God, to lay before Him all our weaknesses and our infirmities, to tell the compassionate Saviour all about these things, believing that He hears our petitions. Sometimes answers to our prayers come immediately; sometimes we have to wait patiently and continue earnestly to plead for the things that we need, our cases being illustrated by the case of the importunate solicitor for bread. "Which of you shall have a friend, and shall go unto him at midnight," etc. This lesson means more than we can imagine. We are to keep on asking, even if we do not realize the immediate response to our prayers. "I say unto you, Ask, and it shall be given you; seek, and ye shall find; knock, and it shall be opened unto you. For everyone that asketh receiveth; and he that seeketh findeth; and to him that knocketh it shall be opened." Luke 11:9, 10.

We need grace, we need divine enlightenment, that through the Spirit we may know how to ask for such things as we need. If our petitions are indited by the Lord they will be answered.—(*Counsels on Health*, 380.)

SIN MUST BE PUT AWAY IF PRAYER FOR HEALING IS TO BE ANSWERED.—To those who desire prayer for their restoration to health, it should be made plain that the violation of God's law, either natural or spiritual, is sin, and that in order for them to receive His blessing, sin must be confessed and forsaken.

The Scripture bids us, "Confess your faults one to another, and pray one for another, that ye may be healed." James 5:16. To the one asking for prayer, let thoughts like these be presented: "We cannot read the heart, or know the secrets of your life. These are known only to yourself and to God. If you repent of your sins, it is your duty to make confession of them."—(*Ministry of Healing*, 228.)

PRESUMPTION LIES CLOSE TO FAITH IN PRAYING FOR THE SICK.—
I have seen so much of carrying matters to extremes, in praying
for the sick, that I have felt that this part of our experience requires much solid, sanctified thinking, lest we shall make movements that we may call faith, but which are really nothing less
than presumption. Persons worn down with affliction need to be
counseled wisely, that they may move discretely; and while they
place themselves before God to be prayed for that they may be
healed, they are not to take the position that methods of restoration to health in accordance with nature's laws are to be neglected.

If they take the position that in praying for healing they must not
use the simple remedies provided by God to alleviate pain and to aid
nature in her work, lest it be a denial of faith, they are taking an
unwise position. This is not a denial of faith; it is in strict harmony
with the plans of God. When Hezekiah was sick, the prophet of God
brought him the message that he should die. He cried unto the Lord,
and the Lord heard His servant and worked a miracle in his behalf,
sending him a message that fifteen years should be added to his life.
Now, one word from God, one touch of the divine finger, would have
cured Hezekiah instantly, but special directions were given to take a
fig and lay it upon the affected part, and Hezekiah was raised to life.
In everything we need to move along the line of God's providence.

The human agent should have faith and should cooperate with
the divine power, using every facility, taking advantage of everything that, according to his intelligence, is beneficial, working in
harmony with natural laws; and in doing this he neither denies
nor hinders faith.—(*Counsels on Health,* 381, 382.)

In the word of God we have instruction relative to special prayer
for the recovery of the sick. But the offering of such prayer is a most
solemn act, and should not be entered upon without careful consideration. In many cases of prayer for the healing of the sick, that
which is called faith is nothing less than presumption.

Many persons bring disease upon themselves by their self-indulgence. They have not lived in accordance with natural law or

the principles of strict purity. Others have disregarded the laws of health in their habits of eating and drinking, dressing, or working. Often some form of vice is the cause of feebleness of mind or body. Should these persons gain the blessing of health, many of them would continue to pursue the same course of heedless transgression of God's natural and spiritual laws, reasoning that if God heals them in answer to prayer, they are at liberty to continue their unhealthful practices and to indulge perverted appetite without restraint. If God were to work a miracle in restoring these persons to health, He would be encouraging sin.

It is labor lost to teach people to look to God as a healer of their infirmities, unless they are taught also to lay aside unhealthful practices. In order to receive His blessing in answer to prayer, they must cease to do evil and learn to do well. Their surroundings must be sanitary, their habits of life correct. They must live in harmony with the law of God, both natural and spiritual.—(*Ministry of Healing*, 227, 228.)

PRAYER FOR MIRACULOUS HEALING CAN LEAD TO FANATICISM.— "Why," asks one and another, "is not prayer offered for the miraculous healing of the sick, instead of so many sanitariums being established?" Should this be done, great fanaticism would arise in our ranks. Those who have much self-confidence would start into action.—(*Evangelism*, 594, 595.)

TAKING PROPER MEASURES IS NOT A DENIAL OF FAITH IN PRAYER FOR HEALING.—Many who seek the Lord's healing mercy think that they must have a direct and immediate answer to their prayers or their faith is defective. For this reason, those who are weakened by disease need to be counseled wisely, that they may act with discretion. They should not disregard their duty to the friends who may survive them, or neglect to employ nature's agencies for the restoration of health.

Often there is danger of error here. Believing that they will be healed in answer to prayer, some fear to do anything that might seem to indicate a lack of faith. But they should not neglect to set their affairs in order as they would desire to do if they expected to be removed by death. Nor should they fear to utter words of encouragement or counsel which at the parting hour they wish to speak to their loved ones.—(*Ministry of Healing*, 231.)

But after I have prayed earnestly for the sick what then? Do I cease to do all I can for their recovery?—No, I work all the more earnestly, with much prayer that the Lord may bless the means which His own hand has provided; that He may give sanctified wisdom to co-operate with Him in the recovery of the sick.—(*Healthful Living*, [1897, 1898] 240).

MEDICAL TREATMENTS TO BE USED ALONG WITH PRAYER FOR HEALING.—Those who seek healing by prayer should not neglect to make use of the remedial agencies within their reach. It is not a denial of faith to use such remedies as God has provided to alleviate pain and to aid nature in her work of restoration. It is no denial of faith to co-operate with God, and to place themselves in the condition most favorable to recovery. God has put it in our power to obtain a knowledge of the laws of life. This knowledge has been placed within our reach for use. We should employ every facility for the restoration of health, taking every advantage possible, working in harmony with natural laws. When we have prayed for the recovery of the sick, we can work with all the more energy, thanking God that we have the privilege of co-operating with Him, and asking His blessing on the means which He Himself has provided.—(*Ministry of Healing*, 231, 232.)

TRUST GOD WHATEVER THE OUTCOME OF PRAYER.—When we have prayed for the recovery of the sick, whatever the outcome of the case, let us not lose faith in God. If we are called upon to meet bereavement, let us accept the bitter cup, remembering that a Father's hand holds it to our lips. But should health be restored, it should not be forgotten that the recipient of healing mercy is placed under renewed obligation to the Creator.—(*Ministry of Healing*, 233.)

CHAPTER

23

Prayer for Forgiveness

THE PRAYER FOR FORGIVENESS IS ALWAYS ANSWERED IMMEDI-ATELY.—When we pray for earthly blessings, the answer to our prayer may be delayed, or God may give us something other than we ask, but not so when we ask for deliverance from sin. It is His will to cleanse us from sin, to make us His children, and to enable us to live a holy life. Christ "gave Himself for our sins, that He might deliver us from this present evil world, according to the will of God and our Father." Gal. 1:4. And "this is the confidence that we have in Him, that, if we ask anything according to His will, He heareth us: and if we know that He hear us, whatsoever we ask, we know that we have the petitions that we desired of Him." 1 John 5:14, 15. "If we confess our sins, He is faithful and just to forgive us our sins, and to cleanse us from all unrighteousness." 1 John 1:9.—(*The Desire of Ages,* 266.)

No sooner does the child of God approach the mercy seat than he becomes the client of the great Advocate. At his first ut-terance of penitence and appeal for pardon Christ espouses his case and makes it His own, presenting the supplication before His

Father as His own request.—(*Testimonies for the Church,* vol. 6, 364.)

Tell Jesus your wants in the sincerity of your soul. You are not required to hold a long controversy with, or preach a sermon to, God, but with a heart of sorrow for your sins, say, "Save me, Lord, or I perish." There is hope for such souls. They will seek, they will ask, they will knock, and they will find. When Jesus has taken away the burden of sin that is crushing the soul, you will experience the blessedness of the peace of Christ.—(*Our High Calling,* 131.)

As, seeing the sinfulness of sin, we fall helpless before the cross, asking forgiveness and strength, our prayer is heard and answered. Those who present their petitions to God in Christ's name will never be turned away. The Lord says, "Him that cometh to Me I will in nowise cast out." "He will regard the prayer of the destitute." Our help comes from Him who holds all things in His hands. The peace that He sends is the assurance of His love to us.

Nothing can be more helpless and yet more invincible than the soul that feels its nothingness, and relies wholly upon the merits of a crucified and risen Saviour. God would send every angel in heaven to the aid of the one who places his whole dependence on Christ, rather than allow him to be overcome.—(*Signs of the Times,* October 29, 1902.)

THOSE SEEKING FORGIVENESS MUST THEMSELVES HAVE A FORGIVING ATTITUDE.—When we come to ask mercy and blessing from God we should have a spirit of love and forgiveness in our own hearts. How can we pray, "Forgive us our debts, as we forgive our debtors," and yet indulge an unforgiving spirit? Matthew 6:12. If we expect our own prayers to be heard we must forgive others in the same manner and to the same extent as we hope to be forgiven.—(*Steps to Christ,* 97.)

After completing the Lord's Prayer, Jesus added: "If ye forgive men their trespasses, your heavenly Father will also forgive you: but if ye forgive not men their trespasses, neither will your Father forgive your trespasses." Matt. 6:14, 15. He who is unforgiving cuts off the very channel through which alone he can receive mercy from God. We should not think that unless those who have injured us confess the wrong we are justified in withholding from them our forgiveness. It is their part, no doubt, to humble their hearts by repentance and confession; but we are to have a spirit of compassion toward those who have trespassed against us, whether or not they confess their faults.—(*The Faith I Live By*, 131.)

In the prayer that Christ taught His disciples was the request: Forgive us our trespasses as we forgive those who trespass against us. We cannot repeat this prayer from the heart and dare to be unforgiving, for we ask the Lord to forgive our trespasses against Him in the same manner that we forgive those who trespass against us. But few realize the true import of this prayer. If those who are unforgiving did comprehend the depth of its meaning they would not dare to repeat it and ask God to deal with them as they deal with their fellow mortals.—(*Testimonies for the Church*, vol. 3, 95.)

We need to examine our hearts as a preparation for coming before God in prayer, that we may know what manner of spirit we are of. If we do not forgive those who have trespassed against us, our prayers for forgiveness will not be heard. "Forgive us our debts, as we forgive our debtors." When as sinners we approach the mercy-seat, we cannot express the sentiment of this petition without forgiveness in our hearts for all who have done us an injury. Upon this petition Jesus makes a comment: "For if ye forgive men their trespasses, your heavenly Father will also forgive you; but if ye forgive not men their trespasses, neither will your Father forgive your trespasses."—(*Signs of the Times*, August 21, 1884.)

CONFESSION MUST BE SPECIFIC.—True confession is always of a specific character, and acknowledges particular sins. They may be of such a nature as only to be brought before God, they may be wrongs that should be confessed before individuals who have suffered injury through them, or they may be of a general kind that should be made known in the congregation of the people. But all confession should be definite and to the point, acknowledging the very sins of which you are guilty.—(*Testimonies for the Church,* vol. 5, 639.)

JESUS HEARS THE SIMPLE PRAYER FOR FORGIVENESS.—It is not essential that all shall be able to specify to a certainty when their sins were forgiven. The lesson to be taught the children is that their errors and mistakes are to be brought to Jesus in their very childhood of life. Teach them to ask His forgiveness daily for any wrong that they have done, and that Jesus does hear the simple prayer of the penitent heart, and will pardon, and receive them, just as He received the children brought to Him when He was upon earth.—(*Child Guidance,* 494, 495.)

Then, children, come to Jesus. Give to God the most precious offering that it is possible for you to make; give Him your heart. He speaks to you saying, "My son, My daughter, give Me thine heart. Though your sins be as scarlet, I will make them white as snow; for I will cleanse you with My own blood. I will make you members of My family—children of the heavenly King. Take My forgiveness, My peace which I freely give you. I will clothe you with My own righteousness,—the wedding garment,—and make you fit for the marriage supper of the Lamb. When clothed in My righteousness, through prayer, through watchfulness, through diligent study of My word, you will be able to reach a high standard. You will understand the truth, and your character will be moulded by a divine influence; for this is the will of God, even your sanctification." —(*The SDA Bible Commentary,* vol. 3, 1162.)

It is very necessary that we should pray in order that we may have strength from above to see and resist the temptations of the enemy; but Satan ever seeks to prevent men from praying, by filling up their time with business or pleasure, or by leading them into such wickedness that they will have no desire to pray. The Lord Jesus has made heaven accessible to all who will come unto Him, and He invites the children and the youth to come. He said, "Suffer the little children to come unto me, and forbid them not; for of such is the kingdom of God." Jesus would have the children and the youth come to Him with the same confidence with which they go to their parents. As a child asks his mother or father for bread when he is hungry, so the Lord would have you ask Him for the things which you need. If your sins are heavy upon your heart, you are to come to God and say, "For Christ's sake, forgive my sins." Every sincere prayer will be heard in heaven, and every earnest petition for grace and strength will be answered.—(*The Youth's Instructor,* July 7, 1892.)

THE PRAYER FOR FORGIVENESS MUST BE SHOWN TO BE SINCERE.— "Cast me not away from thy presence, and take not thy Holy Spirit from me." Repentance as well as forgiveness is the gift of God through Christ. It is through the influence of the Holy Spirit that we are convinced of sin, and feel our need of pardon. None but the contrite are forgiven; but it is the grace of the Lord that makes the heart penitent. He is acquainted with all our weaknesses and infirmities, and He will help us. He will hear the prayer of faith; but the sincerity of prayer can be proved only by our efforts to bring ourselves into harmony with the great moral standard which will test every man's character. We need to open our hearts to the influence of the Spirit, and to experience its transforming power.— (*Review and Herald,* June 24, 1884.)

"Ask, and it shall be given you; seek and ye shall find; knock, and it shall be opened unto you," Why is it that we do not take God at His word? Asking and receiving are closely linked together. If you ask in faith for the things that God has promised, you will receive. Look to Jesus for the things that you need. Ask Him for forgiveness of sins, and as you ask in faith your heart will be softened, and you will forgive those who have injured you, and your petitions will go up to God fragrant with love. With praying comes watching unto prayer, and every thought and word and act will be in harmony with your earnest petition for reformation in life. The prayer of faith will bring corresponding returns. But a mere form of words, without earnest sincerity and fervent desire for help, with no expectation of receiving, will avail nothing. Let not such a petitioner think he shall receive anything of the Lord. Those who come to God must believe that He is, and that He is a rewarder of them that diligently seek Him.—(*Review and Herald,* March 28, 1912.)

24

Intercessory Prayer

PRAY FOR OTHERS.—Let us strive to walk in the light as Christ is in the light. The Lord turned the captivity of Job when he prayed, not only for himself, but for those who were opposing him. When he felt earnestly desirous that the souls that had trespassed against him might be helped, he himself received help. Let us pray, not only for ourselves, but for those who have hurt us, and are continuing to hurt us. Pray, pray, especially in your mind. Give not the Lord rest; for His ears are open to hear sincere, importunate prayers, when the soul is humbled before Him.— (*SDA Bible Commentary,* vol. 3, 1141.)

You are to be the agent through whom God will speak to the soul. Precious things will be brought to your remembrance, and with a heart overflowing with the love of Jesus, you will speak words of vital interest and import. Your simplicity and sincerity will be the highest eloquence, and your words will be registered in the books of heaven as fit words, which are like apples of gold in pictures of silver. God will make them a healing flood of heavenly influence, awakening conviction and desire, and Jesus will add

His intercession to your prayers, and claim for the sinner the gift of the Holy Spirit, and pour it upon his soul. And there will be joy in the presence of the angels of God over one sinner that repenteth.—(*Sons and Daughters of God,* 274.)

There are those all around you who have woes, who need words of sympathy, love, and tenderness, and our humble, pitying prayers.—(*Testimonies for the Church,* vol. 3, 530.)

In calling God our Father, we recognize all His children as our brethren. We are all a part of the great web of humanity, all members of one family. In our petitions we are to include our neighbors as well as ourselves. No one prays aright who seeks a blessing for himself alone.—(*Sons and Daughters of God,* 267.)

As we seek to win others to Christ, bearing the burden of souls in our prayers, our own hearts will throb with the quickening influence of God's grace; our own affections will glow with more divine fervor; our whole Christian life will be more of a reality, more earnest, more prayerful.—(*Christ's Object Lessons,* 354.)

There are souls who have lost their courage; speak to them, pray for them. There are those who need the bread of life. Read to them from the Word of God. There is a soul sickness no balm can reach, no medicine heal. Pray for these, and bring them to Jesus Christ. And in all your work Christ will be present to make impressions upon human hearts.—(*Welfare Ministry,* 71.)

Let those who are spiritual converse with these souls. Pray with and for them. Let much time be spent in prayer and close searching of the word. Let all obtain the real facts of faith in their own souls through belief that the Holy Spirit will be imparted to them because they have a real hungering and thirsting after righteousness.—(*Testimonies for the Church,* vol. 6, 65.)

When self dies, there will be awakened an intense desire for the salvation of others,—a desire which will lead to persevering efforts to do good. There will be a sowing beside all waters; and earnest supplication, importunate prayers, will enter heaven in behalf of perishing souls.—(*Gospel Workers,* 470.)

Oh, that the earnest prayer of faith may arise everywhere, Give me souls buried now in the rubbish of error, or I die! Bring them to the knowledge of the truth as it is in Jesus.—(*This Day With God,* 171.)

Begin to pray for souls; come near to Christ, close to His bleeding side. Let a meek and quiet spirit adorn your lives, and let your earnest, broken, humble petitions ascend to Him for wisdom that you may have success in saving not only your own soul, but the souls of others.—(*Testimonies for the Church,* vol. 1, 513.)

There are many from whom hope has departed. Bring back the sunshine to them. Many have lost their courage. Speak to them words of cheer. Pray for them.—(*Prophets and Kings,* 719.)

Souls are to be sought for, prayed for, labored for. Earnest appeals are to be made. Fervent prayers are to be offered. Our tame, spiritless petitions are to be changed into petitions of intense earnestness.—(*Testimonies for the Church,* vol. 7, 12.)

This work requires you to watch for souls as they that must give an account. The tenderness of Christ must pervade the heart of the worker. If you have a love for souls you will reveal a tender solicitude for them. You will offer humble, earnest, heartfelt prayers for those whom you visit. The fragrance of Christ's love will be revealed in your work. He who gave His own life for the life of the world will co-operate with the unselfish worker to make an impression upon human hearts.—(*Testimonies for the Church,* vol. 6, 75, 76.)

Let us work upon this plan, and pray for one another, bringing one another right into the presence of God by living faith.— (*Review and Herald,* August 28, 1888.)

PRAY FOR BLESSINGS IN ORDER TO BLESS OTHERS.—Our prayers are not to be a selfish asking, merely for our own benefit. We are to ask that we may give. The principle of Christ's life must be the principle of our lives. "For their sakes," He said, speaking of His disciples, "I sanctify Myself, that they also might be sanctified." John 17:19. The same devotion, the same self-sacrifice, the same subjection to the claims of the word of God, that were manifest in Christ, must be seen in His servants. Our mission to the world is not to serve or please ourselves; we are to glorify God by co-operating with Him to save sinners. We are to ask blessings from God that we may communicate to others. The capacity for receiving is preserved only by imparting. We cannot continue to receive heavenly treasure without communicating to those around us.—(*Christ's Object Lessons,* 142, 143.)

When we pray, "Give us this day our daily bread," we ask for others as well as ourselves. And we acknowledge that what God gives us is not for ourselves alone. God gives to us in trust, that we may feed the hungry.—(*Thoughts From the Mount of Blessing,* 111, 112.)

INTERCEDE FOR OTHERS IN PRIVATE PRAYER.—In private prayer all have the privilege of praying as long as they desire and of being as explicit as they please. They can pray for all their relatives and friends. The closet is the place to tell all their private difficulties, and trials, and temptations. A common meeting to worship God is not the place to open the privacies of the heart.—(*Testimonies for the Church,* vol. 2, 578.)

PRAY FOR THOSE WHO PREACH AND MINISTER.—Among God's people there should be at this time frequent seasons of sincere, earnest prayer. The mind should be constantly in a prayerful attitude. In the home and in the church let earnest prayers be offered in behalf of those who have given themselves to the preaching of the Word.—(*In Heavenly Places,* 87.)

As young men go forth to preach the truth, you should have seasons of prayer for them. Pray that God will connect them with Himself and give them wisdom, grace, and knowledge. Pray that they may be guarded from the snares of Satan and kept pure in thought and holy in heart. I entreat you who fear the Lord to waste no time in unprofitable talk or in needless labor to gratify pride or to indulge the appetite. Let the time thus gained be spent in wrestling with God for your ministers. Hold up their hands as did Aaron and Hur the hands of Moses.—(*Testimonies for the Church,* vol. 5, 162.)

PRAY FOR THE YOUTH OF THE CHURCH.—Let those older in experience watch over the younger ones; and when they see them tempted, take them aside, and pray with them and for them.—(*Messages to Young People,* 18.)

SABBATH SCHOOL TEACHERS PRAY FOR YOUR CLASS MEMBERS.—As workers for God we want more of Jesus and less of self. We should have more of a burden for souls, and should pray daily that strength and wisdom may be given us for the Sabbath. Teachers, meet with your classes. Pray with them, and teach them how to pray. Let the heart be softened, and the petitions short and simple, but earnest.—(*Counsels on Sabbath School Work,* 125.)

STUDENTS TO PRAY FOR TEACHERS.—Students should have their own seasons of prayer, where they may offer fervent, simple petitions that God shall bless the president of the school with physical strength, mental clearness, moral power, and spiritual discernment, and that every teacher shall be qualified by the grace of God to do His work.—(*Fundamentals of Christian Education,* 293.)

PRAY FOR FELLOW CHRISTIANS.—Too often we forget that our fellow laborers are in need of strength and cheer. In times of special perplexity and burden, take care to assure them of your interest and sympathy. While you try to help them by your prayers, let them know that you do it. Send along the line God's message to His workers: "Be strong and of a good courage." Joshua 1:6.—(*Testimonies for the Church,* vol. 7, 185.)

PARENTS TO PRAY FOR THEIR CHILDREN.—God has promised to give wisdom to those that ask in faith, and He will do just as He said He would. He is pleased with the faith that takes Him at His word. The mother of Augustine prayed for her son's conversion. She saw no evidence that the Spirit of God was impressing his heart, but she was not discouraged. She laid her finger upon the texts, presenting before God His own words, and pleaded as only a mother can. Her deep humiliation, her earnest importunities, her unwavering faith, prevailed, and the Lord gave her the desire of her heart. Today He is just as ready to listen to the petitions of His people. His "hand is not shortened that it cannot save, neither His ear heavy that it cannot hear;" and if Christian parents seek Him earnestly, He will fill their mouths with arguments, and, for His name's sake, will work mightily in their behalf in the conversion of their children.—(*Testimonies for the Church,* vol. 5, 322, 323.)

We should pray to God much more than we do. There is great strength and blessing in praying together in our families, with and for our children.—(*Child Guidance,* 525.)

Let Christ find you His helping hand to carry out His purposes. By prayer you may gain an experience that will make your ministry for your children a perfect success.—(*Child Guidance,* 69.)

You did not consider hard labor a burden if the way would only open that you might care for your children and shield them from the iniquity prevailing in this age of the world. It was the burden of your heart that you might see them turning to the Lord. You pleaded before God for your children with strong cries and tears. Their conversion you so much desired. Sometimes your heart would despond and faint, and you would fear that your prayers would not be answered; then again you would consecrate your children to God afresh, and your yearning heart would lay them anew upon the altar.

When they went into the army, your prayers followed them. They were wonderfully preserved from harm. They called it good luck; but a mother's prayers from an anxious, burdened soul, as she felt the peril of her children and the danger of their being cut off in their youth without hope in God, had much to do with their preservation. How many prayers were lodged in heaven that these sons might be preserved to obey God, to devote their lives to His glory! In your anxiety for your children you pleaded with God to return them to you again, and you would seek more earnestly to lead them in the path of holiness.—(*Testimonies for the Church,* vol. 2, 274, 275.)

He [God] will not refuse to hear the parents' earnest prayer, that is seconded by persevering labor, that their children may be blessed of Him, and become faithful workers in His cause. When parents do their duty in God's appointed way, they may be sure that their requests for His help in their home work will be granted.—(*Signs of the Times,* May 4, 1888.)

Watch continually to cut off the current and roll back the weight of evil Satan is pressing in upon your children. The children cannot do this of themselves. Parents can do much. By earnest prayer and living faith, great victories will be gained.—(*Spiritual Gifts,* bk. 4b, 139.)

To do her work as it should be done requires talent and skill and patient, thoughtful care. It calls for self-distrust and earnest prayer. Let every mother strive by persevering effort to fulfill her obligations. Let her bring her little ones to Jesus in the arms of faith, telling Him her great need, and asking for wisdom and grace.—(*Counsels to Parents, Teachers, and Students,* 128.)

Painstaking effort, prayer and faith, when united with a correct example, will not be fruitless. Bring your children to God in faith, and seek to impress their susceptible minds with a sense of their obligations to their heavenly Father.—(*Temperance,* 157, 158.)

Do not expect a change to be wrought in your children without patient, earnest labor, mingled with fervent prayer. To study and understand their varied characters, and day by day to mould them after the divine Model, is a work demanding great diligence and perseverance, and much prayer, with an abiding faith in God's promises.—(*Signs of the Times,* May 4, 1888.)

Even the babe in its mother's arms may dwell as under the shadow of the Almighty through the faith of the praying mother.— (*The Desire of Ages,* 512.)

Fathers and mothers, will you not lay hold of your work with energy, perseverance, and love? Sow the precious seed daily, with earnest prayer that God will water it with the dews of grace, and grant you an abundant harvest. The Son of God died to redeem a sinful, rebellious race. Shall we shrink from any toil or sacrifice to save our own dear children?—(*Signs of the Times,* November 24, 1881.)

After you have done your duty faithfully to your children, then carry them to God and ask Him to help you. Tell Him that you have done your part, and then in faith ask God to do His part, that which you cannot do.—(*Child Guidance,* 256.)

CHAPTER

25

Angels and Prayer

ANGELS RECORD EVERY SINCERE PRAYER.—We should now acquaint ourselves with God by proving His promises. Angels record every prayer that is earnest and sincere. We should rather dispense with selfish gratifications than neglect communion with God. The deepest poverty, the greatest self-denial, with His approval, is better than riches, honors, ease, and friendship without it. We must take time to pray. (*The Great Controversy,* 622.)

Let the recording angels write the history of the holy struggles and conflicts of the people of God, let them record their prayers and tears; but let not God be dishonored by the proclamation from human lips, declaring, "I am sinless. I am holy." Sanctified lips will never give utterance to such presumptuous words.—(*Signs of the Times,* May 23, 1895.)

ANGELS CAN HEAR OUR PRAYERS.—Could men see with heavenly vision, they would behold companies of angels that excel in strength stationed about those who have kept the word of Christ's patience. With sympathizing tenderness, angels have witnessed their distress and have heard their prayers.—(*The Great Controversy,* 630.)

ANGELS BEAR OUR PRAYERS TO HEAVEN.—A well-disciplined family, who love and obey God, will be cheerful and happy. The father when he returns from his daily labor, will not bring his perplexities to his home. He will feel that home, and the family circle, are too sacred to be marred with unhappy perplexities. When he left his home, he did not leave his Saviour and his religion behind. Both were his companions. The sweet influence of his home, the blessing of his wife, and the love of his children, make his burdens light; and he returns with peace in his heart, and cheerful, encouraging words for his wife and children, who are waiting joyfully to welcome his coming. As he bows with his family at the altar of prayer to offer up his grateful thanks to God for His preserving care of himself and loved ones through the day, angels of God hover in the room, and bear the fervent prayers of God-fearing parents to heaven, as sweet incense, which are answered by returning blessings.—(*Selected Messages,* bk. 2, 439, 440.)

Angels hear the offering of praise and the prayer of faith, and they bear the petitions to Him who ministers in the sanctuary for His people, and pleads His merits in their behalf. True prayer takes hold upon Omnipotence, and gives men the victory. Upon his knees the Christian obtains strength to resist temptation.—(*Review and Herald,* February 1, 1912.)

God does not leave His erring children who are weak in faith, and who make many mistakes. The Lord hearkens and hears their prayer and their testimony. Those who look unto Jesus day by day and hour by hour, who watch unto prayer, are drawing nigh to Jesus. Angels with wings outspread wait to bear their contrite prayers to God, and to register them in the books of heaven.—(*SDA Bible Commentary,* vol. 4, 1184.)

ANGELS WAIT TO RESPOND TO OUR PRAYERS.—Often in the care of the suffering, much attention is given to minor matters, while the patients' need of the great all-saving truths of the gospel, which would minister to both soul and body, is forgotten. When you neglect to offer prayer for the sick, you deprive them of great blessings; for angels of God are waiting to minister to these souls in response to your petitions.—(*Medical Ministry,* 195.)

Before leaving the house for labor, all the family should be called together; and the father, or the mother in the father's absence, should plead fervently with God to keep them through the day. Come in humility, with a heart full of tenderness, and with a sense of the temptations and dangers before yourselves and your children; by faith bind them upon the altar, entreating for them the care of the Lord. Ministering angels will guard children who are thus dedicated to God.—(*Child Guidance,* 519.)

SPECIFIC ANGELS ARE APPOINTED TO ANSWER PRAYERS.—Heavenly beings are appointed to answer the prayers of those who are working unselfishly for the interests of the cause of God. The very highest angels in the heavenly courts are appointed to work out the prayers which ascend to God for the advancement of the cause of God. Each angel has his particular post of duty, which he is not permitted to leave for any other place. If he should leave, the powers of darkness would gain an advantage. . . .

Day by day the conflict between good and evil is going on. Why is it that those who have had many opportunities and advantages do not realize the intensity of this work? They should be intelligent in regard to this. God is the Ruler. By His supreme power He holds in check and controls earthly potentates. Through His agencies He does the work which was ordained before the foundation of the world.

As a people we do not understand as we should the great conflict going on between invisible agencies, the controversy between loyal and disloyal angels. Evil angels are constantly at work, planning their line of attack, controlling as commanders, kings, and rulers, the disloyal human forces. . . . I call upon the ministers of Christ to press home upon the understanding of all who come within the reach of their voice, the truth of the ministration of angels. Do not indulge in fanciful speculations. The written Word is our only safety. We must pray as did Daniel, that we may be guarded by heavenly intelligences. As ministering spirits angels are sent forth to minister to those who shall be heirs of salvation. Pray, my brethren, pray as you have never prayed before. We are not prepared for the Lord's coming. We need to make thorough work for eternity.—(*SDA Bible Commentary,* vol. 4, 1173.)

God has appointed the angels that do His will to respond to the prayers of the meek of the earth, and to guide His ministers with counsel and judgment. Heavenly agencies are constantly seeking to impart grace and strength and counsel to God's faithful children, that they may act their part in the work of communicating light to the world.—(*Testimonies to Ministers,* 484.)

Ministering angels are waiting about the throne to instantly obey the mandate of Jesus Christ to answer every prayer offered in earnest, living faith.—(*Selected Messages,* bk. 2, 377.)

Oh, that we could all realize the nearness of heaven to earth! When the earthborn children know it not, they have the angels of light as their companions; for the heavenly messengers are sent forth to minister to those who shall be heirs of salvation. A silent witness guards every soul that lives, seeking to win and draw him to Christ. The angels never leave the tempted one a prey to the enemy who would destroy the souls of men if permitted to do so. As long as there is hope, until they resist the Holy Spirit to their eternal ruin, men are guarded by heavenly intelligences.

Oh, that all could behold our precious Saviour as He is, a Saviour. Let His hand draw aside the veil which conceals His glory from our eyes. It shows Him in His high and holy place. What do we see? Our Saviour, not in a position of silence and inactivity. He is surrounded with heavenly intelligences, cherubim, and seraphim, ten thousand times ten thousand of angels. All these heavenly beings have one object above all others, in which they are intensely interested—His church in a world of corruption. . . . They are working for Christ under His commission, to save to the utter-most all who look to Him and believe in Him.

Heavenly angels are commissioned to watch the sheep of Christ's pasture. When Satan with his deceptive snares would deceive if possible the very elect, these angels set in operation influences that will save the tempted souls if they will take heed to the Word of the Lord, realize their danger, and say, "No, I will not enter into that scheme of Satan. I have an Elder Brother on the throne in heaven, who has shown that He has a tender interest in me, and I will not grieve His heart of love."

Living amid these opposing forces, we may through the exercise of faith and prayer, call to our side a retinue of heavenly angels, who will guard us from every corrupting influence.—(*Our High Calling*, 23.)

ANGELS MARK OUR PRAYERS AND PROVIDE HELP.—When you rise in the morning, do you feel your helplessness, and your need of strength from God? and do you humbly, heartily make known your wants to your heavenly Father? If so, angels mark your prayers, and if these prayers have not gone forth out of feigned lips, when you are in danger of unconsciously doing wrong, and exerting an influence which will lead others to do wrong, your guardian angel will be by your side, prompting you to a better course, choosing your words for you, and influencing your actions.

If you feel in no danger, and if you offer no prayer for help and strength to resist temptations, you will be sure to go astray; your neglect of duty will be marked in the book of God in heaven, and you will be found wanting in the trying day.—(*Messages to Young People*, 90.)

GOD SENDS REINFORCEMENTS OF ANGELS TO OUR AID IN ANSWER TO PRAYER.—If Satan sees that he is in danger of losing one soul, he will exert himself to the utmost to keep that one. And when the individual is aroused to his danger, and, with distress and fervor, looks to Jesus for strength, Satan fears that he will lose a captive, and he calls a reinforcement of his angels to hedge in the poor soul, and form a wall of darkness around him, that heaven's light may not reach him. But if the one in danger perseveres, and in his helplessness casts himself upon the merits of the blood of Christ, our Saviour listens to the earnest prayer of faith, and sends a reinforcement of those angels that excel in strength to deliver him. Satan cannot endure to have his powerful rival appealed to, for he fears and trembles before His strength and majesty. At the sound of fervent prayer, Satan's whole host trembles. He continues to call legions of evil angels to accomplish his object. And when angels, all-powerful, clothed with the armory of heaven, come to the help of the fainting, pursued soul, Satan and his host fall back, well knowing that their battle is lost. The willing subjects of Satan are faithful, active, and united in one object. And although they hate and war with one another, yet they improve every opportunity to advance their common interest. But the great Commander in heaven and earth has limited Satan's power. (*Testimonies for the Church,* vol. 1, 345, 346.)

The guardianship of the heavenly host is granted to all who will work in God's ways and follow His plans. We may in earnest, contrite prayer call the heavenly helpers to our side. Invisible armies of light and power will work with the humble, meek, and lowly one.—(*Selected Messages,* bk. 1, 97.)

I saw some, with strong faith and agonizing cries, pleading with God. Their countenances were pale and marked with deep anxiety, expressive of their internal struggle. Firmness and great earnestness was expressed in their countenances; large drops of perspiration fell from their foreheads. Now and then their faces would light up with the marks of God's approbation, and again the same solemn, earnest, anxious look would settle upon them.

Evil angels crowded around, pressing darkness upon them to shut out Jesus from their view, that their eyes might be drawn to the darkness that surrounded them, and thus they be led to distrust God and murmur against Him. Their only safety was in keeping their eyes directed upward. Angels of God had charge over His people, and as the poisonous atmosphere of evil angels was pressed around these anxious ones, the heavenly angels were continually wafting their wings over them to scatter the thick darkness.

As the praying ones continued their earnest cries, at times a ray of light from Jesus came to them, to encourage their hearts and light up their countenances. Some, I saw, did not participate in this work of agonizing and pleading. They seemed indifferent and careless. They were not resisting the darkness around them, and it shut them in like a thick cloud. The angels of God left these and went to the aid of the earnest, praying ones. I saw angels of God hasten to the assistance of all who were struggling with all their power to resist the evil angels and trying to help themselves by calling upon God with perseverance. But His angels left those who made no effort to help themselves, and I lost sight of them.—(*Early Writings*, 269, 270.)

LONG PRAYERS WEARY THE ANGELS.—Long, prosy talks and prayers are out of place anywhere, and especially in the social meeting. They weary the angels as well as the people who listen to them. Our prayers should be short, and right to the point.—(*Review and Herald*, October 10, 1882.)

ANGELS WILL TEACH US HOW TO PRAY.—Church members, young and old, should be educated to go forth to proclaim this last message to the world. If they go in humility, angels of God will go with them, teaching them how to lift up the voice in prayer, how to raise the voice in song, and how to proclaim the gospel message for this time.—(*Messages to Young People*, 217.)

ANGELS SURPRISED THAT HUMANS PRAY SO LITTLE.—What can the angels of heaven think of poor helpless human beings, who are subject to temptation, when God's heart of infinite love yearns toward them, ready to give them more than they can ask or think, and yet they pray so little, and have so little faith? The angels love to bow before God; they love to be near Him. They regard communion with God as their highest joy; and yet the children of earth, who need so much the help that God only can give, seem satisfied to walk without the light of His Spirit, the companionship of His presence.—(*Steps to Christ*, 94.)

26

Counterfeit Prayers

DO NOT APPROACH GOD LIGHTLY IN PRAYER.—Humility and reverence should characterize the deportment of all who come into the presence of God. In the name of Jesus we may come before Him with confidence, but we must not approach Him with the boldness of presumption, as though He were on a level with ourselves. There are those who address the great and all-powerful and holy God, who dwelleth in light unapproachable, as they would address an equal, or even an inferior. There are those who conduct themselves in His house as they would not presume to do in the audience chamber of an earthly ruler. These should remember that they are in His sight whom seraphim adore, before whom angels veil their faces.—(*Patriarchs and Prophets,* 252.)

PRAYERS OF HYPOCRISY.—The prayers that are offered to God to tell Him of all our wretchedness, when we do not feel wretched at all, are the prayers of hypocrisy. It is the contrite prayer that the Lord regards. "For thus saith the high and lofty One that inhabiteth eternity, whose name is Holy; I dwell in the high and holy place, and with him also that is of a contrite and humble spirit, to revive the spirit of the humble, and to revive the heart of the contrite ones."

Prayer is not intended to work any change in God; it brings us into harmony with God. It does not take the place of duty.— (*Messages to Young People,* 247, 248.)

PRAYERS THAT CAST A CHILLY SHADOW.—There are some, I fear, who do not take their troubles to God in private prayer, but reserve them for the prayer meeting, and there do up their praying for several days. Such may be named conference and prayer meeting killers. They emit no light; they edify no one. Their cold, frozen prayers and long, backslidden testimonies cast a shadow. All are glad when they get through, and it is almost impossible to throw off the chill and darkness which their prayers and exhortations bring into the meeting. From the light which I have received, our meetings should be spiritual and social, and not too long. Reserve, pride, vanity, and fear of man should be left at home. Little differences and prejudices should not be taken with us to these meetings. As in a united family, simplicity, meekness, confidence, and love should exist in the hearts of brethren and sisters who meet to be refreshed and invigorated by bringing their lights together.—(*Testimonies for the Church,* vol. 2, 578, 579.)

TO EXPECT THAT OUR PRAYERS WILL ALWAYS BE ANSWERED IN JUST THE WAY WE WANT IS PRESUMPTION.—The prayer of faith is never lost; but to claim that it will be always answered in the very way and for the particular thing we have expected, is presumption. (*Testimonies for the Church,* vol. 1, 231.)

When our prayers seem not to be answered, we are to cling to the promise; for the time of answering will surely come, and we shall receive the blessing we need most. But to claim that prayer will always be answered in the very way and for the particular thing that we desire, is presumption. God is too wise to err, and too good to withhold any good thing from them that walk uprightly. Then do not fear to trust Him, even though you do not see the immediate answer to your prayers. Rely upon His sure promise, "Ask, and it shall be given you."—(*Steps to Christ,* 96.)

PRAYER HAS NO MERIT IN ITSELF TO CLEANSE FROM SIN.—The heathen looked upon their prayers as having in themselves merit to atone for sin. Hence the longer the prayer the greater the merit. If they could become holy by their own efforts they would have something in themselves in which to rejoice, some ground for boasting. This idea of prayer is an outworking of the principle of self-expiation which lies at the foundation of all systems of false religion. The Pharisees had adopted this pagan idea of prayer, and it is by no means extinct in our day, even among those who profess to be Christians. The repetition of set, customary phrases, when the heart feels no need of God, is of the same character as the "vain repetitions" of the heathen.

Prayer is not an expiation for sin; it has no virtue or merit of itself. All the flowery words at our command are not equivalent to one holy desire. The most eloquent prayers are but idle words if they do not express the true sentiments of the heart. But the prayer that comes from an earnest heart, when the simple wants of the soul are expressed, as we would ask an earthly friend for a favor, expecting it to be granted—this is the prayer of faith. God does not desire our ceremonial compliments, but the unspoken cry of the heart broken and subdued with a sense of its sin and utter weakness finds its way to the Father of all mercy.—(*Thoughts From the Mount of Blessing,* 86, 87.)

PRAYER IS NO EVIDENCE OF CONVERSION IF THE LIFE IS NOT CHANGED.—Satan leads people to think that because they have felt a rapture of feeling, they are converted. But their experience does not change. Their actions are the same as before. Their lives show no good fruit. They pray often and long, and are constantly referring to the feelings they had at such and such a time. But they do not live the new life. They are deceived. Their experience goes no deeper than feeling. They build upon the sand, and when adverse winds come, their house is swept away.

Many poor souls are groping in darkness, looking for the feelings which others say they have had in their experience. They overlook the fact that the believer in Christ must work out his own salvation with fear and trembling. The convicted sinner has something to do. He must repent and show true faith.

When Jesus speaks of the new heart, He means the mind, the life, the whole being. To have a change of heart is to withdraw the affections from the world, and fasten them upon Christ. To have a new heart is to have a new mind, new purposes, new motives. What is the sign of a new heart?—A changed life. There is a daily, hourly dying to selfishness and pride.—(*Messages to Young People,* 71, 72.)

PRAYER NO SUBSTITUTE FOR OBEDIENCE.—Men and women, in the face of the most positive commands of God, will follow their own inclination, and then dare to pray over the matter, to prevail upon God to consent to allow them to go contrary to His expressed will. God is not pleased with such prayers. Satan comes to their side, as he did to Eve in Eden, and impresses them, and they have an exercise of mind, and this they relate as a most wonderful experience which the Lord has given them.—(*Review and Herald,* July 27, 1886.)

Communion with God imparts to the soul an intimate knowledge of His will. But many who profess the faith know not what true conversion is. They have no experience in communion with the Father through Jesus Christ, and have never felt the power of divine grace to sanctify the heart. Praying and sinning, sinning and praying, their lives are full of malice, deceit, envy, jealousy, and self-love. The prayers of this class are an abomination to God. True prayer engages the energies of the soul and affects the life. He who thus pours out his wants before God feels the emptiness of everything else under heaven.—(*Testimonies for the Church,* vol. 4, 534, 535.)

There are conditions to the fulfillment of God's promises, and prayer can never take the place of duty. "If ye love Me," Christ says, "Keep My commandments." "He that hath My commandments, and keepeth them, he it is that loveth Me; and he that loveth Me shall be loved of My Father, and I will love him, and will manifest Myself to him." John 14:15, 21. Those who bring their petitions to God, claiming His promise while they do not comply with the conditions, insult Jehovah. They bring the name of Christ as their authority for the fulfillment of the promise, but they do not those things that would show faith in Christ and love for Him.—(*Christ's Object Lessons*, 143.)

Prayer is the opening of the heart to God as to a friend. The eye of faith will discern God very near, and the suppliant may obtain precious evidence of the divine love and care for him. But why is it that so many prayers are never answered? Says David: "I cried unto Him with my mouth, and He was extolled with my tongue. If I regard iniquity in my heart, the Lord will not hear me." By another prophet the Lord gives us the promise: "Ye shall seek Me, and find Me, when ye shall search for Me with all your heart." Again, he speaks of some who "have not cried unto Me with their heart." Such petitions are prayers of form, lip service only, which the Lord does not accept.—(*Testimonies for the Church,* vol. 4, 533.)

Hurried, occasional prayers are not real communion with God.—Heaven is not closed against the fervent prayers of the righteous. Elijah was a man subject to like passions as we are, yet the Lord heard and in a most striking manner answered his petitions. The only reason for our lack of power with God is to be found in ourselves. If the inner life of many who profess the truth were presented before them, they would not claim to be Christians. They are not growing in grace. A hurried prayer is offered now and then, but there is no real communion with God.

We must be much in prayer if we would make progress in the divine life. When the message of truth was first proclaimed, how much we prayed. How often was the voice of intercession heard in the chamber, in the barn, in the orchard, or the grove. Frequently we spent hours in earnest prayer, two or three together claiming the promise; often the sound of weeping was heard and then the voice of thanksgiving and the song of praise.—(*Testimonies for the Church*, vol. 5, 161, 162.)

GOD ABHORS THE PRAYERS OF THE SELFISH.—I saw that there were some like Judas among those who profess to be waiting for their Lord. Satan controls them, but they know it not. God cannot approve of the least degree of covetousness or selfishness, and He abhors the prayers and exhortations of those who indulge these evil traits. As Satan sees that his time is short, he leads men on to be more and more selfish and covetous, and then exults as he sees them wrapped up in themselves, close, penurious, and selfish. If the eyes of such could be opened, they would see Satan in hellish triumph, exulting over them and laughing at the folly of those who accept his suggestions and enter his snares.—(*Early Writings*, 268.)

DRY, STALE PRAYERS HELP NO ONE.—The church needs the fresh, living experience of members who have habitual communion with God. Dry, stale testimonies and prayers, without the manifestation of Christ in them, are no help to the people. If everyone who claims to be a child of God were filled with faith and light and life, what a wonderful witness would be given to those who come to hear the truth! And how many souls might be won to Christ!—(*Testimonies for the Church*, vol. 6, 64.)

All the treasures of heaven were committed to Jesus Christ, that He might impart these precious gifts to the diligent, persevering seeker. He "is made unto us wisdom, and righteousness, and sanctification, and redemption." I Corinthians 1:30. But even the prayers of many are so formal that they carry with them no influence for good. They are not a savor of life.

If teachers would humble their hearts before God and realize the responsibilities they have accepted in taking charge of the youth with the object of educating them for the future immortal life, a marked change would soon be seen in their attitude. Their prayers would not be dry and lifeless, but they would pray with the earnestness of souls who feel their peril.—(*Counsels to Parents, Teachers, and Students,* 371, 372.)

WARNING AGAINST PRAYERS THAT HAVE SELF AS THEIR SOURCE.— Our petitions to God should not proceed from hearts that are filled with selfish aspirations. God exhorts us to choose those gifts that will redound to His glory. He would have us choose the heavenly instead of the earthly. He throws open before us the possibilities and advantages of a heavenly commerce. He gives encouragement to our loftiest aims, security to our choicest treasure. When the worldly possession is swept away, the believer will rejoice in his heavenly treasure, the riches that cannot be lost in any earthly disaster.—(*Sons and Daughters of God,* 188.)

GENUINE AND COUNTERFEIT PRAYERS CONTRASTED.—The poor publican who prayed, "God be merciful to me a sinner" (Luke 18:13), regarded himself as a very wicked man, and others looked upon him in the same light; but he felt his need, and with his burden of guilt and shame he came before God, asking for His mercy. His heart was open for the Spirit of God to do its gracious work and set him free from the power of sin. The Pharisee's boastful, self-righteous prayer showed that his heart was closed against the influence of the Holy Spirit. Because of his distance from God, he had no sense of his own defilement, in contrast with the perfection of the divine holiness. He felt no need, and he received nothing.—(*Steps to Christ,* 30, 31.)

There are two kinds of prayer—the prayer of form and the prayer of faith. The repetition of set, customary phrases when the heart feels no need of God, is formal prayer. . . . We should be extremely careful in all our prayers to speak the wants of the heart and to say only what we mean. All the flowery words at our command are not equivalent to one holy desire. The most eloquent prayers are but vain repetitions if they do not express the true sentiments of the heart. But the prayer that comes from an earnest heart, when the simple wants of the soul are expressed just as we would ask an earthly friend for a favor, expecting that it would be granted—this is the prayer of faith. The publican who went up to the temple to pray is a good example of a sincere, devoted worshiper. He felt that he was a sinner, and his great need led to an outburst of passionate desire, "God be merciful to me a sinner."—(*My Life Today,* 19.)

Of Christ it is said: "And being in an agony He prayed more earnestly." In what contrast to this intercession by the Majesty of heaven are the feeble, heartless prayers that are offered to God. Many are content with lip service, and but few have a sincere, earnest, affectionate longing after God.

Communion with God imparts to the soul an intimate knowledge of His will. But many who profess the faith know not what true conversion is. They have no experience in communion with the Father through Jesus Christ, and have never felt the power of divine grace to sanctify the heart. Praying and sinning, sinning and praying, their lives are full of malice, deceit, envy, jealousy, and self-love. The prayers of this class are an abomination to God. True prayer engages the energies of the soul and affects the life. He who thus pours out his wants before God feels the emptiness of everything else under heaven. "All my desire is before Thee," said David, "and my groaning is not hid from Thee." "My soul thirsteth for God, for the living God: when shall I come and appear before God?" "When I remember these things, I pour out my soul in me."—(*Testimonies for the Church,* vol. 4, 534, 535.)

CHAPTER

27

Satan and Prayer

SATAN TRIES TO OBSTRUCT OUR PRAYER ACCESS TO GOD.—The darkness of the evil one encloses those who neglect to pray. The whispered temptations of the enemy entice them to sin; and it is all because they do not make use of the privileges that God has given them in the divine appointment of prayer. Why should the sons and daughters of God be reluctant to pray, when prayer is the key in the hand of faith to unlock heaven's storehouse, where are treasured the boundless resources of Omnipotence? Without unceasing prayer and diligent watching we are in danger of growing careless and of deviating from the right path. The adversary seeks continually to obstruct the way to the mercy seat, that we may not by earnest supplication and faith obtain grace and power to resist temptation.—(*Steps to Christ,* 94, 95.)

There is a mighty power in prayer. Our great adversary is constantly seeking to keep the troubled soul away from God. An appeal to heaven by the humblest saint is more to be dreaded by Satan than the decrees of cabinets or the mandates of kings.—(*SDA Bible Commentary,* vol. 2, 1008.)

The enemy holds many of you from prayer, by telling you that you do not feel your prayers, and that you would better wait until you realize more of the spirit of intercession, lest your prayers should be a mockery. But you must say to Satan, "It is written" that "men ought always to pray, and not to faint." We should pray until we do have the burden of our wants upon our souls; and if we persevere, we shall have it. The Lord will imbue us with His Holy Spirit. The Lord knows, and the Devil knows, that we cannot resist the temptations of Satan without power from on high. For this reason the evil one seeks to hinder us from laying hold upon Him who is mighty to save. Our Lord made it our duty, as well as our privilege, to connect our weakness, our ignorance, our need, with His strength, His wisdom, His righteousness. He unites His infinite power with the effort of finite beings, that they may be more than victors in the battle with the enemy of their souls.

Let no one be discouraged, for Jesus lives to make intercession for us. There is a heaven to gain, and a hell to escape, and Christ is interested in our welfare. He will help all those who call upon Him. We must mingle faith with all our prayers. We cannot bring Christ down, but, through faith, we can lift ourselves up into unity and harmony with the perfect standard of righteousness. We have a wily foe to meet and to conquer, but we can do it in the name of the Mighty One.—(*Review and Herald,* October 30, 1888.)

DON'T LET SATAN'S SUGGESTIONS KEEP YOU FROM PRAYING.— We are not to be so overwhelmed with the thought of our sins and errors that we shall cease to pray. Some realize their great weakness and sin, and become discouraged. Satan casts his dark shadow between them and the Lord Jesus, their atoning sacrifice. They say, It is useless for me to pray. My prayers are so mingled with evil thoughts that the Lord will not hear them.

These suggestions are from Satan. In His humanity Christ met and resisted this temptation, and He knows how to succor those who are thus tempted. In our behalf, He "offered up prayers and supplications with strong crying and tears" (Heb. 5:7).

Many, not understanding that their doubts come from Satan, become fainthearted and are defeated in the conflict. Do not, because your thoughts are evil, cease to pray. If we could in our own wisdom and strength pray aright, we could also live aright, and would need no atoning sacrifice. But imperfection is upon all humanity. Educate and train the mind that you may in simplicity tell the Lord what you need. As you offer your petitions to God, seeking for forgiveness for sin, a purer and holier atmosphere will surround your soul.—(*In Heavenly Places,* 78.)

PRAYER BAFFLES SATAN'S STRONGEST EFFORTS.—Man is Satan's captive and is naturally inclined to follow his suggestions and do his bidding. He has in himself no power to oppose effectual resistance to evil. It is only as Christ abides in him by living faith, influencing his desires and strengthening him with strength from above, that man may venture to face so terrible a foe. Every other means of defense is utterly vain. It is only through Christ that Satan's power is limited. This is a momentous truth that all should understand. Satan is busy every moment, going to and fro, walking up and down in the earth, seeking whom he may devour. But the earnest prayer of faith will baffle his strongest efforts. Then take "the shield of faith," brethren, "wherewith ye shall be able to quench all the fiery darts of the wicked."—(*Testimonies for the Church,* vol. 5, 294.)

PRAYER TURNS ASIDE SATAN'S ATTACKS.—Prayer unites us with one another and with God. Prayer brings Jesus to our side, and gives to the fainting, perplexed soul new strength to overcome the world, the flesh, and the devil. Prayer turns aside the attacks of Satan.—(*Christ's Object Lessons,* 250.)

We must have on the whole armor of God and be ready at any moment for a conflict with the powers of darkness. When temptations and trials rush in upon us, let us go to God and agonize with Him in prayer. He will not turn us away empty, but will give us grace and strength to overcome, and to break the power of the enemy.—(*Early Writings,* 46.)

SATAN TREMBLES AT THE SOUND OF PRAYER.—If Satan sees that he is in danger of losing one soul, he will exert himself to the utmost to keep that one. And when the individual is aroused to his danger, and, with distress and fervor, looks to Jesus for strength, Satan fears that he will lose a captive, and he calls a reinforcement of his angels to hedge in the poor soul, and form a wall of darkness around him, that heaven's light may not reach him. But if the one in danger perseveres, and in his helplessness casts himself upon the merits of the blood of Christ, our Saviour listens to the earnest prayer of faith, and sends a reinforcement of those angels that excel in strength to deliver him. Satan cannot endure to have his powerful rival appealed to, for he fears and trembles before His strength and majesty. At the sound of fervent prayer, Satan's whole host trembles. He continues to call legions of evil angels to accomplish his object. And when angels, all-powerful, clothed with the armory of heaven, come to the help of the fainting, pursued soul, Satan and his host fall back, well knowing that their battle is lost. The willing subjects of Satan are faithful, active, and united in one object. And although they hate and war with one another, yet they improve every opportunity to advance their common interest. But the great Commander in heaven and earth has limited Satan's power.—(*Testimonies for the Church,* vol. 1, 345, 346.)

SATAN DREADS PRAYER BY THE HUMBLEST SAINT.—There is a mighty power in prayer. Our great adversary is constantly seeking to keep the troubled soul away from God. An appeal to heaven by the humblest saint is more to be dreaded by Satan than the decrees of cabinets or the mandates of kings.—(*SDA Bible Commentary,* vol. 2, 1008.)

PRAYER IS A WEAPON AGAINST SATAN.—Beware how you neglect secret prayer and a study of God's word. These are your weapons against him who is striving to hinder your progress heavenward. The first neglect of prayer and Bible study makes easier the second neglect. The first resistance to the Spirit's pleading prepares the way for the second resistance. Thus the heart is hardened, and the conscience seared.—(*Messages to Young People*, 96.)

PRAYER BREAKS THE SNARE OF SATAN.—When we feel the least inclined to commune with Jesus, let us pray the most. By so doing we shall break Satan's snare, the clouds of darkness will disappear, and we shall realize the sweet presence of Jesus.—(*Lift Him Up*, 372.)

PRAYER PREVAILS AGAINST SATAN.—The prayer of faith is the great strength of the Christian, and will assuredly prevail against Satan. This is why he insinuates that we have no need of prayer. The name of Jesus, our Advocate, he detests; and when we earnestly come to Him for help, Satan's host is alarmed. It serves his purpose well if we neglect the exercise of prayer, for then his lying wonders are more readily received.—(*Testimonies for the Church*, vol. 1, p. 296.)

PRAYER ESPECIALLY NECESSARY AT CRITICAL MOMENTS IN OUR CONFLICT WITH SATAN.—In the conflict with satanic agencies there are decisive moments that determine the victory either on the side of God or on the side of the prince of this world. If those engaged in the warfare are not wide awake, earnest, vigilant, praying for wisdom, watching unto prayer, . . . Satan comes off victor, when he might have been vanquished by the armies of the Lord. . . . God's faithful sentinels are to give the evil powers no advantage.—(*SDA Bible Commentary*, vol. 6, 1094.)

SATAN ENRAGED BY FERVENT PRAYER.—Satan leads many to believe that prayer to God is useless and but a form. He well knows how needful are meditation and prayer to keep Christ's followers aroused to resist his cunning and deception. By his devices he would divert the mind from these important exercises, that the soul may not lean for help upon the Mighty One and obtain strength from Him to resist his attacks. I was pointed to the fervent, effectual prayers of God's people anciently. "Elias was a man subject to like passions as we are, and he prayed earnestly." Daniel prayed unto his God three times a day. Satan is enraged at the sound of fervent prayer, for he knows that he will suffer loss.— (*Testimonies for the Church,* vol. 1, 295.)

SATAN REJOICES WHEN PRAYERS ARE SPOKEN INDISTINCTLY.—Let those who pray and those who speak pronounce their words properly and speak in clear, distinct, even tones. Prayer, if properly offered, is a power for good. It is one of the means used by the Lord to communicate to the people the precious treasures of truth. But prayer is not what it should be, because of the defective voices of those who utter it. Satan rejoices when the prayers offered to God are almost inaudible. Let God's people learn how to speak and pray in a way that will properly represent the great truths they possess. Let the testimonies borne and the prayers offered be clear and distinct. Thus God will be glorified.—(*Testimonies for the Church,* vol. 6, 382.)

SATAN TRIES TO CONVINCE US THAT PRAYER IS NOT NECESSARY.— The idea that prayer is not essential is one of Satan's most successful devices to ruin souls. Prayer is communion with God, the Fountain of wisdom, the Source of strength, and peace, and happiness.—(*Child Guidance,* 518.)

Satan sees the Lord's servants burdened because of the spiritual darkness that enshrouds the people. He hears their earnest prayers for divine grace and power to break the spell of indifference, carelessness, and indolence. Then with renewed zeal he plies his arts. He tempts men to the indulgence of appetite or to some other form of self-gratification, and thus benumbs their sensibilities so that they fail to hear the very things which they most need to learn.

Satan well knows that all whom he can lead to neglect prayer and the searching of the Scriptures, will be overcome by his attacks. Therefore he invents every possible device to engross the mind. There has ever been a class professing godliness, who, instead of following on to know the truth, make it their religion to seek some fault of character or error of faith in those with whom they do not agree. Such are Satan's right-hand helpers. Accusers of the brethren are not few, and they are always active when God is at work and His servants are rendering Him true homage. They will put a false coloring upon the words and acts of those who love and obey the truth. They will represent the most earnest, zealous, self-denying servants of Christ as deceived or deceivers. It is their work to misrepresent the motives of every true and noble deed, to circulate insinuations, and arouse suspicion in the minds of the inexperienced. In every conceivable manner they will seek to cause that which is pure and righteous to be regarded as foul and deceptive.—(*The Great Controversy,* 519.)

CHAPTER

28

Prayer in the Last Days

THOSE LIVING IN THE LAST DAYS ESPECIALLY NEED TO PRAY.—If the Saviour of men, with His divine strength, felt the need of prayer, how much more should feeble, sinful mortals feel the necessity of prayer—fervent, constant prayer! When Christ was the most fiercely beset by temptation, He ate nothing. He committed Himself to God, and through earnest prayer, and perfect submission to the will of His Father, came off conqueror. Those who profess the truth for these last days, above every other class of professed Christians, should imitate the great Exemplar in prayer.—(*Counsels on Diet and Foods,* 52, 53.)

GOD'S PEOPLE HAVE A RESPONSIBILITY TO PRAY FOR A FEW MORE YEARS OF GRACE BEFORE THE END COMES.—There must be more spirituality, a deeper consecration to God, and a zeal in His work that has never yet been reached. Much time should be spent in prayer, that our garments of character may be washed and made white in the blood of the Lamb.

Especially should we, with unwavering faith, seek God for grace and power to be given to His people now. We do not believe that the time has fully come when He would have our liberties restricted.

The prophet saw "four angels standing on the four corners of the earth, holding the four winds of the earth, that the wind should not blow on the earth, nor on the sea, nor on any tree." Another angel, ascending from the east, cried to them, saying: "Hurt not the earth, neither the sea, nor the trees, till we have sealed the servants of our God in their foreheads." This points out the work we have now to do. A vast responsibility is devolving upon men and women of prayer throughout the land to petition that God will sweep back the cloud of evil and give a few more years of grace in which to work for the Master. Let us cry to God that the angels may hold the four winds until missionaries shall be sent to all parts of the world and shall proclaim the warning against disobeying the law of Jehovah.—(*Testimonies for the Church,* vol. 5, 717, 718.)

PRAYER IN TIMES OF PEACE WILL PREPARE GOD'S PEOPLE FOR TIMES OF TROUBLE AT THE END.—The servants of Christ were to prepare no set speech to present when brought to trial. Their preparation was to be made day by day in treasuring up the precious truths of God's word, and through prayer strengthening their faith. When they were brought into trial, the Holy Spirit would bring to their remembrance the very truths that would be needed.

A daily, earnest striving to know God, and Jesus Christ whom He has sent, would bring power and efficiency to the soul. The knowledge obtained by diligent searching of the Scriptures would be flashed into the memory at the right time. But if any had neglected to acquaint themselves with the words of Christ, if they had never tested the power of His grace in trial, they could not expect that the Holy Spirit would bring His words to their remembrance. They were to serve God daily with undivided affection, and then trust Him.—(*The Desire of Ages,* 355.)

We are living in the most solemn period of this world's history. The destiny of earth's teeming multitudes is about to be decided. Our own future well-being, and also the salvation of other souls, depend upon the course which we now pursue. We need to be guided by the Spirit of truth. Every follower of Christ should earnestly inquire, "Lord, what wilt Thou have me to do?" We need to humble ourselves before the Lord, with fasting and prayer, and to meditate much upon His Word, especially upon the scenes of the judgment. We should now seek a deep and living experience in the things of God. We have not a moment to lose. Events of vital importance are taking place around us; we are on Satan's enchanted ground.—(*The Great Controversy*, 601.)

The season of distress and anguish before us will require a faith that can endure weariness, delay, and hunger—a faith that will not faint though severely tried. The period of probation is granted to all to prepare for that time. Jacob prevailed because he was persevering and determined. His victory is an evidence of the power of importunate prayer. All who will lay hold of God's promises, as he did, and be as earnest and persevering as he was, will succeed as he succeeded. Those who are unwilling to deny self, to agonize before God, to pray long and earnestly for His blessing, will not obtain it. Wrestling with God—how few know what it is! How few have ever had their souls drawn out after God with intensity of desire until every power is on the stretch. When waves of despair which no language can express sweep over the suppliant, how few cling with unyielding faith to the promises of God.—(*The Great Controversy*, 621.)

PRAYER TO BE A SAFEGUARD UNTIL THE END.—Till the conflict is ended, there will be those who will depart from God. Satan will so shape circumstances that unless we are kept by divine power, they will almost imperceptibly weaken the fortifications of the soul. We need to inquire at every step, "Is this the way of the Lord?" So long as life shall last, there will be need of guarding the affections and the passions with a firm purpose. Not one moment can we be secure except as we rely upon God, the life hidden with Christ. Watchfulness and prayer are the safeguards of purity.

All who enter the City of God will enter through the strait gate— by agonizing effort; for "there shall in no wise enter into it anything that defileth." Revelation 21:27. But none who have fallen need give up to despair. Aged men, once honored of God, may have defiled their souls, sacrificing virtue on the altar of lust; but if they repent, forsake sin, and turn to God, there is still hope for them. He who declares, "Be thou faithful unto death, and I will give thee a crown of life," also gives the invitation, "Let the wicked forsake his way, and the unrighteous man his thoughts: and let him return unto the Lord, and He will have mercy upon him; and to our God, for He will abundantly pardon." Revelation 2:10; Isaiah 55:7. God hates sin, but He loves the sinner. "I will heal their backsliding," He declares; "I will love them freely." Hosea 14:4.—(*Prophets and Kings,* 83, 84.)

A SMALL GROUP WILL BE PRAYING FOR THE CHURCH IN THE TIME OF HER GREATEST DANGER.—The leaven of godliness has not entirely lost its power. At the time when the danger and depression of the church are greatest, the little company who are standing in the light will be sighing and crying for the abominations that are done in the land. But more especially will their prayers arise in behalf of the church because its members are doing after the manner of the world.

The earnest prayers of this faithful few will not be in vain. When the Lord comes forth as an avenger, He will also come as a protector of all those who have preserved the faith in its purity and kept themselves unspotted from the world. It is at this time that God has promised to avenge His own elect which cry day and night unto Him, though He bear long with them.—(*Testimonies for the Church,* vol. 5, 209, 210.)

PRAY FOR THE SPIRIT IN THE TIME OF THE LATTER RAIN.—We cannot depend upon form or external machinery. What we need is the quickening influence of the Holy Spirit of God. "Not by might, nor by power, but by my Spirit, saith the Lord of Hosts." Pray without ceasing, and watch by working in accordance with your prayers. As you pray, believe, trust in God. It is the time of the latter rain, when the Lord will give largely of his Spirit. Be fervent in prayer, and watch in the Spirit.—(*Review and Herald,* March 2, 1897.)

PRAYER THE CHRISTIAN'S ONLY SAFETY AT THE END.—I saw some, with strong faith and agonizing cries, pleading with God. Their countenances were pale and marked with deep anxiety, expressive of their internal struggle. Firmness and great earnestness was expressed in their countenances; large drops of perspiration fell from their foreheads. Now and then their faces would light up with the marks of God's approbation, and again the same solemn, earnest, anxious look would settle upon them.

Evil angels crowded around, pressing darkness upon them to shut out Jesus from their view, that their eyes might be drawn to the darkness that surrounded them, and thus they be led to distrust God and murmur against Him. Their only safety was in keeping their eyes directed upward. Angels of God had charge over His people, and as the poisonous atmosphere of evil angels was pressed around these anxious ones, the heavenly angels were continually wafting their wings over them to scatter the thick darkness.

As the praying ones continued their earnest cries, at times a ray of light from Jesus came to them, to encourage their hearts and light up their countenances. Some, I saw, did not participate in this work of agonizing and pleading. They seemed indifferent and careless. They were not resisting the darkness around them, and it shut them in like a thick cloud. The angels of God left these and went to the aid of the earnest, praying ones. I saw angels of God hasten to the assistance of all who were struggling with all their power to resist the evil angels and trying to help themselves by calling upon God with perseverance. But His angels left those who made no effort to help themselves, and I lost sight of them.—(*Early Writings,* 269, 270.)

GOD'S PEOPLE WILL PRAY AND PREVAIL AT THE END AS DID JACOB.— Jacob and Esau represent two classes; Jacob the righteous, and Esau the wicked. Jacob's distress when he learned that Esau was marching against him with four hundred men, represents the trouble of the righteous as the decree goes forth to put them to death, just before the coming of the Lord. As the wicked gather about them they will be filled with anguish, for like Jacob they can see no escape for their lives. The angel placed himself before Jacob, and he took hold of the angel and held him, and wrestled with him all night. So also will the righteous, in their time of trouble and anguish, wrestle in prayer with God, as Jacob wrestled with the angel. Jacob in his distress prayed all night for deliverance from the hand of Esau. The righteous in their mental anguish will cry to God day and night for deliverance from the hand of the wicked who surround them.

Jacob confessed his unworthiness. "I am not worthy of the least of all thy mercies, and of all the truth which thou hast showed unto thy servant." The righteous, in their distress, will have a deep sense of their unworthiness, and with many tears will acknowledge their utter unworthiness, and like Jacob will plead the promises of God through Christ, made to just such dependent, helpless, repenting sinners.

Jacob took firm hold of the angel in his distress, and would not let him go. As he made supplication with tears, the angel reminded him of his past wrongs, and endeavored to escape from Jacob, to test him and prove him. So will the righteous, in the day of their anguish, be tested, proved, and tried, to manifest their strength of faith, their perseverance and unshaken confidence in the power of God to deliver them.

Jacob would not be turned away. He knew that God was merciful, and he appealed to His mercy. He pointed back to his past sorrow and repentance of his wrongs, and urged his petition for deliverance from the hand of Esau. Thus his importuning continued all night. As he reviewed his past wrongs, he was driven almost to despair. But he knew that he must have help from God or perish. He held fast the angel, and urged his petition with agonizing, earnest cries, until he prevailed. Thus will it be with the righteous. As they review the events of their past life, their hopes will almost sink. But as they realize that it is a case of life or death, they will earnestly cry unto God, and appeal to Him in regard to their past sorrow and humble repentance of their many sins, and then will refer to His promise, "Let him take hold of My strength, and make peace with Me, and he shall make peace with Me." Thus will their earnest petitions be offered to God day and night.—(*Spiritual Gifts*, vol. 3, 131-133.)

29

The Privilege
of Prayer*

Through nature and revelation, through His providence, and by the influence of His Spirit, God speaks to us. But these are not enough; we need also to pour out our hearts to Him. In order to have spiritual life and energy, we must have actual intercourse with our heavenly Father. Our minds may be drawn out toward Him; we may meditate upon His works, His mercies, His blessings; but this is not, in the fullest sense, communing with Him. In order to commune with God, we must have something to say to Him concerning our actual life.

Prayer is the opening of the heart to God as to a friend. Not that it is necessary in order to make known to God what we are, but in order to enable us to receive Him. Prayer does not bring God down to us, but brings us up to Him.

When Jesus was upon the earth, He taught His disciples how to pray. He directed them to present their daily needs before God, and to cast all their care upon Him. And the assurance He gave them that their petitions should be heard, is assurance also to us.

Jesus Himself, while He dwelt among men, was often in prayer. Our Saviour identified Himself with our needs and weakness, in that He became a suppliant, a petitioner, seeking from His Father fresh supplies of strength, that He might come forth braced for duty and trial. He is our example in all things. He is a brother in our infirmities, "in all points tempted like as we are;" but as the sinless one His nature recoiled from evil; He endured struggles and torture of soul in a world of sin. His humanity made prayer a necessity and a privilege. He found comfort and joy in communion with His Father. And if the Saviour of men, the Son of God, felt the need of prayer, how much more should feeble, sinful mortals feel the necessity of fervent, constant prayer.

Our heavenly Father waits to bestow upon us the fullness of His blessing. It is our privilege to drink largely at the fountain of boundless love. What a wonder it is that we pray so little! God is ready and willing to hear the sincere prayer of the humblest of His children, and yet there is much manifest reluctance on our part to make known our wants to God. What can the angels of heaven think of poor helpless human beings, who are subject to temptation, when God's heart of infinite love yearns toward them, ready to give them more than they can ask or think, and yet they pray so little and have so little faith? The angels love to bow before God; they love to be near Him. They regard communion with God as their highest joy; and yet the children of earth, who need so much the help that God only can give, seem satisfied to walk without the light of His Spirit, the companionship of His presence.

The darkness of the evil one encloses those who neglect to pray. The whispered temptations of the enemy entice them to sin; and it is all because they do not make use of the privileges that God has given them in the divine appointment of prayer. Why should the sons and daughters of God be reluctant to pray, when prayer is the key in the hand of faith to unlock heaven's storehouse, where are treasured the boundless resources of Omnipotence? Without unceasing prayer and diligent watching we are in danger of growing careless and of deviating from the right path. The adversary seeks continually to obstruct the way to the mercy seat, that we may not by earnest supplication and faith obtain grace and power to resist temptation.

There are certain conditions upon which we may expect that God will hear and answer our prayers. One of the first of these is that we feel our need of help from Him. He has promised, "I will pour water upon him that is thirsty, and floods upon the dry ground." Isaiah 44:3. Those who hunger and thirst after righteousness, who long after God, may be sure that they will be filled. The heart must be open to the Spirit's influence, or God's blessing cannot be received.

Our great need is itself an argument and pleads most eloquently in our behalf. But the Lord is to be sought unto to do these things for us. He says, "Ask, and it shall be given you." And "He that spared not His own Son, but delivered Him up for us all, how shall He not with Him also freely give us all things?" Matthew 7:7; Romans 8:32.

If we regard iniquity in our hearts, if we cling to any known sin, the Lord will not hear us; but the prayer of the penitent, contrite soul is always accepted. When all known wrongs are righted, we may believe that God will answer our petitions. Our own merit will never commend us to the favor of God; it is the worthiness of Jesus that will save us, His blood that will cleanse us; yet we have a work to do in complying with the conditions of acceptance.

Another element of prevailing prayer is faith. "He that cometh to God must believe that He is, and that He is a rewarder of them that diligently seek Him." Hebrews 11:6. Jesus said to His disciples, "What things soever ye desire, when ye pray, believe that ye receive them, and ye shall have them." Mark 11:24. Do we take Him at His word?

The assurance is broad and unlimited, and He is faithful who has promised. When we do not receive the very things we asked for, at the time we ask, we are still to believe that the Lord hears and that He will answer our prayers. We are so erring and short-sighted that we sometimes ask for things that would not be a blessing to us, and our heavenly Father in love answers our prayers by giving us that which will be for our highest good—that which we ourselves would desire if with vision divinely enlightened we could see all things as they really are. When our prayers seem not to be answered, we are to cling to the promise; for the time of answering will surely come, and we shall receive the blessing we need most. But to claim that prayer will always be answered in the very way and for the particular thing that we desire, is presumption. God is too wise to err, and too good to withhold any good thing from them that walk uprightly. Then do not fear to trust Him, even though you do not see the immediate answer to your prayers. Rely upon His sure promise, "Ask, and it shall be given you."

If we take counsel with our doubts and fears, or try to solve everything that we cannot see clearly, before we have faith, perplexities will only increase and deepen. But if we come to God, feeling helpless and dependent, as we really are, and in humble, trusting faith make known our wants to Him whose knowledge is infinite, who sees everything in creation, and who governs everything by His will and word, He can and will attend to our cry, and will let light shine into our hearts. Through sincere prayer we are brought into connection with the mind of the Infinite. We may have no remarkable evidence at the time that the face of our Redeemer is bending over us in compassion and love, but this is even so. We may not feel His visible touch, but His hand is upon us in love and pitying tenderness.

When we come to ask mercy and blessing from God we should have a spirit of love and forgiveness in our own hearts. How can we pray, "Forgive us our debts, as we forgive our debtors," and yet indulge an unforgiving spirit? Matthew 6:12. If we expect our own prayers to be heard we must forgive others in the same manner and to the same extent as we hope to be forgiven.

Perseverance in prayer has been made a condition of receiving. We must pray always if we would grow in faith and experience. We are to be "instant in prayer," to "continue in prayer, and watch in the same with thanksgiving." Romans 12:12; Colossians 4:2. Peter exhorts believers to be "sober, and watch unto prayer." 1 Peter 4:7. Paul directs, "In everything by prayer and supplication with thanksgiving let your requests be made known unto God."

Philippians 4:6. "But ye, beloved," says Jude, "praying in the Holy Ghost, keep yourselves in the love of God." Jude 20, 21. Unceasing prayer is the unbroken union of the soul with God, so that life from God flows into our life; and from our life, purity and holiness flow back to God.

There is necessity for diligence in prayer; let nothing hinder you. Make every effort to keep open the communion between Jesus and your own soul. Seek every opportunity to go where prayer is wont to be made. Those who are really seeking for communion with God will be seen in the prayer meeting, faithful to do their duty and earnest and anxious to reap all the benefits they can gain. They will improve every opportunity of placing themselves where they can receive the rays of light from heaven.

We should pray in the family circle, and above all we must not neglect secret prayer, for this is the life of the soul. It is impossible for the soul to flourish while prayer is neglected. Family or public prayer alone is not sufficient. In solitude let the soul be laid open to the inspecting eye of God. Secret prayer is to be heard only by the prayer-hearing God. No curious ear is to receive the burden of such petitions. In secret prayer the soul is free from surrounding influences, free from excitement. Calmly, yet fervently, will it reach out after God. Sweet and abiding will be the influence emanating from Him who seeth in secret, whose ear is open to hear the prayer arising from the heart. By calm, simple faith the soul holds communion with God and gathers to itself rays of divine light to strengthen and sustain it in the conflict with Satan. God is our tower of strength.

Pray in your closet, and as you go about your daily labor let your heart be often uplifted to God. It was thus that Enoch walked with God. These silent prayers rise like precious incense before the throne of grace. Satan cannot overcome him whose heart is thus stayed upon God.

There is no time or place in which it is inappropriate to offer up a petition to God. There is nothing that can prevent us from lifting up our hearts in the spirit of earnest prayer. In the crowds of the street, in the midst of a business engagement, we may send up a petition to God and plead for divine guidance, as did Nehemiah when he made his request before King Artaxerxes. A closet of communion may be found wherever we are. We should have the door of the heart open continually and our invitation going up that Jesus may come and abide as a heavenly guest in the soul.

Although there may be a tainted, corrupted atmosphere around us, we need not breathe its miasma, but may live in the pure air of heaven. We may close every door to impure imaginings and unholy thoughts by lifting the soul into the presence of God through sincere prayer. Those whose hearts are open to receive the support and blessing of God will walk in a holier atmosphere than that of earth and will have constant communion with heaven.

We need to have more distinct views of Jesus and a fuller comprehension of the value of eternal realities. The beauty of holiness is to fill the hearts of God's children; and that this may be accomplished, we should seek for divine disclosures of heavenly things.

Let the soul be drawn out and upward, that God may grant us a breath of the heavenly atmosphere. We may keep so near to God that in every unexpected trial our thoughts will turn to Him as naturally as the flower turns to the sun.

Keep your wants, your joys, your sorrows, your cares, and your fears before God. You cannot burden Him; you cannot weary Him. He who numbers the hairs of your head is not indifferent to the wants of His children. "The Lord is very pitiful, and of tender mercy." James 5:11. His heart of love is touched by our sorrows and even by our utterances of them. Take to Him everything that perplexes the mind. Nothing is too great for Him to bear, for He holds up worlds, He rules over all the affairs of the universe. Nothing that in any way concerns our peace is too small for Him to notice. There is no chapter in our experience too dark for Him to read; there is no perplexity too difficult for Him to unravel. No calamity can befall the least of His children, no anxiety harass the soul, no joy cheer, no sincere prayer escape the lips, of which our heavenly Father is unobservant, or in which He takes no immediate interest. "He healeth the broken in heart, and bindeth up their wounds." Psalm 147:3. The relations between God and each soul are as distinct and full as though there were not another soul upon the earth to share His watchcare, not another soul for whom He gave His beloved Son.

Jesus said, "Ye shall ask in My name: and I say not unto you, that I will pray the Father for you: for the Father Himself loveth you." "I have chosen you: . . . that whatsoever ye shall ask of the Father in My name, He may give it you." John 16:26, 27; 15:16. But to pray in the name of Jesus is something more than a mere mention of that name at the beginning and the ending of a prayer. It is to pray in the mind and spirit of Jesus, while we believe His promises, rely upon His grace, and work His works.

God does not mean that any of us should become hermits or monks and retire from the world in order to devote ourselves to acts of worship. The life must be like Christ's life—between the mountain and the multitude. He who does nothing but pray will soon cease to pray, or his prayers will become a formal routine. When men take themselves out of social life, away from the sphere of Christian duty and cross bearing; when they cease to work earnestly for the Master, who worked earnestly for them, they lose the subject matter of prayer and have no incentive to devotion. Their prayers become personal and selfish. They cannot pray in regard to the wants of humanity or the upbuilding of Christ's kingdom, pleading for strength wherewith to work.

We sustain a loss when we neglect the privilege of associating together to strengthen and encourage one another in the service of God. The truths of His word lose their vividness and importance in our minds. Our hearts cease to be enlightened and aroused by their sanctifying influence, and we decline in spirituality. In our association as Christians we lose much by lack of sympathy with one another. He who shuts himself up to himself is not filling the position that God designed he should. The proper cultivation of the social elements in our nature brings us into sympathy with others and is a means of development and strength to us in the service of God.

If Christians would associate together, speaking to each other of the love of God and of the precious truths of redemption, their own hearts would be refreshed and they would refresh one another. We may be daily learning more of our heavenly Father, gaining a fresh experience of His grace; then we shall desire to speak of His love; and as we do this, our own hearts will be warmed and encouraged. If we thought and talked more of Jesus, and less of self, we should have far more of His presence.

If we would but think of God as often as we have evidence of His care for us we should keep Him ever in our thoughts and should delight to talk of Him and to praise Him. We talk of temporal things because we have an interest in them. We talk of our friends because we love them; our joys and our sorrows are bound up with them. Yet we have infinitely greater reason to love God than to love our earthly friends; it should be the most natural thing in the world to make Him first in all our thoughts, to talk of His goodness and tell of His power. The rich gifts He has bestowed upon us were not intended to absorb our thoughts and love so much that we should have nothing to give to God; they are constantly to remind us of Him and to bind us in bonds of love and gratitude to our heavenly Benefactor. We dwell too near the lowlands of earth. Let us raise our eyes to the open door of the sanctuary above, where the light of the glory of God shines in the face of Christ, who "is able also to save them to the uttermost that come unto God by Him." Hebrews 7:25.

We need to praise God more "for His goodness, and for His wonderful works to the children of men." Psalm 107:8. Our devotional exercises should not consist wholly in asking and receiving. Let us not be always thinking of our wants and never of the benefits we receive. We do not pray any too much, but we are too sparing of giving thanks. We are the constant recipients of God's mercies, and yet how little gratitude we express, how little we praise Him for what He has done for us.

Anciently the Lord bade Israel, when they met together for His service, "Ye shall eat before the Lord your God, and ye shall rejoice in all that ye put your hand unto, ye and your households, wherein the Lord thy God hath blessed thee." Deuteronomy 12:7. That which is done for the glory of God should be done with cheerfulness, with songs of praise and thanksgiving, not with sadness and gloom.

Our God is a tender, merciful Father. His service should not be looked upon as a heart-saddening, distressing exercise. It should be a pleasure to worship the Lord and to take part in His work. God would not have His children, for whom so great salvation has been provided, act as if He were a hard, exacting taskmaster. He is their best friend; and when they worship Him, He expects to be with them, to bless and comfort them, filling their hearts with joy and love. The Lord desires His children to take comfort in His service and to find more pleasure than hardship in His work. He desires that those who come to worship Him shall carry away with them precious thoughts of His care and love, that they may be cheered in all the employments of daily life, that they may have grace to deal honestly and faithfully in all things.

We must gather about the cross. Christ and Him crucified should be the theme of contemplation, of conversation, and of our most joyful emotion. We should keep in our thoughts every blessing we receive from God, and when we realize His great love we should be willing to trust everything to the hand that was nailed to the cross for us.

The soul may ascend nearer heaven on the wings of praise. God is worshiped with song and music in the courts above, and as we express our gratitude we are approximating to the worship of the heavenly hosts. "Whoso offereth praise glorifieth" God. Psalm 50:23. Let us with reverent joy come before our Creator, with "thanksgiving, and the voice of melody." Isaiah 51:3.

---

*[This chapter appears in *Steps to Christ* pages, 93-104.]

CHAPTER

30

The Lord's
Prayer*

"After this manner therefore pray ye."
Matthew 6:9.

The Lord's Prayer was twice given by our Saviour, first to the multitude in the Sermon on the Mount, and again, some months later, to the disciples alone. The disciples had been for a short time absent from their Lord, when on their return they found Him absorbed in communion with God. Seeming unconscious of their presence, He continued praying aloud. The Saviour's face was irradiated with a celestial brightness. He seemed to be in the very presence of the Unseen, and there was a living power in His words as of one who spoke with God.

The hearts of the listening disciples were deeply moved. They had marked how often He spent long hours in solitude in communion with His Father. His days were passed in ministry to the crowds that pressed upon Him, and in unveiling the treacherous sophistry of the rabbis, and this incessant labor often left Him so utterly wearied that His mother and brothers, and even His disciples, had feared that His life would be sacrificed. But as He returned from the hours of prayer that closed the toilsome day, they marked the look of peace upon His face, the sense of refreshment that seemed to pervade His presence. It was from hours spent with God that He came forth, morning by morning, to bring the light of heaven to men. The disciples had come to connect His hours of prayer with the power of His words and works. Now, as they listened to His supplication, their hearts were awed and humbled. As He ceased praying, it was with a conviction of their own deep need that they exclaimed, "Lord, teach us to pray." Luke 11:1.

Jesus gives them no new form of prayer. That which He has before taught them He repeats, as if He would say, You need to understand what I have already given. It has a depth of meaning you have not yet fathomed.

The Saviour does not, however, restrict us to the use of these exact words. As one with humanity, He presents His own ideal of prayer, words so simple that they may be adopted by the little child, yet so comprehensive that their significance can never be fully grasped by the greatest minds. We are taught to come to God with our tribute of thanksgiving, to make known our wants, to confess our sins, and to claim His mercy in accordance with His promise.

"When ye pray, say Our Father."
Luke 11:2.

Jesus teaches us to call His Father our Father. He is not ashamed to call us brethren. Hebrews 2:11. So ready, so eager, is the Saviour's heart to welcome us as members of the family of God, that in the very first words we are to use in approaching God He places the assurance of our divine relationship, "Our Father."

Here is the announcement of that wonderful truth, so full of encouragement and comfort, that God loves us as He loves His Son. This is what Jesus said in His last prayer for His disciples, Thou "hast loved them, as Thou hast loved Me." John 17:23.

The world that Satan has claimed and has ruled over with cruel tyranny, the Son of God has, by one vast achievement, encircled in His love and connected again with the throne of Jehovah. Cherubim and seraphim, and the unnumbered hosts of all the unfallen worlds, sang anthems of praise to God and the Lamb when this triumph was assured. They rejoiced that the way of salvation had been opened to the fallen race and that the earth would be redeemed from the curse of sin. How much more should those rejoice who are the objects of such amazing love!

How can we ever be in doubt and uncertainty, and feel that we are orphans? It was in behalf of those who had transgressed the law that Jesus took upon Him human nature; He became like unto us, that we might have everlasting peace and assurance. We have an Advocate in the heavens, and whoever accepts Him as a personal Saviour is not left an orphan to bear the burden of his own sins.

"Beloved, now are we the sons of God." "And if children, then heirs; heirs of God, and joint heirs with Christ; if so be that we suffer with Him, that we may be also glorified together." "It doth not yet appear what we shall be: but we know that, when He shall appear, we shall be like Him; for we shall see Him as He is." 1 John 3:2; Romans 8:17.

The very first step in approaching God is to know and believe the love that He has to us (1 John 4:16); for it is through the drawing of His love that we are led to come to Him.

The perception of God's love works the renunciation of selfishness. In calling God our Father, we recognize all His children as our brethren. We are all a part of the great web of humanity, all members of one family. In our petitions we are to include our neighbors as well as ourselves. No one prays aright who seeks a blessing for himself alone.

The infinite God, said Jesus, makes it your privilege to approach Him by the name of Father. Understand all that this implies. No earthly parent ever pleaded so earnestly with an erring child as He who made you pleads with the transgressor. No human, loving interest ever followed the impenitent with such tender invitations. God dwells in every abode; He hears every word that is spoken, listens to every prayer that is offered, tastes the sorrows and disappointments of every soul, regards the treatment that is given to father, mother, sister, friend, and neighbor. He cares for our necessities, and His love and mercy and grace are continually flowing to satisfy our need.

But if you call God your Father you acknowledge yourselves His children, to be guided by His wisdom and to be obedient in all things, knowing that His love is changeless. You will accept His plan for your life. As children of God, you will hold His honor, His character, His family, His work, as the objects of your highest interest. It will be your joy to recognize and honor your relation to your Father and to every member of His family. You will rejoice to do any act, however humble, that will tend to His glory or to the well-being of your kindred.

"Which art in heaven." He to whom Christ bids us look as "our Father" "is in the heavens: He hath done whatsoever He hath pleased." In His care we may safely rest, saying, "What time I am afraid, I will trust in Thee." Psalms 115:3; 56:3.

"Hallowed be Thy name." Matthew 6:9.

To hallow the name of the Lord requires that the words in which we speak of the Supreme Being be uttered with reverence. "Holy and reverend is His name." Psalm 111:9. We are never in any manner to treat lightly the titles or appellations of the Deity. In prayer we enter the audience chamber of the Most High; and we should come before Him with holy awe. The angels veil their faces in His presence. The cherubim and the bright and holy seraphim approach His throne with solemn reverence. How much more should we, finite, sinful beings, come in a reverent manner before the Lord, our Maker!

But to hallow the name of the Lord means much more than this. We may, like the Jews in Christ's day, manifest the greatest outward reverence for God, and yet profane His name continually. "The name of the Lord" is "merciful and gracious, long-suffering, and abundant in goodness and truth, . . . forgiving iniquity and transgression and sin." Exodus 34:5-7. Of the church of Christ it is written, "This is the name wherewith she shall be called, The Lord our Righteousness." Jeremiah 33:16. This name is put upon every follower of Christ. It is the heritage of the child of God. The family are called after the Father. The prophet Jeremiah, in the time of Israel's sore distress and tribulation, prayed, "We are called by Thy name; leave us not." Jeremiah 14:9.

This name is hallowed by the angels of heaven, by the inhabitants of unfallen worlds. When you pray, "Hallowed be Thy name," you ask that it may be hallowed in this world, hallowed in you. God has acknowledged you before men and angels as His child; pray that you may do no dishonor to the "worthy name by which ye are called." James 2:7. God sends you into the world as His representative. In every act of life you are to make manifest the name of God. This petition calls upon you to possess His character. You cannot hallow His name, you cannot represent Him to the world, unless in life and character you represent the very life and character of God. This you can do only through the acceptance of the grace and righteousness of Christ.

"Thy kingdom come." Matthew 6:10.

God is our Father, who loves and cares for us as His children; He is also the great King of the universe. The interests of His kingdom are our interests, and we are to work for its upbuilding.

The disciples of Christ were looking for the immediate coming of the kingdom of His glory, but in giving them this prayer Jesus taught that the kingdom was not then to be established. They were to pray for its coming as an event yet future. But this petition was also an assurance to them. While they were not to behold the coming of the kingdom in their day, the fact that Jesus bade them pray for it is evidence that in God's own time it will surely come.

The kingdom of God's grace is now being established, as day by day hearts that have been full of sin and rebellion yield to the sovereignty of His love. But the full establishment of the kingdom of His glory will not take place until the second coming of Christ to this world. "The kingdom and dominion, and the greatness of the kingdom under the whole heaven," is to be given to "the people of the saints of the Most High." Daniel 7:27. They shall inherit the kingdom prepared for them "from the foundation of the world." Matthew 25:34. And Christ will take to Himself His great power and will reign.

The heavenly gates are again to be lifted up, and with ten thousand times ten thousand and thousands of thousands of holy ones, our Saviour will come forth as King of kings and Lord of lords. Jehovah Immanuel "shall be king over all the earth: in that day shall there be one Lord, and His name one." "The tabernacle of God" shall be with men, "and He will dwell with them, and they shall be His people, and God Himself shall be with them, and be their God." Zechariah 14:9; Revelation 21:3.

But before that coming, Jesus said, "This gospel of the kingdom shall be preached in all the world for a witness unto all nations." Matthew 24:14. His kingdom will not come until the good tidings of His grace have been carried to all the earth. Hence, as we give ourselves to God, and win other souls to Him, we hasten the coming of His kingdom. Only those who devote themselves to His service, saying, "Here am I; send me" (Isaiah 6:8), to open blind eyes, to turn men "from darkness to light and from the power of Satan unto God, that they may receive forgiveness of sins and inheritance among them which are sanctified" (Acts 26:18)—they alone pray in sincerity, "Thy kingdom come."

*"Thy will be done in earth, as it is
in heaven." Matthew 6:10.*

The will of God is expressed in the precepts of His holy law, and the principles of this law are the principles of heaven. The angels of heaven attain unto no higher knowledge than to know the will of God, and to do His will is the highest service that can engage their powers.

But in heaven, service is not rendered in the spirit of legality. When Satan rebelled against the law of Jehovah, the thought that there was a law came to the angels almost as an awakening to something unthought of. In their ministry the angels are not as servants, but as sons. There is perfect unity between them and their Creator. Obedience is to them no drudgery. Love for God makes their service a joy. So in every soul wherein Christ, the hope of glory, dwells, His words are re-echoed, "I delight to do Thy will, O My God: yea, Thy law is within My heart." Psalm 40:8.

The petition, "Thy will be done in earth, as it is in heaven," is a prayer that the reign of evil on this earth may be ended, that sin may be forever destroyed, and the kingdom of righteousness be established. Then in earth as in heaven will be fulfilled "all the good pleasure of His goodness." 2 Thessalonians 1:11.

"Give us this day our daily bread."
Matthew 6:11.

The first half of the prayer Jesus has taught us is in regard to the name and kingdom and will of God—that His name may be honored, His kingdom established, His will performed. When you have thus made God's service your first interest, you may ask with confidence that your own needs may be supplied. If you have renounced self and given yourself to Christ you are a member of the family of God, and everything in the Father's house is for you. All the treasures of God are opened to you, both the world that now is and that which is to come. The ministry of angels, the gift of His Spirit, the labors of His servants—all are for you. The world, with everything in it, is yours so far as it can do you good. Even the enmity of the wicked will prove a blessing by disciplining you for heaven. If "ye are Christ's," "all things are yours." 1 Corinthians 3:23, 21.

But you are as a child who is not yet placed in control of his inheritance. God does not entrust to you your precious possession, lest Satan by his wily arts should beguile you, as he did the first pair in Eden. Christ holds it for you, safe beyond the spoiler's reach. Like the child, you shall receive day by day what is required for the day's need. Every day you are to pray, "Give us this day our daily bread." Be not dismayed if you have not sufficient for tomorrow. You have the assurance of His promise, "So shalt thou dwell in the land, and verily thou shalt be fed." David says, "I have been young, and now am old; yet have I not seen the righteous forsaken, nor his seed begging bread." Psalm 37:3, 25. That God who sent the ravens to feed Elijah by the brook Cherith will not pass by one of His faithful, self-sacrificing children. Of him that walketh righteously it is written: "Bread shall be given him; his waters shall be sure." "They shall not be ashamed in the evil time: and in the days of famine they shall be satisfied." "He that spared not His own Son, but delivered Him up for us all, how shall He not with Him also freely give us all things?" Isaiah 33:16; Psalm 37:19; Romans 8:32. He who lightened the cares and anxieties of His widowed mother and helped her to provide for the household at Nazareth, sympathizes with every mother in her struggle to provide her children food. He who had compassion on the multitude because they "fainted, and were scattered abroad" (Matthew 9:36), still has compassion on the suffering poor. His hand is stretched out toward them in blessing; and in the very prayer which He gave His disciples, He teaches us to remember the poor.

When we pray, "Give us this day our daily bread," we ask for others as well as ourselves. And we acknowledge that what God gives us is not for ourselves alone. God gives to us in trust, that we may feed the hungry. Of His goodness He has prepared for the poor. Psalm 68:10. And He says, "When thou makest a dinner or a supper, call not thy friends, nor thy brethren, neither thy kinsmen, nor thy rich neighbors. . . . But when thou makest a feast, call the poor, the maimed, the lame, the blind: and thou shalt be blessed; for they cannot recompense thee: for thou shalt be recompensed at the resurrection of the just." Luke 14:12-14.

"God is able to make all grace abound toward you; that ye, always having all sufficiency in all things, may abound to every good work." "He which soweth sparingly shall reap also sparingly; and he which soweth bountifully shall reap also bountifully." 2 Corinthians 9:8, 6.

The prayer for daily bread includes not only food to sustain the body, but that spiritual bread which will nourish the soul unto life everlasting. Jesus bids us, "Labor not for the meat which perisheth, but for that meat which endureth unto everlasting life." John 6:27. He says, "I am the living bread which came down from heaven: if any man eat of this bread, he shall live forever." Verse 51. Our Saviour is the bread of life, and it is by beholding His love, by receiving it into the soul, that we feed upon the bread which came down from heaven.

We receive Christ through His word, and the Holy Spirit is given to open the word of God to our understanding, and bring home its truths to our hearts. We are to pray day by day that as we read His word, God will send His Spirit to reveal to us the truth that will strengthen our souls for the day's need.

In teaching us to ask every day for what we need—both temporal and spiritual blessings—God has a purpose to accomplish for our good. He would have us realize our dependence upon His constant care, for He is seeking to draw us into communion with Himself. In this communion with Christ, through prayer and the study of the great and precious truths of His word, we shall as hungry souls be fed; as those that thirst, we shall be refreshed at the fountain of life.

> *"Forgive us our sins; for we also forgive
> everyone that is indebted
> to us." Luke 11:4.*

Jesus teaches that we can receive forgiveness from God only as we forgive others. It is the love of God that draws us unto Him, and that love cannot touch our hearts without creating love for our brethren.

After completing the Lord's Prayer, Jesus added: "If ye forgive men their trespasses, your heavenly Father will also forgive you: but if ye forgive not men their trespasses, neither will your Father forgive your trespasses." He who is unforgiving cuts off the very channel through which alone he can receive mercy from God. We should not think that unless those who have injured us confess the wrong we are justified in withholding from them our forgiveness. It is their part, no doubt, to humble their hearts by repentance and confession; but we are to have a spirit of compassion toward those who have trespassed against us, whether or not they confess their faults. However sorely they may have wounded us, we are not to cherish our grievances and sympathize with ourselves over our injuries; but as we hope to be pardoned for our offenses against God we are to pardon all who have done evil to us.

But forgiveness has a broader meaning than many suppose. When God gives the promise that He "will abundantly pardon," He adds, as if the meaning of that promise exceeded all that we could comprehend: "My thoughts are not your thoughts, neither are your ways My ways, saith the Lord. For as the heavens are higher than the earth, so are My ways higher than your ways, and My thoughts than your thoughts." Isaiah 55:7-9. God's forgiveness is not merely a judicial act by which He sets us free from condemnation. It is not only forgiveness for sin, but reclaiming from sin. It is the outflow of redeeming love that transforms the heart. David had the true conception of forgiveness when he prayed, "Create in me a clean heart, O God; and renew a right spirit within me." Psalm 51:10. And again he says, "As far as the east is from the west, so far hath He removed our transgressions from us." Psalm 103:12.

God in Christ gave Himself for our sins. He suffered the cruel death of the cross, bore for us the burden of guilt, "the just for the unjust," that He might reveal to us His love and draw us to Himself. And He says, "Be ye kind one to another, tenderhearted, forgiving each other, even as God also in Christ forgave you." Ephesians 4:32, R.V. Let Christ, the divine Life, dwell in you and through you reveal the heaven-born love that will inspire hope in the hopeless and bring heaven's peace to the sin-stricken heart. As we come to God, this is the condition which meets us at the threshold, that, receiving mercy from Him, we yield ourselves to reveal His grace to others.

The one thing essential for us in order that we may receive and impart the forgiving love of God is to know and believe the love that He has to us. 1 John 4:16. Satan is working by every deception he can command, in order that we may not discern that love. He will lead us to think that our mistakes and transgressions have been so grievous that the Lord will not have respect unto our prayers and will not bless and save us. In ourselves we can see nothing but weakness, nothing to recommend us to God, and Satan tells us that it is of no use; we cannot remedy our defects of character. When we try to come to God, the enemy will whisper, It is of no use for you to pray; did not you do that evil thing? Have you not sinned against God and violated your own conscience? But we may tell the enemy that "the blood of Jesus Christ His Son cleanseth us from all sin." 1 John 1:7. When we feel that we have sinned and cannot pray, it is then the time to pray. Ashamed we may be and deeply humbled, but we must pray and believe. "This is a faithful saying, and worthy of all acceptation, that Christ Jesus came into the world to save sinners; of whom I am chief." 1 Timothy 1:15. Forgiveness, reconciliation with God, comes to us, not as a reward for our works, it is not bestowed because of the merit of sinful men, but it is a gift unto us, having in the spotless righteousness of Christ its foundation for bestowal.

We should not try to lessen our guilt by excusing sin. We must accept God's estimate of sin, and that is heavy indeed. Calvary alone can reveal the terrible enormity of sin. If we had to bear our own guilt, it would crush us. But the sinless One has taken our place; though undeserving, He has borne our iniquity. "If we confess our sins," God "is faithful and just to forgive us our sins, and to cleanse us from all unrighteousness." 1 John 1:9. Glorious truth!—just to His own law, and yet the Justifier of all that believe in Jesus. "Who is a God like unto Thee, that pardoneth iniquity, and passeth by the transgression of the remnant of His heritage? He retaineth not His anger forever, because He delighteth in mercy." Micah 7:18.

"Bring us not into temptation, but
deliver us from the evil one."
Matthew 6:13, R.V.

Temptation is enticement to sin, and this does not proceed from God, but from Satan and from the evil of our own hearts. "God cannot be tempted with evil, and He Himself tempteth no man." James 1:13, R.V.

Satan seeks to bring us into temptation, that the evil of our characters may be revealed before men and angels, that he may claim us as his own. In the symbolic prophecy of Zechariah, Satan is seen standing at the right hand of the Angel of the Lord, accusing Joshua, the high priest, who is clothed in filthy garments, and resisting the work that the Angel desires to do for him. This represents the attitude of Satan toward every soul whom Christ is seeking to draw unto Himself. The enemy leads us into sin, and then he accuses us before the heavenly universe as unworthy of the love of God. But "the Lord said unto Satan, The Lord rebuke thee, O Satan; even the Lord that hath chosen Jerusalem rebuke thee: is not this a brand plucked out of the fire?" And unto Joshua He said, "Behold, I have caused thine iniquity to pass from thee, and I will clothe thee with change of raiment." Zechariah 3:1-4.

God in His great love is seeking to develop in us the precious graces of His Spirit. He permits us to encounter obstacles, persecution, and hardships, not as a curse, but as the greatest blessing of our lives. Every temptation resisted, every trial bravely borne, gives us a new experience and advances us in the work of character building. The soul that through divine power resists temptation reveals to the world and to the heavenly universe the efficiency of the grace of Christ.

But while we are not to be dismayed by trial, bitter though it be, we should pray that God will not permit us to be brought where we shall be drawn away by the desires of our own evil hearts. In offering the prayer that Christ has given, we surrender ourselves to the guidance of God, asking Him to lead us in safe paths. We cannot offer this prayer in sincerity, and yet decide to walk in any way of our own choosing. We shall wait for His hand to lead us; we shall listen to His voice, saying, "This is the way, walk ye in it." Isaiah 30:21.

It is not safe for us to linger to contemplate the advantages to be reaped through yielding to Satan's suggestions. Sin means dishonor and disaster to every soul that indulges in it; but it is blinding and deceiving in its nature, and it will entice us with flattering presentations. If we venture on Satan's ground we have no assurance of protection from his power. So far as in us lies, we should close every avenue by which the tempter may find access to us.

The prayer, "Bring us not into temptation," is itself a promise. If we commit ourselves to God we have the assurance, He "will not suffer you to be tempted above that ye are able; but will with the temptation also make a way to escape, that ye may be able to bear it." 1 Corinthians 10:13.

The only safeguard against evil is the indwelling of Christ in the heart through faith in His righteousness. It is because selfishness exists in our hearts that temptation has power over us. But when we behold the great love of God, selfishness appears to us in its hideous and repulsive character, and we desire to have it expelled from the soul. As the Holy Spirit glorifies Christ, our hearts are softened and subdued, the temptation loses its power, and the grace of Christ transforms the character.

Christ will never abandon the soul for whom He has died. The soul may leave Him and be overwhelmed with temptation, but Christ can never turn from one for whom He has paid the ransom of His own life. Could our spiritual vision be quickened, we should see souls bowed under oppression and burdened with grief, pressed as a cart beneath sheaves and ready to die in discouragement. We should see angels flying swiftly to aid these tempted ones, who are standing as on the brink of a precipice. The angels from heaven force back the hosts of evil that encompass these souls, and guide them to plant their feet on the sure foundation. The battles waging between the two armies are as real as those fought by the armies of this world, and on the issue of the spiritual conflict eternal destinies depend.

To us, as to Peter, the word is spoken, "Satan hath desired to have you, that he may sift you as wheat: but I have prayed for thee, that thy faith fail not." Luke 22:31, 32. Thank God, we are not left alone. He who "so loved the world, that He gave His only-begotten Son, that whosoever believeth in Him should not perish,

but have everlasting life" (John 3:16), will not desert us in the
battle with the adversary of God and man. "Behold," He says, "I
give unto you power to tread on serpents and scorpions, and over
all the power of the enemy: and nothing shall by any means hurt
you." Luke 10:19.

Live in contact with the living Christ, and He will hold you
firmly by a hand that will never let go. Know and believe the love
that God has to us, and you are secure; that love is a fortress im-
pregnable to all the delusions and assaults of Satan. "The name of
the Lord is a strong tower: the righteous runneth into it, and is
safe." Proverbs 18:10.

> *"Thine is the kingdom, and the power,*
> *and the glory." Matthew 6:13.*

The last like the first sentence of the Lord's Prayer, points to our
Father as above all power and authority and every name that is named.
The Saviour beheld the years that stretched out before His disciples,
not, as they had dreamed, lying in the sunshine of worldly prosperity
and honor, but dark with the tempests of human hatred and satanic
wrath. Amid national strife and ruin, the steps of the disciples would
be beset with perils, and often their hearts would be oppressed by fear.
They were to see Jerusalem a desolation, the temple swept away, its
worship forever ended, and Israel scattered to all lands, like wrecks on
a desert shore. Jesus said, "Ye shall hear of wars and rumors of wars."
"Nation shall rise against nation, and kingdom against kingdom: and
there shall be famines, and pestilences, and earthquakes, in divers
places. All these are the beginning of sorrows." Matthew 24:6-8. Yet
Christ's followers were not to fear that their hope was lost or that God
had forsaken the earth. The power and the glory belong unto Him
whose great purposes would still move on unthwarted toward their
consummation. In the prayer that breathes their daily wants, the disciples of Christ were directed to look above all the power and dominion of evil, unto the Lord their God, whose kingdom ruleth over all
and who is their Father and everlasting Friend.

The ruin of Jerusalem was a symbol of the final ruin that shall overwhelm the world. The prophecies that received a partial fulfillment in the overthrow of Jerusalem have a more direct application to the last days. We are now standing on the threshold of great and solemn events. A crisis is before us, such as the world has never witnessed. And sweetly to us, as to the first disciples, comes the assurance that God's kingdom ruleth over all. The program of coming events is in the hands of our Maker. The Majesty of heaven has the destiny of nations, as well as the concerns of His church, in His own charge. The divine Instructor is saying to every agent in the accomplishment of His plans, as He said to Cyrus, "I girded thee, though thou hast not known Me." Isaiah 45:5.

In the vision of the prophet Ezekiel there was the appearance of a hand beneath the wings of the cherubim. This is to teach His servants that it is divine power which gives them success. Those whom God employs as His messengers are not to feel that His work is dependent upon them. Finite beings are not left to carry this burden of responsibility. He who slumbers not, who is continually at work for the accomplishment of His designs, will carry forward His own work. He will thwart the purposes of wicked men, and will bring to confusion the counsels of those who plot mischief against His people. He who is the King, the Lord of hosts, sitteth between the cherubim, and amid the strife and tumult of nations He guards His children still. He who ruleth in the heavens is our Saviour. He measures every trial, He watches the furnace fire that must test every soul. When the strongholds of kings shall be overthrown, when the arrows of wrath shall strike through the hearts of His enemies, His people will be safe in His hands.

"Thine, O Lord, is the greatness, and the power, and the glory, and the victory, and the majesty: for all that is in the heaven and in the earth is Thine. . . . In Thine hand is power and might; and in Thine hand it is to make great, and to give strength unto all." 1 Chronicles 29:11, 12.

---

*[This chapter appears in *Thoughts From the Mount of Blessing,* pages 102-122.]

31

Asking to Give*

Christ was continually receiving from the Father that He might communicate to us. "The word which ye hear," He said, "is not Mine, but the Father's which sent Me." John 14:24. "The Son of man came not to be ministered unto, but to minister." Matt. 20:28. Not for Himself, but for others, He lived and thought and prayed. From hours spent with God He came forth morning by morning, to bring the light of heaven to men. Daily He received a fresh baptism of the Holy Spirit. In the early hours of the new day the Lord awakened Him from His slumbers, and His soul and His lips were anointed with grace, that He might impart to others. His words were given Him fresh from the heavenly courts, words that He might speak in season to the weary and oppressed. "The Lord God hath given Me," He said, "the tongue of the learned, that I should know how to speak a word in season to him that is weary: He wakeneth morning by morning, He wakeneth Mine ear to hear as the learned." Isa. 50:4.

Christ's disciples were much impressed by His prayers and by His habit of communion with God. One day after a short absence from their Lord, they found Him absorbed in supplication. Seeming unconscious of their presence, He continued praying aloud. The hearts of the disciples were deeply moved. As He ceased praying, they exclaimed, "Lord, teach us to pray."

In answer, Christ repeated the Lord's prayer, as He had given it in the sermon on the mount. Then in a parable He illustrated the lesson He desired to teach them.

"Which of you," He said, "shall have a friend, and shall go unto him at midnight, and say unto him, Friend, lend me three loaves; for a friend of mine in his journey is come to me, and I have nothing to set before him? And he from within shall answer and say, Trouble me not; the door is now shut, and my children are with me in bed: I cannot rise and give thee. I say unto you, Though he will not rise and give him because he is his friend, yet because of his importunity he will rise and give him as many as he needeth."

Here Christ represents the petitioner as asking that he may give again. He must obtain the bread, else he cannot supply the necessities of a weary, belated wayfarer. Though his neighbor is unwilling to be troubled, he will not desist his pleading; his friend must be relieved; and at last his importunity is rewarded, his wants are supplied.

In like manner the disciples were to seek blessings from God. In the feeding of the multitude and in the sermon on the bread from heaven, Christ had opened to them their work as His representatives. They were to give the bread of life to the people. He who had appointed their work, saw how often their faith would be tried. Often they would be thrown into unexpected positions, and would realize their human insufficiency. Souls that were hungering for the bread of life would come to them, and they would feel themselves to be destitute and helpless. They must receive spiritual food, or they would have nothing to impart. But they were not to turn one soul away unfed. Christ directs them to the source of supply. The man whose friend came to him for entertainment, even at the unseasonable hour of midnight, did not turn him away. He had nothing to set before him, but he went to one who had food and pressed his request until the neighbor supplied his need. And would not God, who had sent His servants to feed the hungry, supply their need for His own work?

But the selfish neighbor in the parable does not represent the character of God. The lesson is drawn, not by comparison, but by contrast. A selfish man will grant an urgent request, in order to rid himself of one who disturbs his rest. But God delights to give. He is full of compassion, and He longs to grant the requests of those who come unto Him in faith. He gives to us that we may minister to others and thus become like Himself.

Christ declares, "Ask, and it shall be given you; seek, and ye shall find; knock, and it shall be opened unto you. For every one that asketh receiveth; and he that seeketh findeth; and to him that knocketh it shall be opened."

The Saviour continues: "If a son shall ask bread of any of you that is a father, will he give him a stone? or if he ask a fish, will he for a fish give him a serpent? or if he shall ask an egg, will he offer him a scorpion? If ye then, being evil, know how to give good gifts unto your children, how much more shall your heavenly Father give the Holy Spirit to them that ask Him?"

In order to strengthen our confidence in God, Christ teaches us to address Him by a new name, a name entwined with the dearest associations of the human heart. He gives us the privilege of calling the infinite God our Father. This name, spoken to Him and of Him, is a sign of our love and trust toward Him, and a pledge of His regard and relationship to us. Spoken when asking His favor or blessing, it is as music in His ears. That we might not think it presumption to call Him by this name, He has repeated it again and again. He desires us to become familiar with the appellation.

God regards us as His children. He has redeemed us out of the careless world and has chosen us to become members of the royal family, sons and daughters of the heavenly King. He invites us to trust in Him with a trust deeper and stronger than that of a child in his earthly father. Parents love their children, but the love of

God is larger, broader, deeper, than human love can possibly be. It is immeasurable. Then if earthly parents know how to give good gifts to their children, how much more shall our Father in heaven give the Holy Spirit to those who ask Him?

Christ's lessons in regard to prayer should be carefully considered. There is a divine science in prayer, and His illustration brings to view principles that all need to understand. He shows what is the true spirit of prayer, He teaches the necessity of perseverance in presenting our requests to God, and assures us of His willingness to hear and answer prayer.

Our prayers are not to be a selfish asking, merely for our own benefit. We are to ask that we may give. The principle of Christ's life must be the principle of our lives. "For their sakes," He said, speaking of His disciples, "I sanctify Myself, that they also might be sanctified." John 17:19. The same devotion, the same self-sacrifice, the same subjection to the claims of the word of God, that were manifest in Christ, must be seen in His servants. Our mission to the world is not to serve or please ourselves; we are to glorify God by co-operating with Him to save sinners. We are to ask blessings from God that we may communicate to others. The capacity for receiving is preserved only by imparting. We cannot continue to receive heavenly treasure without communicating to those around us.

In the parable the petitioner was again and again repulsed, but he did not relinquish his purpose. So our prayers do not always seem to receive an immediate answer; but Christ teaches that we should not cease to pray. Prayer is not to work any change in God; it is to bring us into harmony with God. When we make request of Him, He may see that it is necessary for us to search our hearts and repent of sin. Therefore He takes us through test and trial, He brings us through humiliation, that we may see what hinders the working of His Holy Spirit through us.

There are conditions to the fulfillment of God's promises, and prayer can never take the place of duty. "If ye love Me," Christ says, "Keep My commandments." "He that hath My commandments, and keepeth them, he it is that loveth Me; and he that loveth Me shall be loved of My Father, and I will love him, and will manifest Myself to him." John 14:15, 21. Those who bring their petitions to God, claiming His promise while they do not comply with the conditions, insult Jehovah. They bring the name of Christ as their authority for the fulfillment of the promise, but they do not those things that would show faith in Christ and love for Him.

Many are forfeiting the condition of acceptance with the Father. We need to examine closely the deed of trust wherewith we approach God. If we are disobedient, we bring to the Lord a note to be cashed when we have not fulfilled the conditions that would make it payable to us. We present to God His promises, and ask Him to fulfill them, when by so doing He would dishonor His own name.

The promise is "If ye abide in Me, and My words abide in you, ye shall ask what ye will, and it shall be done unto you." John 15:7. And John declares: "Hereby we do know that we know Him, if we keep His commandments. He that saith, I know Him, and keepeth not His commandments, is a liar, and the truth is not in him. But whoso keepeth His word, in him verily is the love of God perfected." 1 John 2:3-5.

One of Christ's last commands to His disciples was "Love one another as I have loved you." John 13:34. Do we obey this command, or are we indulging sharp, unchristlike traits of character? If we have in any way grieved or wounded others, it is our duty to confess our fault and seek for reconciliation. This is an essential preparation that we may come before God in faith, to ask His blessing.

There is another matter too often neglected by those who seek the Lord in prayer. Have you been honest with God? By the prophet Malachi the Lord declares, "Even from the days of your fathers ye are gone away from Mine ordinances, and have not kept them. Return unto Me, and I will return unto you, saith the Lord of hosts. But ye said, Wherein shall we return? Will a man rob God?

Yet ye have robbed Me. But ye say, Wherein have we robbed Thee? In tithes and offerings." Mal. 3:7, 8.

As the Giver of every blessing, God claims a certain portion of all we possess. This is His provision to sustain the preaching of the gospel. And by making this return to God, we are to show our appreciation of His gifts. But if we withhold from Him that which is His own, how can we claim His blessing? If we are unfaithful stewards of earthly things, how can we expect Him to entrust us with the things of heaven? It may be that here is the secret of unanswered prayer.

But the Lord in His great mercy is ready to forgive, and He says, "Bring ye all the tithes into the storehouse, that there may be meat in Mine house, and prove Me now herewith, . . . if I will not open you the windows of heaven, and pour you out a blessing, that there shall not be room enough to receive it. And I will rebuke the devourer for your sakes, and he shall not destroy the fruits of your ground; neither shall your vine cast her fruit before the time in the field. . . . And all nations shall call you blessed; for ye shall be a delightsome land, saith the Lord of hosts." Mal. 3:10-12.

So it is with every other one of God's requirements. All His gifts are promised on condition of obedience. God has a heaven full of blessings for those who will co-operate with Him. All who obey Him may with confidence claim the fulfillment of His promises.

But we must show a firm, undeviating trust in God. Often He delays to answer us in order to try our faith or test the genuineness of our desire. Having asked according to His word, we should believe His promise and press our petitions with a determination that will not be denied.

God does not say, Ask once, and you shall receive. He bids us ask. Unwearyingly persist in prayer. The persistent asking brings the petitioner into a more earnest attitude, and gives him an increased desire to receive the things for which he asks. Christ said to Martha at the grave of Lazarus, "If thou wouldest believe, thou shouldest see the glory of God." John 11:40.

But many have not a living faith. This is why they do not see more of the power of God. Their weakness is the result of their unbelief. They have more faith in their own working than in the working of God for them. They take themselves into their own keeping. They plan and devise, but pray little, and have little real trust in God. They think they have faith, but it is only the impulse of the moment. Failing to realize their own need, or God's willingness to give, they do not persevere in keeping their requests before the Lord.

Our prayers are to be as earnest and persistent as was the petition of the needy friend who asked for the loaves at midnight. The more earnestly and steadfastly we ask, the closer will be our spiritual union with Christ. We shall receive increased blessings because we have increased faith.

Our part is to pray and believe. Watch unto prayer. Watch, and co-operate with the prayer-hearing God. Bear in mind that "we are labourers together with God." 1 Cor. 3:9. Speak and act in harmony with your prayers. It will make an infinite difference with you whether trial shall prove your faith to be genuine, or show that your prayers are only a form.

When perplexities arise, and difficulties confront you, look not for help to humanity. Trust all with God. The practice of telling our difficulties to others only makes us weak, and brings no strength to them. It lays upon them the burden of our spiritual infirmities, which they cannot relieve. We seek the strength of erring, finite man, when we might have the strength of the unerring, infinite God.

You need not go to the ends of the earth for wisdom, for God is near. It is not the capabilities you now possess or ever will have that will give you success. It is that which the Lord can do for you. We need to have far less confidence in what man can do and far more confidence in what God can do for every believing soul. He longs to have you reach after Him by faith. He longs to have you expect great things from Him. He longs to give you understanding in temporal as well as in spiritual matters. He can sharpen the intellect. He can give tact and skill. Put your talents into the work, ask God for wisdom, and it will be given you.

Take the word of Christ as your assurance. Has He not invited you to come unto Him? Never allow yourself to talk in a hopeless, discouraged way. If you do you will lose much. By looking at appearances and complaining when difficulties and pressure come, you give evidence of a sickly, enfeebled faith. Talk and act as if your faith was invincible. The Lord is rich in resources; He owns the world. Look heavenward in faith. Look to Him who has light and power and efficiency.

There is in genuine faith a buoyancy, a steadfastness of principle, and a fixedness of purpose that neither time nor toil can weaken. "Even the youths shall faint and be weary, and the young men shall utterly fall: but they that wait upon the Lord shall renew their strength; they shall mount up with wings as eagles; they shall run, and not be weary; and they shall walk, and not faint." Isa. 40:30, 31.

There are many who long to help others, but they feel that they have no spiritual strength or light to impart. Let them present their petitions at the throne of grace. Plead for the Holy Spirit. God stands back of every promise He has made. With your Bible in your hands say, I have done as Thou hast said. I present Thy promise, "Ask, and it shall be given you; seek, and ye shall find; knock, and it shall be opened unto you."

We must not only pray in Christ's name, but by the inspiration of the Holy Spirit. This explains what is meant when it is said that the Spirit "maketh intercession for us, with groanings which cannot be uttered." Rom. 8:26. Such prayer God delights to answer. When with earnestness and intensity we breathe a prayer in the name of Christ, there is in that very intensity a pledge from God that He is about to answer our prayer "exceeding abundantly above all that we ask or think." Eph. 3:20.

Christ has said, "What things soever ye desire, when ye pray, believe that ye receive them, and ye shall have them." Mark 11:24. "Whatsoever ye shall ask in My name, that will I do, that the

Father may be glorified in the Son." John 14:13. And the beloved
John, under the inspiration of the Holy Spirit, speaks with great
plainness and assurance: "If we ask anything according to His will,
He heareth us: and if we know that He hear us, whatsoever we
ask, we know that we have the petitions that we desired of Him."
1 John 5:14, 15. Then press your petition to the Father in the
name of Jesus. God will honor that name.

The rainbow round about the throne is an assurance that God
is true, that in Him is no variableness, neither shadow of turning.
We have sinned against Him, and are undeserving of His favor;
yet He Himself has put into our lips that most wonderful of pleas,
"Do not abhor us, for Thy name's sake; do not disgrace the throne
of Thy glory; remember, break not Thy covenant with us." Jer.
14:21. When we come to him confessing our unworthiness and
sin, He has pledged Himself to give heed to our cry. The honor of
His throne is staked for the fulfillment of His word unto us.

Like Aaron, who symbolized Christ, our Saviour bears the
names of all His people on His heart in the holy place. Our great
High Priest remembers all the words by which He has encouraged
us to trust. He is ever mindful of His covenant.

All who seek of Him shall find. All who knock will have the
door opened to them. The excuse will not be made, Trouble Me
not; the door is closed; I do not wish to open it. Never will one be
told, I cannot help you. Those who beg at midnight for loaves to
feed the hungry souls will be successful.

In the parable, he who asks bread for the stranger, receives "as
many as he needeth." And in what measure will God impart to us
that we may impart to others? "According to the measure of the
gift of Christ." Eph. 4:7. Angels are watching with intense interest
to see how man is dealing with his fellow men. When they see one
manifest Christlike sympathy for the erring, they press to his side
and bring to his remembrance words to speak that will be as the
bread of life to the soul. So "God shall supply all your need according to His riches in glory by Christ Jesus." Phil. 4:19. Your
testimony in its genuineness and reality He will make powerful in

the power of the life to come. The word of the Lord will be in your mouth as truth and righteousness.

Personal effort for others should be preceded by much secret prayer; for it requires great wisdom to understand the science of saving souls. Before communicating with men, commune with Christ. At the throne of heavenly grace obtain a preparation for ministering to the people.

Let your heart break for the longing it has for God, for the living God. The life of Christ has shown what humanity can do by being partaker of the divine nature. All that Christ received from God we too may have. Then ask and receive. With the persevering faith of Jacob, with the unyielding persistence of Elijah, claim for yourself all that God has promised.

Let the glorious conceptions of God possess your mind. Let your life be knit by hidden links to the life of Jesus. He who commanded the light to shine out of darkness is willing to shine in your heart, to give the light of the knowledge of the glory of God in the face of Jesus Christ. The Holy Spirit will take the things of God and show them unto you, conveying them as a living power into the obedient heart. Christ will lead you to the threshold of the Infinite. You may behold the glory beyond the veil, and reveal to men the sufficiency of Him who ever liveth to make intercession for us.

---

*[This chapter appears in *Christ's Object Lessons,* pages 139-149.]

32

Faith and Prayer*

Faith is trusting God—believing that He loves us and knows best what is for our good. Thus, instead of our own, it leads us to choose His way. In place of our ignorance, it accepts His wisdom; in place of our weakness, His strength; in place of our sinfulness, His righteousness. Our lives, ourselves, are already His; faith acknowledges His ownership and accepts its blessing. Truth, uprightness, purity, have been pointed out as secrets of life's success. It is faith that puts us in possession of these principles.

Every good impulse or aspiration is the gift of God; faith receives from God the life that alone can produce true growth and efficiency.

How to exercise faith should be made very plain. To every promise of God there are conditions. If we are willing to do His will, all His strength is ours. Whatever gift He promises, is in the promise itself. "The seed is the word of God." Luke 8:11. As surely as the oak is in the acorn, so surely is the gift of God in His promise. If we receive the promise, we have the gift.

Faith that enables us to receive God's gifts is itself a gift, of which some measure is imparted to every human being. It grows as exercised in appropriating the word of God. In order to strengthen faith, we must often bring it in contact with the word.

In the study of the Bible the student should be led to see the power of God's word. In the creation, "He spake, and it was done; He commanded, and it stood fast." He "calleth those things which be not as though they were" (Psalm 33:9; Romans 4:17); for when He calls them, they are.

How often those who trusted the word of God, though in themselves utterly helpless, have withstood the power of the whole world—Enoch, pure in heart, holy in life, holding fast his faith in the triumph of righteousness against a corrupt and scoffing generation; Noah and his household against the men of his time, men of the greatest physical and mental strength and the most debased in morals; the children of Israel at the Red Sea, a helpless, terrified multitude of slaves, against the mightiest army of the mightiest nation on the globe; David, a shepherd lad, having God's promise of the throne, against Saul, the established monarch, bent on holding fast his power; Shadrach and his companions in the fire, and Nebuchadnezzar on the throne; Daniel among the lions, his enemies in the high places of the kingdom; Jesus on the cross, and the Jewish priests and rulers forcing even the Roman governor to work their will; Paul in chains led to a criminal's death, Nero the despot of a world empire.

Such examples are not found in the Bible only. They abound in every record of human progress. The Vaudois and the Huguenots, Wycliffe and Huss, Jerome and Luther, Tyndale and Knox, Zinzendorf and Wesley, with multitudes of others, have witnessed to the power of God's word against human power and policy in support of evil. These are the world's true nobility. This is its royal line. In this line the youth of today are called to take their places.

Faith is needed in the smaller no less than in the greater affairs of life. In all our daily interests and occupations the sustaining strength of God becomes real to us through an abiding trust.

Viewed from its human side, life is to all an untried path. It is a path in which, as regards our deeper experiences, we each walk alone. Into our inner life no other human being can fully enter. As the little child sets forth on that journey in which, sooner or later, he must choose his own course, himself deciding life's issues for eternity, how earnest should be the effort to direct his trust to the sure Guide and Helper!

As a shield from temptation and an inspiration to purity and truth, no other influence can equal the sense of God's presence. "All things are naked and opened unto the eyes of Him with whom we have to do." He is "of purer eyes than to behold evil, and canst not look on iniquity." Hebrews 4:13; Habakkuk 1:13. This thought was Joseph's shield amidst the corruptions of Egypt. To the allurements of temptation his answer was steadfast: "How . . . can I do this great wickedness, and sin against God?" Genesis 39:9. Such a shield, faith, if cherished, will bring to every soul.

Only the sense of God's presence can banish the fear that, for the timid child, would make life a burden. Let him fix in his memory the promise, "The angel of the Lord encampeth round about them that fear Him, and delivereth them." Psalm 34:7. Let him read that wonderful story of Elisha in the mountain city, and, between him and the hosts of armed foemen, a mighty encircling band of heavenly angels. Let him read how to Peter, in prison and condemned to death, God's angel appeared; how, past the armed guards, the massive doors and great iron gateway with their bolts and bars, the angel led God's servant forth in safety. Let him read of that scene on the sea, when the tempest-tossed soldiers and seamen, worn with labor and watching and long fasting, Paul the prisoner, on his way to trial and execution, spoke those grand words of courage and hope: "Be of good cheer: for there shall be no loss of any man's life among you. . . . For there stood by me this night the angel of God, whose I am, and whom I serve, saying, Fear not, Paul; thou must be brought before Caesar: and, lo, God hath given thee all them that sail with thee." In the faith of this promise Paul assured his companions, "There shall not an hair fall from the head of any of you." So it came to pass. Because there was in that ship one man through whom God could work, the whole shipload of heathen soldiers and sailors was preserved. "They escaped all safe to land." Acts 27:22-24, 34, 44.

These things were not written merely that we might read and wonder, but that the same faith which wrought in God's servants of old might work in us. In no less marked a manner than He wrought then will He work now wherever there are hearts of faith to be channels of His power.

Let the self-distrustful, whose lack of self-reliance leads them to shrink from care and responsibility, be taught reliance upon God. Thus many a one who otherwise would be but a cipher in the world, perhaps only a helpless burden, will be able to say with the apostle Paul, "I can do all things through Christ which strengtheneth me." Philippians 4:13.

For the child also who is quick to resent injuries, faith has precious lessons. The disposition to resist evil or to avenge wrong is often prompted by a keen sense of justice and an active, energetic spirit. Let such a child be taught that God is the eternal guardian of right. He has a tender care for the beings whom He has so loved as to give His dearest Beloved to save. He will deal with every wrongdoer.

"For he that toucheth you toucheth the apple of His eye." Zechariah 2:8.

"Commit thy way unto the Lord; trust also in Him; and He shall bring it to pass. . . . He shall bring forth thy righteousness as the light, and thy judgment as the noonday." Psalm 37:5, 6.

"The Lord also will be a refuge for the oppressed, a refuge in times of trouble. And they that know Thy name will put their trust in Thee: for Thou, Lord, hast not forsaken them that seek Thee." Psalm 9:9, 10.

The compassion that God manifests toward us, He bids us manifest toward others. Let the impulsive, the self-sufficient, the revengeful, behold the meek and lowly One, led as a lamb to the slaughter, unretaliating as a sheep dumb before her shearers. Let them look upon Him whom our sins have pierced and our sorrows burdened, and they will learn to endure, to forbear, and to forgive.

Through faith in Christ, every deficiency of character may be supplied, every defilement cleansed, every fault corrected, every excellence developed.

"Ye are complete in Him." Colossians 2:10.

Prayer and faith are closely allied, and they need to be studied together. In the prayer of faith there is a divine science; it is a science that everyone who would make his lifework a success must understand. Christ says, "What things soever ye desire, when ye pray, believe that ye receive them, and ye shall have them." Mark 11:24. He makes it plain that our asking must be according to God's will; we must ask for the things that He has promised, and whatever we receive must be used in doing His will. The conditions met, the promise is unequivocal.

For the pardon of sin, for the Holy Spirit, for a Christlike temper, for wisdom and strength to do His work, for any gift He has promised, we may ask; then we are to believe that we receive, and return thanks to God that we have received.

We need look for no outward evidence of the blessing. The gift is in the promise, and we may go about our work assured that what God has promised He is able to perform, and that the gift, which we already possess, will be realized when we need it most.

To live thus by the word of God means the surrender to Him of the whole life. There will be felt a continual sense of need and dependence, a drawing out of the heart after God. Prayer is a necessity; for it is the life of the soul. Family prayer, public prayer, have their place; but it is secret communion with God that sustains the soul life.

It was in the mount with God that Moses beheld the pattern of that wonderful building which was to be the abiding place of His glory. It is in the mount with God—in the secret place of communion—that we are to contemplate His glorious ideal for humanity. Thus we shall be enabled so to fashion our character building that to us may be fulfilled His promise, "I will dwell in them, and walk in them; and I will be their God, and they shall be My people." 2 Corinthians 6:16.

It was in hours of solitary prayer that Jesus in His earth life received wisdom and power. Let the youth follow His example in finding at dawn and twilight a quiet season for communion with their Father in heaven. And throughout the day let them lift up their hearts to God. At every step of our way He says, "I the Lord thy God will hold thy right hand, . . . Fear not; I will help thee." Isaiah 41:13. Could our children learn these lessons in the morning of their years, what freshness and power, what joy and sweetness, would be brought into their lives!

These are lessons that only he who himself has learned can teach. It is because so many parents and teachers profess to believe the word of God while their lives deny its power, that the teaching of Scripture has no greater effect upon the youth. At times the youth are brought to feel the power of the word. They see the preciousness of the love of Christ. They see the beauty of His character, the possibilities of a life given to His service. But in contrast they see the life of those who profess to revere God's precepts. Of how many are the words true that were spoken to the prophet Ezekiel:

Thy people "speak one to another, everyone to his brother, saying, Come, I pray you, and hear what is the word that cometh forth from the Lord. And they come unto thee as the people cometh, and they sit before thee as My people, and they hear thy words, but they will not do them: for with their mouth they show much love, but their heart goeth after their covetousness. And, lo, thou art unto them as a very lovely song of one that hath a pleasant voice, and can play well on an instrument: for they hear thy words, but they do them not." Ezekiel 33:30-32.

It is one thing to treat the Bible as a book of good moral instruction, to be heeded so far as is consistent with the spirit of the times and our position in the world; it is another thing to regard it as it really is—the word of the living God, the word that is our life, the word that is to mold our actions, our words, and our thoughts. To hold God's word as anything less than this is to reject it. And this rejection by those who profess to believe it, is foremost among the causes of skepticism and infidelity in the youth.

An intensity such as never before was seen is taking possession of the world. In amusement, in moneymaking, in the contest for power, in the very struggle for existence, there is a terrible force that engrosses body and mind and soul. In the midst of this maddening rush, God is speaking. He bids us come apart and commune with Him. "Be still, and know that I am God." Psalm 46:10.

Many, even in their seasons of devotion, fail of receiving the blessing of real communion with God. They are in too great haste. With hurried steps they press through the circle of Christ's loving presence, pausing perhaps a moment within the sacred precincts, but not waiting for counsel. They have no time to remain with the divine Teacher. With their burdens they return to their work.

These workers can never attain the highest success until they learn the secret of strength. They must give themselves time to think, to pray, to wait upon God for a renewal of physical, mental, and spiritual power. They need the uplifting influence of His Spirit. Receiving this, they will be quickened by fresh life. The wearied frame and tired brain will be refreshed, the burdened heart will be lightened.

Not a pause for a moment in His presence, but personal contact with Christ, to sit down in companionship with Him—this is our need. Happy will it be for the children of our homes and the students of our schools when parents and teachers shall learn in their own lives the precious experience pictured in these words from the Song of Songs:

"As the apple tree among the trees of the wood,
So is my Beloved among the sons.
I sat down under His shadow with great delight,
And His fruit was sweet to my taste.
He brought me to the banqueting house,
And His banner over me was love." Canticles 2:3, 4.

---

*[This chapter appears in *Education*, pages 253-261.]